HALE COUNTY COURT HOUSE
At Plainview, Texas

HISTORY
OF
HALE COUNTY, TEXAS

by
MARY L. COX

Southern Historical Press, Inc.
Greenville, South Carolina

This volume was reproduced
from a personal copy located in
the Publishers private library

All rights reserved. No part of this publication may be reproduced,
stored in a retrieval system, transmitted in any form, posted
on the web in any form or by any means without the
prior written permission of the publisher.

Please direct all correspondence and book orders to:
**SOUTHERN HISTORICAL PRESS, Inc.
1071 Park West Blvd.
Greenville, SC 29611**

Copyright 1937 by:
    Mary L. Cox
ISBN #978-1-63914-635-2
Printed in the United States of America

DEDICATED

To the memory of Lieutenant John C. Hale, in whose honor Hale County was named, in Centennial tribute to the Heroes of Texas Independence

To the Pioneers of Hale County, in Semi-Centennial tribute to the courageous men and women who wrested from the wilderness the fertile acres of Hale County and made the history herein recorded

To Dorothy Cox, whose loyalty and cooperation made the writing of it possible.

HALE

Hale County was so named in honor of Lieutenant John C. Hale, a hero of San Jacinto. A native of Maine, he came to Texas in 1834 and settled with his family in what is now Sabine County. When Captain Benjamin Franklin Bryant organized a company for the purpose of joining General Houston's army in the War for the Independence of Texas, Hale was made First Lieutenant of Company 7, Second Texas Infantry. He was killed while leading his company in the Battle of San Jacinto on April 21, 1836.

FOREWORD

The purpose in writing this book has been to preserve in permanent and tangible form an authentic record of half a century of Hale County's history and development, with the hope that such data will be useful to those in both the present and future who may wish to acquaint themselves with the early history of the county.

The sources from which this material has been compiled are many and varied. Much of the data in this volume has been secured from County records, various official records in State and Federal offices, as well as personally kept records. Data has been secured from the County newspapers, as well as those in the District and State. Texas histories, Gammel's Laws of Texas and many other sources have been consulted. Many pioneers and other individuals have furnished valuable information, and much research has been spent in each separate phase of this history. The work has been exceedingly interesting and fascinating, and has been the occasion of many pleasant contacts and the making of many delightful acquaintances.

The short stories herein contained were given to the author in personal interviews with pioneers and each is intended to portray a separate picture of some phase of early history.

Many persons have contributed to this volume and hundreds have had some part in its making. Most sincere thanks are extended to all who have contributed in any way in the compiling of this history.

CONTENTS

CHAPTER	PAGE
I. EARLY HISTORY	1

Organization—First Acts of Commissioners Court—Erection of Court House

II. SETTLEMENT 7

Post-Indian Pre-Settlement Period—Morrison Ranch—First Settlers—Towns and Post Offices

III. LANDS AND LAND PROBLEMS 30

Distribution of Public Domain—Distribution of Hale County Lands—Early Land Owners

IV. INDUSTRIAL AND AGRICULTURAL DEVELOPMENT 40

Early Industry—Cattle—Dairying—Agriculture—Irrigation—Wheat and Milling Industry—Cotton Industries—Topography—Census, Crop and Weather Reports

V. TRANSPORTATION 63

Early Modes—Railroads—Motor Transportation

VI. HISTORY OF EDUCATION 72

Subscription Schools—Public Schools—Colleges—Public Library—Extension Work

VII. NEWSPAPERS 90

Hale County Newspapers—Their Part in Development

VIII. LEGAL AND JUDICIAL HISTORY 95

Judicial Districts—District Court—Location of County Seat—Prohibition—Woman's Suffrage—Early Hale County Lawyers—Roster of Attorneys—Bar Association—County Officers

IX. FINANCIAL HISTORY 106

Banks—Loan Companies—Credit Bureau

X. MEDICAL HISTORY 115

First Physicians—Early Medical Practice—The Medical Society—Hospitals—Roster of Hale County Doctors—An Old Fashioned Prescription

CONTENTS

CHAPTER	PAGE
XI. RELIGIOUS HISTORY	123

Early Religious Services—Church Histories

XII. LODGES AND FRATERNAL ORGANIZATIONS............138
Histories of Fraternal Orders

XIII. CIVIC ORGANIZATIONS......................149
Civic and Service Clubs

XIV. WOMEN'S CLUBS............................155
Histories of Women's Clubs

XV. MILITARY HISTORY..........................167
Texas National Guards—Distinguished Service Awards—World War Dead—131st Field Artillery—American Legion—Roster of World War Veterans—Memorial

XVI. TALES THE OLD TIMERS TOLD: 177
The Plains Buffalo....................L. S. Kinder
Buffalo Hunting in the Seventies.........Levi Schick
Buffalo Days............................J. W. Smylie
Pioneer Days as a Texas Ranger........W. F. Meador
Chief Lone Wolf Visits the Morrison Ranch........
..................................J. N. Morrison
Moving the Slaughter Cattle..........George D. May
Horatio Graves—First Settler...........Amy Graves
Memory Pictures................Lottie Graves Layer
Frontier Hardships...................D. N. Shepley
Z. T. Maxwell..................William E. Maxwell
E. L. Lowe.................Virginia Lowe Quillen
Thornton Jones' Grocery Store........Thornton Jones
First Visit to Plainview............W. L. Harrington
Those Early Days..............Mrs. J. W. Smylie
Early Business Firms in Plainview.....W. B. Martine
"Uncle John" Pendley, Blacksmith................
..............................Stella Pendley Garner
Surveying Incidents................Col. R. P. Smyth
Why We Organized Hale County........L. G. Wilson
Carrying The Mail in 1888..............W. L. Tharp
The First Public School.........Alice Rosser Buntin
Freighting..............................R. M. Irick
The Old Clisbee Stage Line...........J. H. Lutrick
A Cattle Man Learned to Farm......J. W. Stevens
Pioneer Days As a Sheep Man........R. B. C. Howell
The Mercantile Business in 1890......J. N. Donohoo
Early Medical Practice...........Dr. J. H. Wayland
Frontier Days As a Missionary..........J. W. Winn
Pioneering the "Herald"................J. M. Shafer

CONTENTS

The Grasshopper Plague.................*Anson Cox*
First Business Woman...........*Mrs. J. L. Vaughn*
Talmage's Sermon.................*J. Frank Norfleet*
Early Trial By Jury....................*D. C. Lowe*
The Jumping Off Place.............*Martha Glover*
Early Days In the Cattle Industry......*J. C. Hooper*
Cattle In a Storm.................*R. W. Lemond*
My "Home On the Range"...........*Mrs. J. E. Cox*
The Meteor......................*R. A. McWhorter*
The Indian Scare of 1891........*Mrs. J. O. Oswald*
Why Boys Leave Home..................*M. M. Day*
Moving the Hale City School House...*N. M. Akeson*
Early Social Life ....*Mrs. L. A. Knight*
A Christmas Festivity.............*Mrs. W. A. Lowe*
Early Romance....................*B. H. Towery*
The First Church Wedding........*Mrs. Mary V. Dye*
Starting the Town of Petersburg.......*Ed M. White*
Early Grain Business...................*L. F. Cobb*
A Full Meal.......................*R. W. O'Keefe*
The Coming of the Railroad...*Emma Grigsby Meharg*
The Lantern On the Windmill..........*J. H. Abney*
Looking Backward....................*R. G. Carter*

HISTORY OF HALE COUNTY, TEXAS

CHAPTER I

Early History

Hale County was created by an Act of the Legislature approved August 21, 1876. At that time a map was drawn checkerboard fashion and the whole of northwest Texas was divided into counties, more than fifty of which were carved out of Bexar and Young Counties. Each county so established was named in honor of a Texas hero or pioneer prominent in early Texas history. Prior to 1876 the territory now embraced within the limits of Hale County was a part of Bexar County.

At the time the Constitution of Mexico was adopted, approved March 11, 1827, there were three Departments, ie., Bexar, Monclovia and Saltillo. The Department of Bexar was probably coextensive with the limits of the State beginning with the settlement of San Antonio in 1730. On January 31, 1831, the Congress of Coahuila and Texas divided Texas into two districts, ie., Bexar and Nacogdoches, and in 1834, created another known as Brazos. Later the municipalities of Gonzales, Mina, Austin and Goliad were created out of Bexar.

The only political divisions at the time the Texas Revolution began were Departments and Municipalities. Representatives came from the various Municipalities as the Department was not practicable for a representative form of government. The Municipalities were the nucleus of the first counties created by the First Congress of the Republic of Texas. There were eighteen Municipalities, among which was Bexar, in the Department of Bexar. The area within Hale County's borders remained in Bexar territory until its organization and was never included in any Municipality except Bexar.

Organization

Twelve years after the creation of Hale County found small settlements and ranches thriving scarce fifteen years since the red men inhabited the Staked Plains. The newcomers, whose minds were forever looking into the future, saw visions of a rapidly developing country. The little town of Plainview had sprung up through the efforts of Z. T. Maxwell and E. L. Lowe and was attracting homeseekers. In the summer of 1888, the idea of organizing the county was originated. Unanimously the people of Plainview set out to secure the required 150 signatures on the petition. They combed the prairies to get signers and merchants kept a petition on the counter, and it is said that few customers were served with supplies until the petition had been signed to get the county organized.

On July 4, 1888, the petition was ready to be presented to the Commissioners Court then in session at Estacado, in Crosby County, petitioning the Court to authorize the organization of Hale County. The precious document was entrusted to a group of loyal citizens, ie., E. L. Lowe, Z. T. Maxwell, Henry Moore, J. M. Carter, L. G. Wilson and R. P. Smyth, who celebrated the 4th of July by journeying to Estacado by hack, a distance of thirty miles, to be on hand early in the morning to present the petition.

On July 5th the Commissioners Court met in Estacado in Crosby County with County Judge G. M. Swink presiding, and others present A. W. Lewis, Claud M. Telford, Wm. Harrell, and Harry B. Smith, Commissioners; Paris Cox, County Clerk, and Sid B. Swink, Deputy Sheriff.

The Minutes of the Commissioners Court of Crosby County show the following record: "Then came on to be heard and considered a petition signed by 150 legal voters of Hale County. Whereupon after due consideration, and there being no sufficient cause shown why the prayers of the said petition should not be granted. It is therefore ordered by the Court that the prayers of said petition of the Citizens of said Hale County be and the same is hereby granted."

It was ordered by the Court that an election be held in Hale County on August 4th, 1888, for the purpose of electing county officers and to decide upon the County Seat. The Court divided the county into four precincts and appointed the following citizens for presiding officers at the voting places: John Pendley Sr., Prec. No. 1, in the town of Plainview; C. L. Groff, Prec. No. 2, voting place C. L. Groff's house. Horatio Graves, Prec. No. 3 at Epworth. M. H. Newell, Prec. No. 4 at the Circle Ranch.

The Commissioners Court of Crosby County met in regular session at the Court House in Estacado on Monday, August 13, 1888, with the following officers present: Judge G. M. Swink presiding, A. W. Lewis, Wm. Harrell and Harry B. Smith, Commissioners; M. M. Cox Deputy Clerk and Sid B. Swink Deputy Sheriff. The returns of the Special Election held in reference to the organization of Hale County were opened and counted, which result showed the following County Seat and officers had been chosen: "For County Seat the Town of Plainview; County Judge F. M. Lester; County and District Clerk E. L. Lowe; County Attorney L. G. Wilson; Sheriff and Tax Collector R. A. Ford; Assessor, J. H. Bryan; County Surveyor G. H. Chipman; County Treasurer C. W. Marsalis; Hide and Animal Inspector W. H. Bryan; County Commissioners: Precinct No. 1 John Pendley; Precinct No. 2 Jack Cooper; Precinct No. 3 G. W. Baker, Precinct No. 4 R. W. O'Keefe; Justice Peace Precinct No. 1 A. L. Conkling; Justice Peace Precinct No. 3 L. T. Lester; Constable Precinct No. 1 T. A. Taylor; and Constable Precinct No. 3 J. E. Whitmire."

The records of the Commissioners Court of Hale County show that the following persons served on the first election Board in Hale County: R. L. Stringfellow, Z. T. Maxwell, Thornton Jones, J. T. Matsler, John Vaughn, Horatio Graves, L. A. White, D. L. Shepley, T. C. Overhuls, Ed Powell, F. M. Bradford, Hugh McClelland, W. H. Portwood, P. F. Bryan, T. C. Cooper, M. G. McEntyre, L. T. Lester, D. W. Owens, Tom Miller and Charlie Quillen.

The Commissioners Court met in Plainview in first session in a temporary Court House on August 20, 1888, with Judge F. M. Lester presiding and others present John Pendley, G. W. Baker, J. W. Cooper and R. W. O'Keefe, Commissioners,

E. L. Lowe, Clerk, and R. A. Ford, Sheriff. The bonds of the Officers having been approved by the Court of Crosby County, the officers took the oath of office and Hale County was declared duly organized.

First Acts of Commissioners Court

The salaries of the officers were fixed as follows: County Judge $58.33 per month, Clerk $25.00, Sheriff $25.00 and County Attorney $25.00. $1,305.00 was appropriated to purchase books, stationery and furniture for the various offices. The sum of $109.91 was set apart for the surveying of the county line.

A Jury View to lay out and open roads leading from Plainview to the different lines of Hale County was appointed, composed of D. L. Shepley, C. L. Groff, F. M. Bradford, Sam McEntyre and A. E. Adams.

An ordinance was passed providing that a well should be dug on the Court House Square at a cost of $20 and John Pendley was appointed to supervise the work.

On submission of petitions from School Districts Nos. 1 and 2, it was ordered that an election be held on September 15, 1888, to decide whether a tax of 20¢ on the hundred dollar valuation should be levied for public school purposes. An election for local option was ordered to be held on the same date.

At a second session of the Commissioners Court, the result of the elections held on September 15th showed that the majority of voters in School District No. 1 voted for the levy of tax while District No. 2 voted unanimously against the levy. Local Option carried unanimously.

County Attorney L. G. Wilson was appointed to transcribe the tax records from Crosby County records for the Tax Collector of Hale County.

N. B. Davidson was appointed to survey and select the land set apart by the State for Hale County School Land and L. A. White was appointed to assist in making the selection.

At the session of the Commissioners Court held in October, the election held in September was held null and void on account of irregularities.

EARLY HISTORY

Erection of Court House

At the first session of the Commissioners Court, held on August 20, 1888, the following order was passed:

"In the matter of building a Court House, It is ordered that a Court House of the dimensions of 24 feet by 40 feet be built on the corner of the Public Square in the town of Plainview by and according to the plans and specifications hereafter to be decided upon."

Bonds in the amount of two thousand five hundred dollars were issued to pay for the Court House and a tax levy of fifteen cents on the one hundred dollar valuation was made. No time was lost by the citizens in the erection of the Court House, which was a temporary structure, built, not on the Court House Square, but across the street west of its present location. This was done with a view of selling it to be used as a business house at a later date, when a new and larger Court House could be financed, and the dimensions of the building were designated with that purpose in mind.

In keeping with the structure of buildings at that time, the building was erected on cedar underpinnings and was boxed and batoned, and the partitions were of shiplap placed horizontally. The lumber to build the first Court House was freighted with wagons from Amarillo by a party of citizens composed of County Judge F. M. Lester, County Attorney L. G. Wilson, Henry Moore, A. Vince, W. V. Duncan, Thos. Baird, Chas. Mapes, Poliet Smith, S. M. McEntyre, J. M. Johnson and J. W. Bryan. The labor of erecting the Court House was done by another group of citizens composed of Thornton Jones, W. B. Ford, J. T. Matsler, Poliet Smith, S. R. Perry, J. M. Carter, John Smylie, F. M. Bradford, R. F. Powell and H. Potter. The building was completed and ready for occupancy by the time the regular election took place in November, 1888.

The first County Jail was a small sod building of one room, built on the lot later occupied by J. N. Morrison's Creamery, now the corner of Fifth and Baltimore Streets.

When the County had increased somewhat in population, a move was launched to build a new Court House. Late in 1889, a contract was let to Martin, Byrne and Johnson, of

Colorado City, to erect a two-story frame Court House at a cost of ten thousand six hundred dollars. Diebold Safe and Lock Company was given the contract to build a jail at a cost of three thousand eight hundred dollars. The second Court House was received by the Commissioners Court on November 26, 1890, and rooms were assigned to the county officials. A jail was built on Lots 5 and 6, Block 39, Old Town of Plainview, east of the Court House. This was a one-room building made of two by four inch lumber fastened together with spikes.

The old Court House was rented to Oscar Bryan on December 20, 1890, for a rental of $10.00 per month. The building was sold to Dr. J. W. Wayland on May 10, 1892, for $500.00, to be used for a drug store.

On November 9, 1908, a bond was issued for sixty thousand dollars for the purpose of constructing a brick Court House, and jail combined. The contract was let for the building and fixtures November 23, 1909. W. T. McRae received the contract for the building, and other companies the contracts for fixtures. The total cost when completed was $70,600. A new brick jail was built in 1925 on the southeast corner of the Court House Square at a cost of $48,000.

CHAPTER II

SETTLEMENT

The Post-Indian Pre-Settlement Period

In 1880 Hale County was marking time at a brief interval which may be designated as a Post-Indian Pre-Settlement Period. Her lands were but a waste of windswept prairie, uninhabited by any living creature save and except by a few scattered buffalo, wild-horses, antelopes, coyotes, prairie-dogs and rattlesnakes. The marauding bands of Indians had vanished, most of the buffalo had gone, and the cattlemen had not yet arrived.

The decade that had just passed witnessed the last stand of the red men on the Staked Plains of Texas. General Mackenzie in command of federal troops waged a four years compaign in a seemingly fruitless effort to rid west Texas of the Comanches. Several bands of Indians who refused to go on the reservations still made the Plains their home and hiding place and raided the settlements east of the Caprock. The last outbreak of the Indians on the Plains occurred in the summer of 1874, when six hundred warriors with their families and all their wordly goods left the reservations bound for the Panhandle to join some 1500 Indians in hiding in the Palo Duro Canyon. Mackenzie's troops located them and taking them by surprise routed them from their hiding places in a final battle on September 28, 1874 and sent them hurrying back to the reservations.

Buffalo hunters followed swiftly on the heels of the soldiers and in a few short years they rid the prairies of the ponderous beasts which for centuries had made the Plains a Happy Hunting Ground.

In the spring of 1876, Fort Elliott was established in Wheeler County as a military outpost to protect the coming settlers from the Indians. That year Col. Charles Goodnight drove his 16,000 head of cattle from Colorado into the Palo

Duro Canyon and started the first ranch in the Panhandle. Other ranches were soon started in the north Panhandle and the towns of Mobeetie and Tascosa sprang into existence in 1876, followed shortly by old Clarendon. Hank Smith moved from Fort Griffin to the rock house in Blanco Canyon in 1877, and in 1879, the Quakers founded the colony at Estacado. This was the first settlement on the Staked Plains and was located six miles from the Hale County Line.

The Morrison Ranch

The Morrison Brothers, T. W. and J. N. Morrison, who had come from Illinois in 1880 and started a ranch at Clarendon, purchased a body of scattered land in 1881 some twenty miles square lying in the corners of Hale, Lamb, Castro and Swisher Counties, and started the Cross L. Ranch, or Morrison's Ranch. The Runningwater Draw was a running stream at that time, and this was their incentive for the location of the ranch. The ranch headquarters were located on the draw ten miles above the present site of Runningwater School. Soon after stocking the ranch, Morrison Bros. sold one-half interest in their lands and cattle to W. D. Johnson. The lands in this ranch were railroad sections, and the alternate sections of school lands which lay between the sections gave them access to free grazing of the school lands. Since the State school lands could not be enclosed without first being leased, they built a fence on three sides of the ranch, leaving the north side open. This custom was not unusual in the early days of ranching.

In 1883 Morrison Brothers and Johnson traded one-half interest in their 10,000 acres of land to Col. C. C. Slaughter for one-half interest in 10,000 head of cattle. The Runningwater Land and Cattle Company was organized and was incorporated with $130,000 capital. The name of the ranch was changed from Morrison Bros. and Johnson or the Cross L to the Circle Ranch. R. W. O'Keefe brought the first of the Slaughter cattle to Hale County, arriving with the herd on September 1, 1883, and became the first foreman of the Circle Ranch.

The Runningwater Land and Cattle Company was dissolved in 1890, and Morrison Bros. and Johnson traded their half interest in the lands to C. C. Slaughter for his half interest in the livestock, cattle and horses.

First Settlers

The first permanent settler to come to Hale County was Rev. Horatio Graves who moved with his family from Ausable Forks, New York, in 1882. Mr. Graves first came to the Staked Plains in 1877 with a party of surveyors to locate "Government Scrip" or land allotted to railroad companies as a bonus for the building of railroads in Eastern Texas. He made another trip to Texas in 1878, at which time he purchased for himself sixteen sections of land in the center of Hale County. Four of these sections were the corner sections in four blocks, and in this way Mr. Graves became the owner of four adjoining sections, the center of which was one mile west of the "Bottle Corner" near the center of Hale County. He is said to have been the only man in Hale County who had four sections connected up. His home was built one and one-half miles southwest of the center of the present site of Hale Center.

Mr. Graves left New York with his family on July 4, 1882, enroute to Texas, traveling by rail to Eastland and by covered wagon from Eastland to Estacado, where he arrived the latter part of August. Leaving his wife and three daughters in Estacado, he freighted lumber from Colorado City, a distance of 150 miles, to build his house. His home was a story-and-one-half four-room house, weather-boarded on the outside, lined with adobe brick and sealed inside. He later added a one-story lean-to, making three additional rooms, in one of which was housed the Post Office of Epworth and in another was held the first school.

In March, 1883, Mr. Graves moved his wife and daughters to their new home, they having spent the winter of 1882-1883 in Estacado. Alpheus Dyer, a bachelor whom Mr. Graves had known in New York, and who purchased some land in 1878 came in the fall of 1883 and built a small house near Mr. Graves' home. No other families came until the spring of 1885, when A. E. Adams moved his family to Hale County and built a sod house on a section adjoining Mr. Graves' home section. A. N. Jones was the next settler, bringing his family in the fall of 1885 and settling on land adjoining Mr. Graves on the north. In March, 1886, D. L. Shepley came from Snyder and F. M. and L. T. Lester came from Palo Pinto County and settled near by. The Graves home soon became a community and religious center for the settlers, the cowboys on the Circle Ranch and the ranches farther west to the Pecos River. This was the first settlement in Hale County and was known as the Epworth Community.

TOWNS AND POST OFFICES

Ephraim

The Post Office of Ephraim was established in Hale County on June 27, 1881, with Ephraim H. Cone as Postmaster. Its location is not definitely known; however, it is said that it was situated in a cow camp in the northwest corner of the county on the Morrison Ranch which was established in the spring of 1881. Mail was brought by ox wagon from Old Clarendon by freighters who made the journey to the ranch only when occasion demanded. This Post Office existed for more than a year and was discontinued before the coming of the first settler.

Epworth

Epworth was started in 1883 when Rev. Horatio Graves began carrying the mail from Estacado to his home in Hale County as an accommodation to the cowboys. He named the Post Office "Epworth" in honor of the little village in England that was the birthplace of John Wesley, founder of the Methodist Church. Mail was carried once a month at first, then every two weeks, and finally once a week, the cowboys sometimes lending assistance by making the trip for him. The mail came by way of Plainview after the railroad reached Amarillo in March, 1888. Mr. Graves planned to start a town at Epworth and dreamed of establishing a colony of people of his own religious faith (the "Northern" Methodist) as the Quakers had done at Estacado.

Mr. Graves platted the town of Epworth on April 1, 1887 (as shown by the County Deed Records). The Post Office

FIRST HOME AND HOME BUILDERS

Top: This home was built in 1882-3 by Rev. Horatio Graves 1½ miles southwest of the present site of Hale Center. It housed the Epworth Post Office established in 1884 and the Epworth School in 1886.

Bottom: Rev. and Mrs. Horatio Graves, first settlers.

was officially established on June 3, 1884. Mr. Graves served as Postmaster at Epworth until March 10, 1891, when Frank Y. Lincoln was appointed his successor.

Only two houses beside his own were ever built on the townsite, those being the homes of Alpheus Dyer and J. C. Harlan. Mr. Dyer moved to Estacado in a short time, however, and his home was used by Mr. Graves as a store building in which he kept a small stock of merchandise and supplies which he sold to neighboring settlers and to the cattlemen at the Yellowhouse Division of the XIT Ranch. A number of southern families were among the first to settle near him and some of these were Southern Methodists, therefore his plan for his Northern colony was abandoned.

Hale City and New Epworth

Hale City was started by A. N. Jones in the spring of 1891. The townsite was platted on March 4, 1891, on Jones' home section one-half mile north of Mr. Graves' home, or Epworth. As an inducement to build homes in his town, Mr. Jones gave away parcels of ten lots to every man who would build a house on his townsite. Consequently a number of small buildings sprang up, as a shack eight or ten feet square was all that was required to procure the ten lots.

The name of the Post Office was changed from Epworth to Hale City on April 16, 1891, and the Post Office was moved to Hale City on June 1, 1891. Frank Y. Lincoln, a young man said to be a relative of Abraham Lincoln, served as Postmaster until October 7, 1891, when he resigned and Horatio Graves was reappointed. Mr. Graves served from that date until October 19, 1893. Newcomers added hope to the settlement and for a time the town of Hale City prospered, confident that a railroad would soon be built into the community.

Almost simultaneously with the starting of Hale City, another town was started two miles south of it. The people who lived south of Old Epworth wanted to reclaim the town of Epworth, so the Hale County Townsite Company was organized with a capitol stock of $2000, which stock was sold at $10.00 per share. On March 26, 1891, Mr. Graves donated and deeded to the Townsite Company 320 acres of land, being two quarter sections out of the south two of his four adjoining sections, and the new town was also named Epworth.

For a time newcomers poured in and the two towns vied with each other for supremacy. Each town had its own newspaper, general store, hotel, and livery stable. A Mr. Hampton operated a general store at Hale City, and Mrs. Calloway had a hotel in that town. W. P. Blake published the Hale City Globe, while J. Winford Hunt edited and published the Epworth Chronicle. Dr. L. B. Lovelace practiced medicine at Hale City. Tom Pearson had a hotel at Epworth, Will Donohoo a store and N. C. Payne a livery stable. Each town had a school house where Sunday School and religious services were held. J. Winford Hunt organized a Christian Endeavor Society at Epworth, the first one organized in Hale County. A Methodist Church was organized in the Epworth School House, which was not located at the town of Epworth, in which Mrs. A. N. Jones was one of three charter members.

A drouth in 1892 followed by a plague of grasshoppers devastated the Plains and it soon became apparent that ten lots in town was not sufficient land on which to earn a livelihood. Only those who owned large tracts of land and large herds of cattle were able to stay on, so almost simultaneously the people began to move away. Those who remained saw no use in keeping up two struggling towns two miles apart and they wanted to come together on one townsite.

Hale Center

The town of Hale Center was established in 1893 as the outgrowth of the rivalry between the towns of Hale City and Epworth. Horatio Graves donated and deeded to the Townsite Company one-half section of land for the townsite of Hale Center. The Townsite Company then purchased a half-section of land adjoining it, out of the Harlan tract, and on this 640 acres the town of Hale Center was platted on June 16, 1893. The land in the townsite of Hale City then reverted to Mr. Jones and that in Epworth to Mr. Graves.

The name "Hale Center" was chosen because it was located approximately in the center of Hale County. The buildings from both Hale City and Epworth were then moved to Hale

Center. The Post Office was moved from Hale City on September 19, 1893, and the name was changed to Hale Center. Hopes of securing a railroad gave Hale Center residents courage and enthusiasm, but the depression caused by the drouth affected the town and gradually the people moved away and most of the houses were bought by settlers and moved to the ranches for homes. In 1898 all that remained was two business houses,—W. E. Ivey's Store and that of N. M. Akeson and the residence of Mrs. C. I. Maggard. One store building was moved to Plainview, and later was moved back to Hale Center.

The mail was carried from Plainview to Hale Center by mail hack until the coming of the Santa Fe Railroad into Hale Center on July 14, 1909. The Post Office of Clisbee, established in 1891 at the Clisbee stage stand, was served from the Hale Center Post Office, and later the Post Offices of Copenhagen, Norfleet and Bartonsite were added.

The following persons have served as Mayor of Hale Center: N. M. Akeson, Walter Lemond, and William Harral. The town had a population of 1,007 in 1930.

Plainview

Plainview, the Countyseat of Hale County, is located near the center of the northeast quarter of the county, on the Runningwater Draw.

The history of Plainview dates from the coming of its co-founders, Z. T. Maxwell and E. L. Lowe, in 1886. It is not definitely known when the town of Plainview actually started, but the idea was evidently conceived in the minds of the founders soon after their arrival.

Mr. Maxwell came from Floyd County, in May, 1886, in search of a location for a sheep ranch. He had sold his claim in Floyd County to the Blacker Cattle Company, who owned the H Bar L Ranch, and then traded his herd of cattle for sheep. Following the Mackenzie Trail, he journeyed westward until he reached the two hackberry groves, which was a landmark on the trail and said to be the only trees on the plains. Watered by the underground channel of the Runningwater Draw for no one knows how many years, they had grown to immense size and were a veritable "oasis in the desert." The

Hackberry Groves played their part in the history of Hale County, for they decided the location of the Maxwell homestead, the site of Plainview, and eventually the location of the countyseat. The trees still stand in the corner of the City Park at Plainview and though they have grown taller during the fifty years since Maxwell found them, they have lost their prominence among the thousands of trees now growing in the park and in Plainview.

Before returning to Floyd County, Mr. Maxwell built a sod fence between the two groves for a corral for his sheep and dug a well in the bed of the draw. In the early part of September, he returned with his family and built a dugout home in the bank north of the draw. The front wall of his home was built of sod. Poles were placed across the top and dirt placed thereon for a roof. On the heels of Mr. Maxwell came E. L. Lowe from Arkansas, who filed on the claim immediately north of Maxwell's land. Unloading his prairie schooner, he pitched his tent on the open prairie and with his sister and his two motherless daughters began to make a home.

Postal authorities give the date when the Post Office was established at Plainview as March 18, 1887, at which time Edwin L. Lowe was appointed first Postmaster.

In the spring of 1887, having decided to start a town, Maxwell and Lowe withdrew their homestead claims and pre-empted the land on May 21, 1887. The name "Plainview" is self-explanatory. It is said that the name "Hackberry Groves" was suggested, and also "Runningwater," but Plainview seemed to the founders as most fitting, since they could stand on the townsite and see in every direction as far as the eye could carry with no object to break the view.

The town was started gradually and at first the lots were surveyed only as they were sold. Thornton Jones, of Estacado, was offered a number of lots in the town on condition that he would open a grocery store in Plainview not later than June 1, 1887. In order to comply with the requirements, Jones opened a grocery store in a tent on a vacant lot near the Court House Square, and placed his brother, Will Jones, in charge until he could dispose of his interests in Estacado. Plainview then became a trading post for the few settlers in the vicinity and for travelers who passed along the old Mackenzie Trail.

SETTLEMENT

The townsite of Plainview was surveyed in the fall of 1887, by Col. R. P. Smyth, then a young surveyor who lived at Estacado and who was at that time State Surveyor. Eighty acres out of the north side of the Maxwell land and eighty acres from the south side of Lowe's land constituted the townsite, the section line running east and west through the center of the Court House Square.

During the year 1887 and the early part of 1888, a number of settlers moved to the vicinity and homesteaded land. Among these were Hugh McClelland, Horace Griffin, J. M. Carter, J. W. Smylie, John Pendley, J. H. Bryan, Thornton Jones, Poliet Smith, J. C. Burch and C. W. Marsalis.

On July 3, 1888, a deed of dedication to the land composing the streets, alleys, and public square in the town of Plainview for the benefit of the public was executed by E. L. Lowe, M. A. Lowe, Z. T. Maxwell and wife, Hugh McClelland and wife, T. Jones and wife, and Poliet Smith and wife, and placed of record July 26, 1888, in the office of the County Clerk of Crosby County.

When the County was organized in August, 1888, no united effort was made by the Epworth Community to secure the countyseat. The Plainview settlement had grown faster than that of Epworth for the reason that the lands around Plainview were in the Homestead Strip and divided into quarter sections, while the school and railroad lands around Epworth were in one-section tracts, so Plainview was elected the countyseat.

Settlers poured into Hale County during the few years following and soon the Homestead Strip was exhausted. In 1890 the population of Hale County numbered 721, and Plainview had reached 250. The founders spared neither time nor effort in developing the town in the first years of its existence. E. L. Lowe died in 1890, and Z. T. Maxwell moved away in 1892. The following persons have served as Mayor of Plainview, J. R. Delay (1907-1911), J. L. Dorsett (1912-1915), W. E. Risser (1916-1917), C. F. Vincent (1918-1921), J. M. Waller (1922-1925), W. E. Risser (1926-1927), T. J. Shelton (1928-1929), J. B. Cardwell (1930-1931), R. P. Smyth (1932-1933), T. J. Shelton (1934-).

Petersburg

The town of Petersburg is situated near the southeast corner of Hale County. It derived its name from its first Postmistress, Mrs. Margaret Peters, wife of Captain Z. H. Peters, who secured the appointment in 1891 and kept the Post Office in her home in Floyd County, five miles northeast of the present town of Petersburg. Mr. Peters carried the mail from Plainview twice a week with horse and buggy for the convenience of the settlers in that community.

The town of Petersburg was founded by Ed M. White, who was appointed Postmaster in 1896 when the Peters family moved from the country. Mr. White moved the Post Office to the present site of Petersburg, purchased a stock of merchandise and opened a store in his home in connection with the Post Office. As the country became settled up, he added a stock of hardware, and later operated a hardware store.

The townsite was platted by W. V. Kennedy on March 23, 1909, on lands conveyed by M. J. and E. W. Elliott and Ed M. White, at which time plans for a railroad through Petersburg were under way. The plans for the railroad fell through, however, and almost twenty years passed before Petersburg at last secured a railroad. The Fort Worth and Denver Railroad Company brought the first train into town in October, 1928.

Petersburg has a population of 548. Though the town is small, its residences are all comfortable well built homes. It was incorporated in 1928 with a Mayor-Commission form of government. The following persons have served as Mayor: Tom Davis, E. P. Hildreth, Chas. Schuler, Jr., and Albert R. Clubb.

Wadsworth

Wadsworth was started in 1890 by Dennis Rice, twelve miles northwest of Plainview, north of the Runningwater Draw. Mr. Rice first came to Texas in 1878, and purchased several sections of Railroad land on the Runningwater Draw. The possibility of securing a railroad across his lands and enhancing the value was his incentive for starting a town. He secured a post office on December 8, 1890 and became its first Postmaster. Others became interested in the townsite, but objected to the

SETTLEMENT

name and insisted that it be changed to Runningwater for it was believed the name would call attention to the fact that it was located on a running stream and attract newcomers. The name of the Post Office was changed to Runningwater on January 28, 1891, and Wadsworth ceased to exist.

Runningwater

The town of Runningwater came into existence with the passing of Wadsworth. Mr. Rice organized the Runningwater Townsite and Improvement Company and platted the town on August 26, 1892. The opening of the town was celebrated by a great barbecue and picnic at which all the people in Hale and surrounding counties came together to visit and to boost for the prospective railroad. The town became a community center and a number of homes were built on the townsite. Mr. Rice planned to establish a cheese factory at Runningwater, but the project was abandoned before the plant was put into operation. W. W. Cooper took charge of the Post Office for Mr. Rice until his father, S. T. Cooper, moved from Amarillo and became Postmaster in May, 1893. S. T. Cooper also operated a general store.

The drouth and grasshopper plague affected the Runningwater community as it did others on the plains and the people were compelled to move away. Not until after the Four Section Act was passed in 1897 did Runningwater take on new life. Settlers began coming in and for many years it served as a community center.

Runningwater was doomed to disappointment in regard to the railroad, for when the Fort Worth and Denver Railroad built from Plainview to Dimmitt in 1928, it missed the town about three miles. The Runningwater Post Office was moved to Edmonson Switch on June 15, 1935, to be on the railroad. The name of the Post Office was changed to Edmonson on February 1, 1937. All that remains at Runningwater is the community church, a brick school house and a few residences.

Clisbee

The Post Office of Clisbee was established on August 3, 1891, at the Clisbee stage stand some eighteen miles southwest of Plainview. The mail at that time was carried by stage from

Amarillo to Estacado. Clisbee Brothers of Amarillo had a contract to carry the mail, the stage coach being drawn by relays of wild little mules which raced madly from one stage stand to another. Robert Montgomery, stage driver, was Clisbee's first Postmaster. The Post Office was later moved a few miles northwest to what is now known as the Les Harrington place. Clisbee Post Office was discontinued on September 11, 1894, and mail was carried to Hale Center.

New Clisbee

The Clisbee Post Office was reestablished in 1900 when the country had become more thickly settled. This time it was located two miles north of the Lubbock County Line, five miles east of the present town of Abernathy and was kept in the J. R. Garrison home until it was discontinued in the fall of 1901. Clisbee never became a town or community center, but served the people only as a Post Office.

Stant Rhea Stage Stand

The Stant Rhea Stage Stand was located fifteen miles south of Plainview on a branch line of the Amarillo-Estacado mail route, which led from Plainview to Lubbock via Hale Center and Clisbee (and later Strip). Mr. Rhea carried the mail to Hale Center where it was sorted by the Postmaster and the mail for the people who lived near the stage stand was handed back to the driver. This he placed in a tin bucket in an abandoned dugout near his corrals and the people came there to get their mail, each sorting and taking what belonged to him and leaving that of his neighbors. This unofficial postal service accommodated the people living in the vicinity of the Stant Rhea Stage Stand from 1901 until 1907.

Copenhagen

The Post Office of Copenhagen was established on June 26, 1902, with T. H. Miller as Postmaster. It was located near the Center Plains School, in the home of Mr. Miller.

When application for a Post Office was made, the name "Center Plains" was submitted to the Postal authorities, but it seemed there were other post offices in Texas with similar names, so that name was rejected. Someone in the Post Office

Department at Washington delved into the annals of the Old World and borrowed the name of the Capitol of Denmark for the little Post Office at Center Plains. Thus it was called Copenhagen.

John W. Stevens became the Postmaster two years later and moved the Post Office to his home in the same community. He served until 1907 when the town of Norfleet was started, at which time he moved the Post Office to Norfleet and the name was officially changed to Norfleet.

Copenhagen never became a community center and no town was ever started there.

Ellen

The Post Office of Ellen was established in 1904 some fifteen miles southeast of Plainview. Ed M. White, founder of the town of Petersburg, selected the name "Ellen" in honor of his wife. C. W. Richardson served as Postmaster from the time the Post Office was established until it was discontinued in 1921, keeping it in his home all the while. Mail was supplied from Plainview, Reuben Burris carrying the mail in an open buggy once a week during the first year. The second year it came twice a week and it was eight years before it came every day. It finally was brought twice a day.

In 1905 the Ellen School House was built by the people in the community. Religious services were held in the school house and Ellen served as a community center.

Strip

The Post Office of Strip was established on April 15, 1904, at the home of Jerry M. Turner, its first Postmaster, one mile west of New Clisbee, which had been discontinued. Both these post offices were located in what was known as "the strip," it being a strip of land one and one-half miles wide and fifteen miles long which lay between two blocks of land assigned and patented by the State to Railroad Companies. This narrow strip of land was public domain and was therefore opened to homesteaders. After much of the land had been taken up, there was need of a community center and a post office. Pearce's Chapel had been built for religious services and a cemetery was dedicated before the Post office was established. Several residences were built, and Strip served the settlers in the "homestead strip" as a community center until Abernathy was started five miles farther west. Strip Post Office was discontinued July 15, 1910.

Norfleet

The townsite of Norfleet was platted on July 18, 1907, by the Norfleet Townsite Company, of which Joe Lee Ferguson was president. This company was composed of ten men, as follows: Joe Lee Ferguson, J. W. Stevens, W. B. Jones, A. J. Baker, J. J. Rushing, Bert McWhorter, J. W. Patton, L. H. Triplett, J. Frank Norfleet and J. F. Sageser.

The town was located ten miles west of Hale Center, one mile from the present site of Cotton Center. It was started as a townsite proposition when a railroad was platted across the site. The Panhandle Short Line between Vega and Big Springs was platted through Hale County and construction was begun. This line was intended to connect Vega with Kerrville, to connect up with the road that ran from San Antonio to Kerrville.

The Post Office of Copenhagen was moved to the new townsite and was operated for several months by J. W. Stevens, after which the name was changed to Norfleet and Barnie Rushing was appointed Postmaster. Mr. Rushing built a large store building and operated a general merchandise store. Moreland Lash Grocery Company put in a stock of groceries, Carter Mercantile Company moved a stock of drygoods to Norfleet, R. C. Ware Hardware Company put in a stock of hardware and McAdams Lumber Company established a branch lumber yard, all under the management of Mr. Rushing. The Center Plains School House was moved to Norfleet. This also served the community as a church. A number of residences were built and the town moved forward during the peak of the real estate boom in the few years that followed the coming of the Santa Fe Railway into Plainview.

The Panhandle Short Line that was under construction was not completed and the project was abandoned. The stockholders of the townsite company ceased development when it became known that the railroad was not forthcoming and the buildings were gradually moved away. The school house was returned to its former location at Center Plains and the store building was moved to Hale Center. T. C. Masterson became Postmaster on January 1, 1911, and moved the Post Office to his farm. The Norfleet Post Office was discontinued in 1913.

Bartonsite

The town of Bartonsite was located thirteen miles northwest of the present site of Abernathy, on the J. J. Barton Ranch. The townsite was platted in July, 1907, when it became known that the Santa Fe Railroad Company planned to build a short line from Plainview to Lubbock and that the route would pass through the Barton Ranch.

The prospect of a railroad created much interest in the town and it was not long until Bartonsite gave promise of a thriving town. A number of business houses were built, among which were a lumber yard managed by Al Horton, The Bartonsite Hotel managed by J. K. Nance, Reed's Grocery Store, a Blacksmith Shop, and the Post Office. Mail was brought daily by horse and buggy from Hale Center. The town had a school house and a church where all denominations worshipped together. Bartonsite became a popular community center and by the end of two years the population of the town had reached 250 people.

A change in the route of the railroad was a death blow to Bartonsite. When Abernathy sprang up in 1909, most of the buildings at Bartonsite were moved to Abernathy. The Post Office of Bartonsite was continued for a number of years,—until 1921. It was never discontinued but became inactive when the patrons of that office were served by a star route out of Hale Center. The church at Bartonsite was moved to Cotton Center and is still in use. Bartonsite holds fond memories for many of the early settlers who knew it in its halcyon days.

Abernathy

Abernathy is situated on the Hale-Lubbock County line, thirty-two miles south of Plainview and seventeen miles north of Lubbock. It was founded by M. G. Abernathy and Dr. M. C. Overton, of Lubbock, who bought a section of land and platted the townsite on July 8, 1909, naming the town for M. G. Abernathy.

The occasion of the starting of the town was the building of the Santa Fe Railroad from Plainview to Lubbock, and the changing of the route which was to have gone through Bartonsite. Later Abernathy and Overton sold the townsite to the railroad company and to M. G. Holland.

The first business firms to locate in Abernathy were the Fulton Lumber Company managed by N. C. Hix, the McAdams Lumber Company with M. S. White, Manager, and F. M. Cranford's Grocery Store. The Barton Supply Company, a stock company owned by J. J. Barton, George M. Arnett and others, was moved from Bartonsite and purchased by J. D. Marsh and J. C. Arnett. After changing hands several times, it is now known as the Struve Mercantile Co. A number of residences were also moved to Abernathy from Bartonsite.

In the fall of 1909 a school building was built by public subscription and the first school was taught by Mrs. Ola Legg, who taught from that time every year save one until her election to the office of County Superintendent of Schools, in 1922. The Tuco plant was built two miles north of Abernathy in 1930.

Abernathy was incorporated in 1925 with F. W. Struve as the first Mayor. Mr. Struve is Mayor at the present time.

Abernathy was supplied by the Strip Post Office until the Post Office at Abernathy was established on January 13, 1910.

The population of the town is 743 persons in Hale County and 115 in Lubbock County.

Freeport

The Post Office of Freeport was established in 1909, two miles north of Plainview in the Seth Ward Addition, to serve the Central Plains College and Conservatory of Music that was established by the Nazarene Church. The Post Office was discontinued when the school became Seth Ward College.

Halfway

Halfway was started as a community center in 1909, when the school was established, which was named "Halfway" by

George L. Mayfield, at that time County Judge and Ex Officio Superintendent of Schools, since it was located at a point halfway between the two countyseats, Plainview and Olton, or about fourteen miles west of Plainview. Edgar Howard opened a store at Halfway and became the first Postmaster.

Unlike some of the towns of Hale County, Halfway was not started by any prospect of a railroad, and until the present time, no effort has been made to secure one. In the beginning, the little store served a community need. Mail was brought by Star Route from Plainview to Olton. When a movement was made to change the route in a way that would miss Halfway, the people applied for a Post Office in order to retain the Star Route. The limited patronage was not sufficient to justify the services of a Postmaster, however, and after a time it was discontinued.

At the present time Halfway is composed of the school house, one store and filling station, a blacksmith shop, a cotton gin, two churches and several residences.

Edmonson

The town of Edmonson was platted by W. W. Edmonson on August 22, 1929, at the Edmonson Switch on the Fort Worth and Denver Railroad. The train, however, does not stop at Edmonson at the present time, and the Post Office which was moved from Runningwater to Edmonson is supplied by Star Route from Kress. The town consists of two elevators, two grocery stores, and filling stations, a blacksmith shop, several residences and the Post Office. The name of the Runningwater Post Office was changed to Edmonson on February 1, 1937.

Cotton Center

Cotton Center became a community center in 1925 when the Anchor, Norfleet and Bartonsite rural schools were consolidated into an Independent School District, known as the Cotton Center School. It is located twelve miles southwest of Hale Center, in the center of a thriving cotton-farming community, not far from the old Norfleet townsite, on a paved highway leading from Plainview to Littlefield.

A $50,000 school building was erected and school opened

in the fall of 1925 with ten teachers, with G. A. Lowrey as Superintendent. The school at the present time has twenty-one and one-half credits with the State Board of Education and ranks among the best rural schools on the Plains.

The Post Office was established at Cotton Center in September, 1935, with Mrs. E. M. Yates as Postmistress. There are now two gins, a barber shop, a cafe, two garages, a church, school house and several residences at Cotton Center.

Post Offices

The record of Post Offices in Hale County with Roster of Postmasters and dates of their appointments is as follows:

Postmaster	P. O. Date Appointed

EPHRAIM

Ephraim H. Cone.........June 27, 1881 (Established)
Discontinued and mail ordered
sent to Clarendon in Donley
County............................October 24, 1882

EPWORTH

Horatio Graves............June 3, 1884 (Established)
Frank Y. Lincoln...................February 6, 1891
The name of this office was changed
to Hale City............................April 16, 1891

PLAINVIEW

Edwin L. Lowe.........March 18, 1887 (Established)
Thornton Jones...................September 13, 1887
Andrew Vince......................October 25, 1888
John G. Davidson.....................July 30, 1890
James M. Presler.....................April 10, 1893
Jesse C. Burch...................December 14, 1895
Hugh McClelland.....................March 17, 1899
Charles McCormack......................May 11, 1901
James C. Newman...............December 16, 1907
George Keck.....................January 28, 1909
B. O. Sanford.......................June 17, 1913
Ernest E. Spencer (Acting)........February 25, 1919
William P. Stockton...................July 28, 1919
Fred L. Brown (Acting)..........November 19, 1922
Fred L. Brown.....................March 1, 1923
Leroy W. Williamson..............November 17, 1932
John C. Terry (Acting)................April 6, 1933
John C. Terry....................February 15, 1935

SETTLEMENT

Postmaster   *P. O.*   *Date Appointed*

WADSWORTH

Dennis Rice..........December 8, 1890 (Established)
The name of this office was
changed to Runningwater...........January 28, 1891

RUNNINGWATER

Dennis Rice............January 28, 1891 (Established)
Samuel T. Cooper......................May 4, 1893
Stephen T. Stone......................June 6, 1896
Adelbert J. Whitney..............December 19, 1896
Addie Winsor.....................September 30, 1901
Sallie Jones......................November 9, 1903
Taylor Fortenberry..............September 26, 1904
James Anderson.....................January 2, 1906
Charley W. Day....................January 18, 1909
Herbert R. Tarwater..............December 30, 1909
Mrs. Anna L. Meisenheimer...........April 26, 1921
Mrs. Lillian Fortenberry.............August 2, 1923
Changed to Edmonson...............February 1, 1937

HALE CITY

Frank Y. Lincoln........April 16, 1891 (Established)
Horatio Graves.....................October 7, 1891
The name of this office was
changed to Hale Center...........September 19, 1893

CLISBEE

Robert Montgomery......August 3, 1891 (Established)
Thomas C. Scott..................November 16, 1891
Robert W. Montgomery...........November 28, 1892
Samuel A. Spears..................October 30, 1893
T. L. Van Vacter......................July 6, 1894
This office was discontinued.......September 11, 1894
Mail was ordered sent to Hale Center.
This office was re-established.............July 16, 1900
James R. Garrison....................July 16, 1900
This office was discontinued.......September 30, 1901
Mail was ordered sent to Petersburg.

PROGRESS

William P. Long.........April 11, 1892 (Established)
Discontinued.........................May 31, 1898
Mail was ordered sent to Plainview

Postmaster P. O. *Date Appointed*

HALE CENTER

Joseph S. Highsmith..September 19, 1893 (Established)
Andrew J. Oliver.................December 13, 1899
Nils M. Akeson.......................June 2, 1900
Rebecca J. Bridges...................April 24, 1907
Mrs. Artie M. Shepard.............October 28, 1914
Miss Matilda Akeson..............November 18, 1921
Mrs. Carolyn A. Moreman (Acting)....July 20, 1934
Mrs. Carolyn A. Moreman.........February 15, 1935

KENNEBUNK

Mortimore E. Merrill.....Aug. 16, 1894 (Established)
Discontinued...........................June 15, 1896
Mail was ordered sent to Hale Center

PETERSBURG

This office was established as Petersburg in Floyd County.
Margaret Peter......September 29, 1891 (Established)
This office was changed into Hale County................................May 16, 1896
Edwin M. White.....................May 16, 1896
Joseph T. J. Stalcup...............November 1, 1907
George T. Stagner......................July 8, 1908
Henry A. White.................September 18, 1909
John B. Gartin....................February 19, 1912
Mack H. Winningham................March 20, 1913
Elias C. Dean....................December 27, 1915
Robert H. Gregory....................April 10, 1917
H. Oran Martin....................October 31, 1925
Mrs. Maggie Thomas (Acting)....September 23, 1927
Mrs. Maggie Thomas...................April 20, 1928
Floyd A. Eaves (Acting).............October 5, 1936

SPEEDWELL

Lafayette E. Speed........April 12, 1901 (Established)
Discontinued...........................June 30, 1902
Mail ordered sent to Petersburg

COPENHAGEN

Thomas H. Miller..........June 26, 1902 (Established)
John W. Stevens.......................July 15, 1904
The name of this office was changed to
Norfleet................................May 23, 1907

SETTLEMENT

Postmaster   *P. O.*   *Date Appointed*

STRIP

Jerry M. Turner..........April 15, 1904 (Established)
Joseph W. St. Clair................December 28, 1907
This office was discontinued..............July 15, 1910
Mail was ordered sent to Abernathy

ELLEN

Carl W. Richardson........May 20, 1904 (Established)
This office was discontinued...........January 31, 1923
Mail was ordered sent to Plainview.

NORFLEET

John W. Stevens..........May 23, 1907 (Established)
Barnie E. Rushing.................November 16, 1907
James P. Flake........................July 16, 1909
Thomas C. Masterson....................July 21, 1910
John A. Hall.........................April 4, 1911
This office was discontinued..............June 30, 1913
Mail was ordered sent to Hale Center

BARTONSITE

G. M. Reed............February 8, 1908 (Established)
Mrs. Sallie J. Smith..................August 31, 1909
Boswell B. Brown..................December 31, 1913
Oliver C. Harraman................December 12, 1917
Winkfrey M. Garrison.............September 14, 1918
This office was discontinued..............April 15, 1921
Mail was ordered sent to Hale Center

EDENVILLE

Walter J. Dunlap........August 7, 1908 (Established)
Discontinued...........................July 31, 1909
Mail was ordered sent to Eden in Concho County

FREEPORT

Clarence C. Smith..........July 10, 1909 (Established)
This office was discontinued..............May 14, 1910
Mail was ordered sent to Plainview

ABERNATHY

J. M. Anderson........January 13, 1910 (Established)
John C. Arnett.....................December 10, 1910
Arthur G. Gilbert....................January 9, 1923
George W. Ragland (Acting)..........October 1, 1927
George W. Ragland................December 15, 1927

| Postmaster | P. O. | Date Appointed |

HALFWAY

Edgar L. Howard..........May 4, 1910 (Established)
Mrs. Cora B. McComas..............January 30, 1912
William W. Pinkerton................March 21, 1913
This office was discontinued..........January 31, 1914
Mail was ordered sent to Runningwater.

COTTON CENTER

Mrs. Eunice P. Yates......Sept. 25, 1935 (Established)

EDMONSON

Mrs. Lillian Fortenberry......Feb. 1, 1937 (Established)

Home Building

The development in home building and construction of business houses has been in keeping with other phases of progress. Most of the homes built prior to 1890 were dugouts. These were temporal abodes and were forerunners of the wooden houses which at first were in primitive form. The dugout was made with little labor and expense, but was all that the frontier justified, when lands sold for 25¢ per acre. They were warm in winter and cool in summer, served their purpose and gave way to better things. The sod house was a happy improvement, and the plank floor added to its comfort. The pioneers of Hale County were young people full of hope and courage and lived in the future rather than the present, and privations were overlooked in the joy in anticipation of building a new country.

Better homes began to appear in Plainview in the nineties though most of the citizens still lived in dugouts. The first wooden home was the box house, boarded and weatherstripped, sometimes called the "plank house." These usually consisted of two rooms and a lean-to. There were few homes in Hale County having more than four rooms prior to 1908. The coming of the railroad and the immigration of settlers brought about what is known as the little wood bungalow. Several aristocratic homes were built during 1908 having eight and ten rooms and these were the first homes with brick chimneys. In 1909 better houses appeared. The first good farm homes are said to have been built in the Menonite community in the Snyder District. Stucco homes were popular for a period. The building boom abated when the railroad built south from Plainview, but in 1912 new and better rural homes were constructed. Building fluctuated for several years. Then from 1919 to 1929 an extensive building period brought about the modern home with all its improvements. The brick veneer homes in attractive plans and types of architecture became more popular and added to the beauty of the towns and country. The primitive fuel gave way to high priced coal which is now largely replaced by natural gas. The creaking windmill on each town lot has been taken down and city water placed at finger tips. Electricity has replaced the tallow candle, the coal-oil lamp, the washboard and the old flat iron. These modern utilities, gas and electricity, have invaded parts of the rural districts. With the wheels of progress still turning, the rural communities will doubtless soon have access to these improvements.

CHAPTER III

Lands and Land Problems

At the time Texas won her independence from Mexico, she claimed as her western boundary the Rio Grande River and from its head to the 42nd parallel of latitude, and for her eastern boundary the line agreed upon between the United States and Mexico in 1819. When the Republic of Texas was admitted into the union as a state, she retained control of all her vast public domain. By the compromise of 1850, the State of Texas relinquished to the United States for the sum of $10,000,000 all that part of this territory now embraced in the states of New Mexico, Oklahoma, Kansas, Colorado and Wyoming, which amounted to approximately one-third of her area at that time. Since Texas was a slave state, and the Mason and Dixon Line was designated as the dividing line between slave and non-slave states, the northern boundary between the 100th and 103rd meridians was moved south to the parallel of 36° 30′, cutting off that strip of land which lay north of the Mason and Dixon Line, now known as the Oklahoma Panhandle.

To encourage the building of railroads in Texas, a law was passed granting to railroad companies sixteen sections (640 acres each) of land for each mile of railroad built and operated in the state. Scrip calling for required number of certificates was issued to railroad companies granting them the right to select at any place upon the public domain one section of land for each certificate held.

In order to get the school lands surveyed, the state required that the railroad companies survey one section of school land for each section of railroad land they surveyed. Each alternate section was given to the railroads and the other section to the schools, the odd numbered sections being railroad land and the even numbers school land. This checkerboard method of distributing the land was intended to promote the settlement of the country. Furthermore, the railroad companies were compelled to dispose of their grants within a certain time or forfeit their claims. Many of the railroad companies evaded this by selling these certificates through their agents through the middle west, while a few of the railroads formed land companies within themselves and sold the lands to the real estate companies so formed. The cost of the railroad land to the settler was approximately 25¢ per acre when all expenses had been paid. The blocks of land so surveyed were named for the patentee rather than the Township system used in other parts of the United States. Blocks of land in Hale County were issued to and named for the following Railroad Companies: Denison and South Eastern Railway Company, East Line and Red River Railroad Company, Tyler Tap Railway Company, Gulf, Colorado and Santa Fe Railroad Company and the Houston, El Paso and West Texas Railroad Company.

Between the blocks of land surveyed in Hale County by the Railroad Companies or their grantees, there remained several narrow strips of land not included in any surveys. This land was given to settlers for homesteads, 160 acres to each head of a family and eighty acres to each unmarried person who would occupy and cultivate it for three years. At the end of that period a patent was granted upon proof of occupancy. A Pre-emption Law permitted a settler to "pre-empt" land, live on it one year, pay $1.25 per acre for it and receive a patent. The first homesteads to be filed upon in Hale County were those of Z. T. Maxwell and E. L. Lowe in 1886, who afterwards pre-empted the land and secured title within one year. In a few years all homestead lands were taken.

An Act of the Legislature provided that four leagues of land out of the public domain should be reserved for each county for free school purposes. As a county was organized, that county was allowed to select four leagues of land at any place where sufficient unappropriated land could be found. Four leagues of land lying in the southwestern part of Hale County was given to Sabine County and two leagues in the southeastern part of the county with two leagues adjoining them in Floyd County were given to Callahan County. Hale County's school lands are located in Bailey County.

The distribution of the public domain made by the State of Texas, as shown by the Report of the Commissioner of the General Land Office 1934-1936, is as follows:

Distribution of the Public Domain

	Acres
Grants by Spain and Mexico	26,280,000
The State University, by the Republic	221,400
The State University (1876) Constitution	1,000,000
The State University (1883) Legislature	1,000,000
Kiamasha Road	27,000
To build the Capitol	3,050,000
Parker County Courthouse	320
Palo Pinto County Courthouse	320
San Jacinto Veteran donation	1,169,382
Disabled Confederates	1,979,852
To Pay Public Debt	1,660,936
Homestead donations (preemption)	4,847,136
Internal Improvements (irrigation, etc.)	4,061,000
Counties for school purposes	4,229,166
Headright and bounties	36,876,492
Colonies (Peters, Mercer, et al.)	4,494,806
Railroads	32,153,878
Asylums (four)	400,000
Public Free School	42,400,556
Total surveyed	165,852,244
Estimated Area	170,936,080

The state school lands were placed on the market first at $1 per acre with thirty years to pay for it, one person being allowed to purchase seven sections, however, some of the large ranchers who desired large bodies of land secured Power of Attorney from their relatives and friends and acquired control of large tracts of land to the exclusion of the actual settlers.

The state school lands in Hale County were first classified as Agricultural Land and placed on the market at $2 per acre on forty years time with 5 per cent interest on deferred payments, each person being allowed to purchase only one section. This law was made by the State Legislators in other parts of the state who wished to promote the settlement of the region of the Staked Plains and Panhandle which had been made habitable by the exit of the Indians in 1874. These terms of sale seemed liberal to the legislators at the time but when settlers began to actually occupy the land they were faced with the uncertainty of farming in a new country where no transportation facilities provided an outlet for the industry and they were

LANDS AND LAND PROBLEMS

forced to turn to cattle-raising as their principal means of livelihood. One section of land proved inadequate for the grazing of sufficient cattle to make a living for a family and to meet the payments of interest and principal on the land.

During the early nineties, drouth and a plague of grasshoppers swept the plains; settlers failed to make crops and the grass was insufficient for the cattle. Many people were forced to leave the country, while others stayed on with their holdings and fought to work out their problems.

Through the efforts of Senator D. F. Goss, of Seymour, an extension of the payment of interest was effected in 1893. This, however, afforded only temporary relief. In 1895 Senator Goss attempted to achieve further relief for the Plains settlers, but legislators over the state were unfamiliar with the existing conditions and all he was able to accomplish was to secure a reduction in the rate of interest from 5 to 3 per cent for grazing land. This afforded no relief to the plainsmen since their land was classed as Agricultural land.

Having agreed among themselves that four sections of land was a reasonable acreage to enable a settler to keep enough livestock to live on, and that $2 per acre was too high a price for land to be used for grazing purposes, the people of the Staked Plains and Panhandle united in an effort to secure more favorable legislation, and Col. R. P. Smyth, of Plainview, was elected as Representative from the Panhandle District to the State Legislature.

Being thoroughly familiar with every phase of the problem, and knowing the minds of his people, Colonel Smyth went to the Legislature in 1897 with plans definitely formulated. His first action was to call a caucus of the western members to consider the changes he wished to make in the Goss Land Bill which was then before the House. This Bill attempted certain changes in the school land laws but which would provide little relief. The most important Amendment the Colonel wished to make was to permit a settler to buy school land without regard to any lease by the state upon the land. This Amendment the western members absolutely refused to grant, but they finally agreed to pass such an amendment to apply only to the Panhandle District of 36 counties. When this point had been settled and many pledges given to support the new bill, the Colonel contacted Senator Goss, and an agreement was reached by which the frame work of the Goss Land Bill was retained but all objectionable provisions were stricken out and the new provisions proposed were substituted. By this means the co-operation of Senator Goss was secured in passing it through the Senate.

The new provisions included the following: (a) The purchase by a settler of a school section without regard to any lease upon the land; (b) provision that a settler could buy four sections, three of which must be within five miles of his home section, and that if at any time the settler was financially unable to carry one or more of the additional sections he could surrender same to the state and his obligations for same would be canceled; (c) that the Commissioners Court of each county should classify the land in their respective counties; (d) that the terms of sale should be one-fortieth paid in cash and the balance in forty years with 3% interest on the deferred payments.

The Attorney General was asked to rewrite the Bill to include the changes agreed upon between Colonel Smyth and Senator Goss. Before the Bill came to a vote in the House, the Colonel secured the consent of members south of his district to move the line which was afterwards popularly known as the "Absolute Lease Line" two counties south, thus placing all counties north of the south line of Lynn County in the territory where the school land was to be leased subject to sale to settlers. This change was made when the Bill came up for final passage in the House, April 29, 1897, where it passed by a unanimous vote. Thus came into being the FOUR SECTION ACT which led to the settlement of the Plains.

All those who had bought school land at $2. per acre under the one section law forfeited their lands. The Commissioners Court of Hale County promptly reclassified the lands as Grazing Land, automatically reducing the price to $1 per acre, and all who had faith in the country and vision to foresee its future values bought four sections each. In a short time after the passing of the Four Section Act, a flood of immigrants came into Hale County and soon the public school lands were all taken up.

LANDS AND LAND PROBLEMS

Distribution of Hale County Land

Original Grants to:	Acres
Railroads	272,049
State School Fund	336,292
Homesteads and Pre-emptions	26,877
War Benefits	3,332
Callahan County School Fund	7,117
Sabine County School Fund	17,373
Total	663,040

Early Land Owners

In order to show the names of as many of the early settlers as possible, a list of the original purchasers of school land and those who filed on homesteads is given below.

Purchaser	Date of Sale	Purchaser	Date of Sale
J. E. Perry	2-21-1890	Alexander Thomas	9-3-1890
W. B. Ford	8-13-1890	J. W. Cox	3-4-1890
Miss Willie Baker	10-16-1891	C. C. Wilkerson	8-5-1890
J. T. Matsler	6-19-1890	J. E. Cox	3-24-1890
W. P. Long	12-2-1890	Wm. W. Humble	2-27-1890
J. B. Neil	7-5-1890	Wm. Lilwall	7-31-1890
J. W. Swink	8-13-1891	J. A. Hooper	3-1-1890
R. D. McCallester	11-14-1891	R. W. O'Keefe	11-12-1889
J. H. Portwood	4-27-1891	A. P. Hill	7-14-1890
J. S. Ray	1-16-1891	W. M. Chandler	9-16-1892
J. F. Ray, Jr.	3-9-1891	J. S. Highsmith	8-12-1890
J. R. Gollaher	4-1-1892	Alex Jones	9-19-1890
L. L. Bush	11-23-1891	G. H. Durham	6-27-1890
M. Stone & P. B. Oats	12-10-1891	C. H. Polen	11-28-1890
W. H. Perdue	6-15-1891	T. L. Pearson	1-12-1891
J. W. Gallant	1-5-1892	W. R. Ferguson	12-13-1890
W. S. Helm	4-5-1892	D. B. Stingily	12-1-1890
Percy L. Robinson	2-12-1892	W. M. Irby	9-15-1890
G. Lohmann	4-1-1892	J. E. Fitzgerald	8-8-1890
E. L. Hardin	5-4-1892	M. J. Ewalt	12-2-1891
C. R. M. Floyd	7-1-1892	J. T. Hill	10-14-1890
L. A. Donaldson	5-7-1892	H. B. Schoonmaker	7-10-1890
Wm. M. Pumphrey	5-14-1892	Harry Austin	4-4-1892
Edwin N. Welter	4-1-1892	Elizabeth Ledbetter	8-25-1891
W. P. Herbert	7-17-1890	W. A. Harral	8-29-1890
A. R. McCriston	9-1-1890	J. R. Harral	8-29-1890
J. D. Green	10-6-1890	R. M. Morris	3-3-1890
J. C. White	3-1-1890	J. A. Phillips	10-2-1891
J. W. Smylie	1-23-1891	W. R. Norfleet	4-17-1893
W. R. Hampton	10-8-1892	W. M. Owens	10-30-1891

HISTORY OF HALE COUNTY, TEXAS

Purchaser	Date of Sale	Purchaser	Date of Sale
W. E. Ivey	4-3-1890	F. L. Blanchard	1-2-1891
J. H. Calvert	3-1-1890	J. V. Matlock	1-5-1891
C. Stone	9-2-1890	A. W. Powers	3-6-1891
S. B. Fannin	8-8-1890	A. D. Hooper	3-4-1892
J. L. Crawford	9-24-1891	M. D. Evans	12-17-1890
W. M. Stone	8-7-1890	Wm. Onyett	4-23-1892
R. A. Hudgins	9-2-1890	J. S. Evans	5-7-1892
D. P. Waggoner	8-8-1890	H. Y. Morrow	5-7-1893
E. S. Renfro	3-1-1892	W. N. Claxton	6-28-1892
N. P. Giles	12-1-1891	D. F. Webb	5-20-1893
F. Browning	8-12-1891	Frank Sageser	12-27-1892
C. H. Van Horn	10-20-1890	Anderson Carter	8-6-1892
W. C. Thomason	8-14-1890	C. H. Marshall	11-6-1890
J. C. Renfrow	4-18-1890	W. E. Helm	11-21-1890
Robt. Montgomery	5-11-1891	I. J. Helm	11-8-1890
J. H. Reed	11-24-1890	A. J. Baker	9-26-1892
W. L. Harrington	8-24-1891	W. D. Robinson	5-4-1892
J. S. Cook	8-24-1891	J. H. Meeks	5-2-1892
Chas. Craft	2-18-1891	J. H. Denson	5-4-1892
W. E. Craft	2-6-1891	E. E. Burden	9-9-1891
W. L. Carry	4-4-1891	G. L. Mayfield	7-4-1892
W. B. Woodruff	1-30-1893	W. P. Ewing	9-9-1891
B. F. Hatchell	3-19-1892	Oscar Hinde	5-25-1891
B. M. Hatchell	2-4-1892	N. Smith	12-28-1891
John Glynn	2-12-1892	J. W. Ivey	8-5-1891
R. C. Hampton	9-3-1892	H. B. Carpenter	9-11-1891
T. M. Lattimore	12-10-1891	W. H. Ragland	9-1-1891
R. V. Jones	12-26-1890	T. Ivey	8-5-1891
W. P. Blake	9-8-1891	W. W. Hassell	12-28-1891
Chas. Scott	12-12-1890	J. W. Reedy	9-1-1891
I. M. Harkey	9-26-1890	A. L. Maupin	2-12-1891
Jno. A. Cassidy	12-20-1890	J. B. Vanvacter	10-1-1891
R. B. Corneuls	7-22-1890	Jno. W. Moore	1-3-1891
J. E. Bryan	8-22-1890	O. Young	4-13-1893
R. C. Ware	12-13-1890	Jo Ray	1-16-1891
N. J. Herbert	10-6-1890	A. L. King	2-21-1891
J. R. True	7-18-1890	W. J. Addo	4-2-1891
I. M. Sowder	4-4-1892	G. C. Sharp	5-6-1891
P. A. Alverson	6-24-1890	Sam T. Ray	1-19-1891
T. W. Canterberry	6-25-1891	R. L. Hooper	4-30-1892
M. A. Merrell	8-30-1890	J. L. Moore	6-11-1892
J. W. Anderson	9-23-1892	W. S. Potter	5-20-1893
W. L. McGehee	12-4-1890	J. E. Ogden	2-11-1892
A. C. Cooper	3-6-1893	Alice Rosser	2-1-1890
G. M. Slaughter	2-2-1891	J. E. Roberts	11-11-1890
W. W. Cooper	5-8-1893	D. L. Baker	7-28-1893
J. S. Boren	5-12-1892	R. E. Snider	4-22-1891

LANDS AND LAND PROBLEMS 37

Purchaser	Date of Sale	Purchaser	Date of Sale
J. L. Blake	8-8-1891	T. H. Miller	1-7-1892
M. L. Landers	12-29-1890	G. H. Morris	9-10-1890
J. T. Landers	8-17-1891	L. A. White	8-8-1889
T. N. McDaniel	1-18-1892	W. T. Lay	9-1-1890
B. F. Kendall	2-12-1891	J. E. Whitmire	8-8-1889
A. T. Howell, Jr.	8-29-1890	F. G. Hudgins	8-25-1890
C. F. Shirley	2-4-1893	F. M. Lester	8-8-1889
W. B. Sheffy	6-30-1893	Jno. E. McEntire	8-15-1890
M. T. Wilson	2-12-1891	J. J. Hamilton	8-8-1890
P. H. Pearson	8-7-1891	L. T. Lester	8-8-1890
J. T. Haynes, Jr.	8-20-1891	W. M. Roberts	12-10-1890
J. T. Haynes, Sr.	12-7-1891	J. J. Barton	2-12-1892
J. A. Jackson	8-7-1891	Richard C. Barton	10-13-1891
J. L. McWilliams	12-4-1894	J. R. Porterfield	8-26-1892
W. H. Ragle, Jr.	1-16-1891	Mrs. Julia A. Barton	10-13-1891
J. E. Hood	9-9-1891	Ed Miller	3-11-1892
Kate Cannon	3-31-1888	M. L. Hatchell	4-18-1892
A. Jones	7-15-1890	H. Vantrees	8-21-1891
L. G. Wilson	11-22-1889	J. H. Hooper	3-4-1892
Crawford Greer	6-10-1893	Eugene Hixon	12-18-1890
W. C. Hill	7-30-1892	J. M. Robinson	4-11-1891
Gust Nelson	7-16-1890	G. Lehman	12-27-1890
T. V. Overhuls	8-18-1890	E. Nixon	12-18-1890
T. W. Morrison	9-7-1889	T. R. Bruce	9-20-1890
W. J. Tidwell	3-22-1890	J. T. Hewlett	9-16-1890
M. D. Hadden	6-20-1890	E. M. McGaugh	8-12-1890
J. E. Peters	4-5-1890	H. Hancock	3-26-1891
J. J. Blythe	6-24-1890	E. J. Roberts	12-12-1890
D. C. Lowe	2-1-1890	Lee Duvall	1-2-1891
Thos. Wilson	5-10-1894	S. T. Cooper	3-6-1893
A. E. Moore	4-10-1890	G. M. Slaughter	12-13-1892
Geo. W. Dismuke	5-17-1890	J. O. Brown	5-30-1893
W. A. Ambler	12-15-1891	D. C. Shelton	2-20-1892
H. J. Pipkin	9-22-1890	J. H. Leaverton	4-22-1892
M. D. Leach	5-15-1890	John Hobbs	9-13-1890
Joel H. Snider	5-31-1890	J. W. Ray	9-13-1890
J. T. Smyer	9-15-1890	Geo. E. Vallade	3-1-1890
J. Q. Turner	6-14-1890	J. E. Walker	5-17-1890
A. D. Wallen	6-16-1890	J. E. Kendall	10-10-1891
C. L. Stone	9-2-1890	R. L. Meyers	12-16-1890
Wm. Morley	8-12-1889	J. M. Presler	10-4-1890
D. L. Shepley	8-8-1889	J. T. Omalier	3-11-1890
A. D. Shepley	8-9-1890	W. H. Morrison	7-31-1890
I. M. Harkey	9-18-1889	C. C. Quillin	12-4-1890
G. D. Allen	8-28-1889	C. E. Epps	8-11-1890
A. E. Allen	8-19-1890	J. L. Waits	12-13-1890
G. W. Baker	8-8-1889	W. F. Hicks	2-7-1891

Purchaser	Date of Sale	Purchaser	Date of Sale
H. R. Isbell	8-8-1895	T. C. Scott	1-2-1891
Seat Turner	11-18-1890	J. W. Baker	8-13-1890
W. O. Morton	10-16-1890	J. M. Upshaw	4-14-1893
W. C. Reagan	8-15-1892	Robt. M. Hood	9-9-1891
Ike Hendley	9-8-1891	C. L. Groff	2-4-1890
J. H. Davis	12-30-1890	M. E. Rosser	8-31-1891
J. V. Allen	5-8-1892	A. E. Adams	2-3-1890
H. G. Wynn	5-28-1891	W. S. Young	2-3-1890
E. M. Harp	5-2-1892	S. P. Strong	4-11-1890
T. R. Alexander	11-21-1890	T. G. Nance	6-28-1890
E. L. Philips	7-22-1890	A. J. Triplett	9-1-1891
M. L. Bryant	7-3-1890	Ed Duncan	8-25-1890
J. J. Browder	5-24-1890	E. W. Dyer	6-18-1893
W. A. Truss	10-20-1890	W. J. Donohoo	11-9-1895
J. K. Haynes	3-26-1890		

Homesteads

Surveyed for:	Date Surveyed	Surveyed for:	Date Surveyed
Ed L. Lowe	5-21-1887	Joshua Pendley	11-8-1888
Z. T. Maxwell	5-21-1887	A. L. Conkling	11-10-1888
Poliet Smith	2-20-1888	C. F. Conkling	11-10-1888
W. H. Portwood	2-20-1888	T. B. Leverett	11-10-1888
Mrs. M. A. Lowe	2-22-1888	J. M. Carter	11-21-1888
H. L. Griffin	3-29-1888	John Pendley	12-11-1888
W. P. Griffin	3-29-1888	S. C. Lewis	12-11-1888
Horace Griffin	3-29-1888	J. W. Smylie	12-12-1888
A. J. Welter	3-4-1888	Hugh McClelland	2-13-1889
T. E. Smith	6-22-1888	John Pendley	4-13-1889
Chas. E. McClelland	6-22-1888	Wm. M. Pendley	4-14-1889
J. C. Burch	7-24-1888	Chas. Pendley	4-14-1889
Hugh Burch	7-26-1888	F. M. Bradford	4-19-1889
I. G. Bowman	7-10-1888	Ed Miller	4-22-1889
Thomas Beard	7-13-1888	Lizzie Whitcher	5-9-1889
Jno. A. Bell	7-20-1888	A. H. Hanson	5-9-1889
E. F. Graham	7-21-1888	H. I. Formway	7-30-1889
J. C. Glenn	7-23-1888	J. M. Snider	7-31-1889
C. H. Harlan	7-23-1888	R. E. Snider	7-31-1889
Sterling P. Leach	7-24-1888	J. T. Chapman	8-1-1889
Chas. J. Mapes	7-25-1888	W. E. Stewart	8-19-1889
J. S. Vaughn	7-30-1888	D. L. Baker	10-21-1889
R. A. Ford	8-9-1888	B. L. Spencer	10-22-1889
W. H. Bryan	8-30-1888	Christian Sander	10-22-1889
Jas. H. Bryan	8-30-1888	J. M. Rosser	12-10-1889
Polk Bryan	8-30-1888	Eli Barks	12-21-1889
J. B. Leach	10-9-1888	Andrew Vince	1-29-1890
M. D. Leach	10-9-1888	Will Bradford	2-8-1890

LANDS AND LAND PROBLEMS 39

Surveyed for:	Date Surveyed	Surveyed for:	Date Surveyed
G. E. Smith	2-10-1890	L. Lee Dye	3-24-1895
Isaac McCormick	2-18-1890	W. B. Ford	3-4-1891
R. M. Crump	2-17-1890	W. M. Glover	2-8-1893
E. J. Turner	2-17-1890	M. D. Glover	2-8-1893
L. S. Kinder	3-12-1890	D. P. Goodwin	5-3-1893
R. G. Oldham	3-13-1890	John Glynn	1-24-1893
R. Holland	6-18-1890	W. V. Hobbs	4-7-1893
J. O. Brown	4-14-1890	A. A. Hobbs	4-7-1893
Tom Murphy	6-24-1890	J. D. Hobbs	4-7-1893
J. H. Garrison	4-15-1890	J. V. Hobbs	4-7-1893
Lee Murphy	7-24-1890	R. F. Hobbs	1-8-1893
J. E. Whitman	10-10-1890	John Kiser	9-12-1889
W. S. Foster	10-10-1890	M. E. Lemaster	2-4-1891
S. L. Tucker	10-9-1890	F. J. Lemaster	2-4-1891
J. H. Dunagan	10-23-1890	R. C. Lemaster	2-15-1891
P. S. Green	10-9-1890	D. A. Meridith	1-27-1891
F. M. Drake	10-29-1890	C. J. Mapes	10-17-1891
J. P. Lattimore	10-29-1890	W. B. Martine	10-16-1891
E. A. Glover	11-1-1890	D. R. McVicker	9-3-1891
E. F. Williams	7-29-1890	S. M. Nations	5-29-1891
L. G. Hoffman	7-26-1890	J. F. Owens	8-29-1891
R. W. Martine	2-28-1891	J. B. Oswald	1-5-1892
J. H. Potter	6-17-1890	J. M. Presler	8-8-1891
S. D. Lemaster	6-3-1890	C. C. Pendley	7-11-1891
Poliet Smith	4-15-1890	W. H. Portwood	4-16-1892
J. P. Ogden	10-6-1890	H. J. Pipkin	5-25-1892
W. V. Ogden	10-6-1890	A. B. Rosser	8-27-1891
M. M. Starkey	12-24-1890	B. L. Ray	1-18-1895
J. W. Christie	1-21-1891	J. M. Shafer	1-28-1891
A. L. Conkling	1-27-1891	W. W. Snell	8-29-1893
C. F. Conkling	1-27-1891	I. B. Shelton	10-8-1892
R. A. Rosson	1-29-1891	J. B. Shelton	10-8-1892
John McNeil	2-2-1891	G. W. Shelton	10-8-1892
J. F. Norfleet	3-26-1895	W. A. Shelton	10-8-1892
C. T. Merrick	12-15-1891	I. A. Shelton	5-29-1893
E. J. Beard	3-27-1891	J. P. Toney	10-14-1891
H. M. Burch	12-14-1891	L. Vallade	12-9-1893
R. E. Burch	12-14-1891	E. L. Vallade	3-31-1892
J. A. Brewster	10-15-1891	M. C. Vallade	3-31-1892
A. J. Brewster	10-15-1891	Ed M. White	2-28-1896
Oscar Bryan	1-18-1892	S. A. White	2-28-1896
J. H. Bryan	9-19-1891	J. E. White	2-28-1896
W. H. Bryan	9-19-1891	H. A. White	2-28-1896
H. A. Counts	10-15-1891	Hamilton West	10-14-1892

CHAPTER IV

INDUSTRIAL AND AGRICULTURAL DEVELOPMENT

Cattle and Dairy Industry

For a quarter of a century, cattle-raising was the only profitable industry of Hale County. The open range afforded free grazing for the stock and when the waters of the streams which then drained the vast prairies proved inadequate, windmills were erected and water was pumped from deep wells into great earthen tanks.

The cattle industry began in Hale County in 1881 when Morrison Brothers started a ranch at Runningwater with a herd of Cross L cattle brought from Old Clarendon. The first cattle were of the Longhorn variety. They were not the original Spanish "Texas Longhorn," whose horns measured from six to eight feet from tip to tip; nevertheless the Cross L cattle had ample means to protect them from the coyotes and they were endowed by nature with all the instincts of self-preservation.

In 1883, white faced cattle brought from the Lazy S Ranch at Big Springs displaced the Cross L Longhorns when C. C. Slaughter and Morrison Brothers and Johnson started the Circle Bar Ranch with ten thousand head of cattle. As a range stock the Herefords ranked high. They were hardy and stood well the strain of the long drives on the trail to market, were not too wild, and were possessed with the instincts that made them good rustlers and enabled them to weather the storms.

The small herds of the early settlers grazed at large upon the open range before the advent of the wire fences. The cattle were often driven by storms and winds as far west as the Pecos River in New Mexico, or as far southeast as the Blanco Canyon, mingling together in one great herd. There they often remained until round up season when the owners joined forces in gathering up their stock. Brands were then

AGRICULTURAL DEVELOPMENT 41

segregated and the calves branded and the cattle were taken in a herd up the trail to Dodge City, Kansas, to market.

When the county's first settler came in 1882, he brought two milk cows from New York for domestic use. He had been told that there was not a cow in Texas that could be milked, which report was more or less true, especially as regarded the Panhandle-Plains cattle. In 1889, another settler in the Hale Center community brought two registered Jersey cows from Ohio. There was no market for dairy products, however, and the butter and cheese made from the Jersey cream was useless beyond the family's own needs.

In 1901 Clements Brothers established the first dairy in Hale County on the farm of W. C. Clements, one mile east of Plainview, with a few range cows, for the purpose of selling milk only. The cows grazed on the open range as there were no fences at that time. Grain sorghums supplemented the prairie grasses for feed in time of storms, but was used only in emergencies. The milk was brought to town in buckets with a hack drawn by mules. An old school bell heralded the coming of the "milk man" and the housewives came out with their pails or pitchers to get their daily supply of milk. Buttermilk and clabber were in equal demand with sweet milk, for light-bread had not yet come into popularity and every housewife was accomplished in the art of biscuit-making.

There were no sanitary regulations or testing of cows until 1911, at which time Dr. I. E. Barr, of Lockney, became the county's first Sanitary Officer. At his orders the milk houses were screened and equipped with concrete floors. In 1912 milk bottles first came into use. The Clements dairy, then composed of thirty-seven milk cows, was sold to Mitchell Dunaway in 1913, who in turn sold it to C. B. Rees in 1919. Mr. Rees was the first to Pasteurize milk in Hale County.

The Plainview Creamery was started in 1902 when J. N. Morrison began the manufacture of the first commercial ice cream. Mr. Morrison had started a bottling works the year before, and the ice cream was added. He purchased all the cream and milk that was produced by the farmers in the country. Until the coming of the railroad five years later, the ice cream was shipped by stage to Lubbock, Tulia, Floydada, Emma, Matador and other points as the mail carrier traveled to the post offices on his route. In 1913 Mr. Morrison began the manufacture of butter as a means of utilizing sour cream, and in this way all the milk and cream available from the farms was used, the output of the creamery being limited only to the raw products in the country. The people in the community did not readily accept creamery butter and for many years there was much prejudice against its use locally. Therefore the entire output was shipped to Amarillo, Kansas City, St. Louis, Chicago, Fort Worth, El Paso and New Orleans. Mr. Morrison operated the Plainview Creamery until 1926, when the plant was sold and the creamery was discontinued.

The development of the dairy industry began on the Plains in 1921 when S. A. Guy started a dairy at Crosbyton with high grade Jersey cattle which he imported from the Isle of Jersey. For some of these cattle Mr. Guy paid as high as $10,000 and $25,000 each. From this herd of high-grade imported Jersey cattle began the dairy industry on the Plains.

In the spring of 1923, the First National Bank of Plainview financed the purchase of eleven high grade registered animals which were sold to the breeders in Hale County, and interest in better dairy cattle was further enhanced.

The Hale County Dairy Association was organized at Hale Center in April, 1923, by Wayne Thomas, County Agricultural Agent. This Association, composed of eight members, originally operated as a shipping association for the marketing of cream and sold cream on the highest bids to the various creameries in Texas, Oklahoma and Kansas, until March, 1929, when a creamery was built at Plainview for the manufacture of butter. 365,000 lbs. of butter was made during the first year that the creamery was operated.

In 1930 a cheese factory was opened at Abernathy in connection with the creamery as an experiment. This was more or less disappointing during the first year, and the operator was inclined to be discouraged. But in 1931, a Mr. Wilson, from Washington, D. C., came to Hale County and proved that cheese could be successfully made on the Plains. After working for a week with the plant at Abernathy, the plant was making a grade of cheese that was accepted on the markets and since that time they have been unable to supply the markets.

DON MISCHIEF 10th, Grand Champion, Iowa State Fair at Des Moines, Iowa, Aug. 27-Sept. 14, 1937 (ten states in competition), Kansas Free State Fair, Topeka, Kansas, Sept. 13-18, 1937, and Minnesota State Fair, St. Paul, Minn., Sept. 4-11, 1937. Don Mischief 10th, calved August 1, 1934, is a Hale County product, grown by Fred Weyl near Plainview.

In 1932 the Hale County Dairy Association was changed to the Plains Cooperative Incorporated, which was a consolidation of a small creamery at Ralls and a cream shipping association at Portales, New Mexico, with the creamery at Plainview. Since this consolidation, the average output has been a million and a quarter pounds of butter per year. The Association erected a second creamery at Portales, New Mexico, in 1933. It now operates cream receiving stations in thirty-five different towns on the Plains of Texas and New Mexico and handles a gross volume each year of about $365,000 business. The manufactured butter is sold principally in Texas, New Mexico and Arizona and some in California.

It is estimated that about one-third or one-fourth of the creamery butter made in Texas is made on the Plains. The Plains region is the one section in Texas that exports butter twelve months in the year. The improvement in the quality of cream and butter has been in keeping with the progress made in the development of the high-grade dairy herds.

The Breeders Extension Service of the A. & M. College and the County Agricultural Agents of the various counties interested the cattlemen in organizing a Dairy Association at a meeting called for that purpose at Tulia on November 19, 1927. This organization was perfected in December of that year under the name of the Annual Panhandle-Plains Dairy Show. These annual dairy shows have been held in Plainview each year since 1928, and have been an important factor in educating the dairymen as to the individual merits of the animals shown. Much benefit has resulted from the advice and help of fellow-breeders. Tests made by the American Jersey Cattle Association as to protein and butter fat content has enabled the dairymen to eliminate animals of low value from the herds.

The program on which the dairymen are now concentrating is general improvement in the grade and price rather than on quantity; however, there is still room for many more dairy cattle on the Plains. The greatest development in the dairy industry has taken place from 1927 to 1933. Since then general conditions have retarded the progress somewhat, but regardless of the drouth and depression, Hale County and plains dairymen have maintained the high standard of the herd.

The new program for soil conservation offers strong encouragement for the dairy industry, for the land taken from the production of surplus crops may be used advantageously for the grazing of dairy cattle. The grass which supplies excellent feed for the cattle also pins down the top soil and prevents soil erosion from the wind. The dairymen have found that the Plains which once was the range for the great herds of buffalo and for the early range cattle is especially adapted to the dairy industry.

Early Minor Industries

Minor and temporary industries prevailed for a time during the early days, such as the bone industry, when the buffalo bones that strewed the prairies were gathered up by the settlers, freighted 150 miles to Colorado City or 90 miles to Amarillo by wagon load and sold to be shipped to eastern markets to be ground into fertilizer. The buffalo bones brought $20 per ton at railroad terminals, and afforded the settlers with ready cash to supply their needs. The taming of the wild horses was another remunerative but short lived industry, and soon all the wild droves had been gathered and driven by trail to the markets. Some of the early settlers owned herds of sheep, which were quite successful on the plains; however, cattle-raising appealed to a much larger number of citizens.

The first settler raised no cattle, but experimented with farming on the newly broken sod. His efforts proved successful and his sorghum grains beyond his needs were readily sold to the cattlemen for use in time of storms. Farming began on a small scale on the homesteads around Plainview, where the settlers experimented with garden stuffs and grain sorghums for their own use only. The cattlemen did not try farm or raise gardens. In fact, they had contempt for the industry and resented any deviation from what they considered the only legitimate industry on the plains.

A Changing Era

At the coming of the railroad into Plainview on January 1, 1907, a new era was ushered in. Simultaneously with the advent of the railway the automobile first made its appearance.

AGRICULTURAL DEVELOPMENT

Hale County had progressed considerably during the twenty-five years prior to that time. The top buggy and surry had displaced the side-saddle and the two-wheel cart as modes of transportation, though the covered wagon was still in use.

A healthy boom started in 1907 and lasted for several years. A flood of immigrants poured in from all parts of the United States, and these, like the earlier settlers, were the best class of citizens, homeseekers, intelligent and industrious, who have done much for the development of the country.

Real estate dealers brought several automobiles into the country to convey the prospectors about the country. Railroad companies cooperated by giving special excursion rates to homeseekers, and prospectors were brought in by train loads. The price of land jumped rapidly, and many of the newcomers began speculating in land when they found they could make more money by buying and selling land than they could produce by farming the land.

Beginning of Agriculture

As the early ranchmen were not interested in farming, the industry was given but little attention during the year 1907. Until that time farming was limited almost entirely to the growing of milo maize and kafir corn. Crops planted on the newly broken sod required no cultivation as there were no weeds in the soil. It was the custom to allow the land to revert to grass after the first year's use and to plow a fresh piece of sod for the next crop in order to avoid the necessity of cultivation. No further attention was given the crop after planting until the harvest, and this made it possible to tend a much larger acreage than could be done under cultivation.

In 1908 there was shipped from Plainview 1400 cars of cattle, 15 cars of hogs, 30 cars of grain and 3 cars of wheat. These were not entirely Hale County's products, but included shipments from adjoining counties.

Period of Experimentation

The ten years following the coming of the railroad was an era of experimentation. The people who came from farming regions of the north and east began to plant and to cultivate the crops to which they were accustomed. They found that such crops could be successfully grown, and soon experiments were made in the growing of practically every known field crop, fruit and vegetable.

In 1909 Hale County's first entry in the State Fair was awarded first prize. This was one bale of alfalfa, and the people were elated. It stimulated interest in the raising of prize products, and in 1910 the Annual County Fair was inaugurated. Large displays were also entered at the Panhandle Fair in Amarillo as well as at the State Fair in Dallas.

In 1911 Hale County entered 26 exhibits at the State Fair and was awarded 19 first and 7 second prizes. In 1912 the record was 36 firsts and 16 seconds. 1913 entries brought 70 awards, being 37 firsts and 33 seconds. These prizes were awarded for exhibits in wheat, oats, speltz, alfalfa, millet, sorghum, milo maize, kafir corn, cow pea hay, tobacco, flax seed, buckwheat, mill products, potatoes, sweet potatoes, beets, sugar beets, beans, parsnips, carrots, kershaw and winter squash, watermelons, canteloupes, Bermuda onions, turnips, peppers and many varieties of apples, pears and peaches. During the five years,—1909 to 1913 inclusive,—alfalfa hay held first place at the Dallas Fair.

In 1913 the County was awarded first place at Oklahoma City over an exhibit collected by the Great Northern Railroad from five northwestern states, including an exhibit from the national government of Canada.

In 1915 Hale County was awarded the Gold Medal offered by the International Dry Farming Congress in Denver for the best bushel of hard winter wheat. This wheat was grown by the dry-farming method by Fred Weyl eight miles south of Plainview and an average yield of forty bushels per acre was made on an eighty acre field. This prize was won in competition with the products of all the counties, provinces and states of the world. Hale County was awarded 114 premiums out of 120 entries, being 50 firsts, 38 seconds, 18 thirds, 7 medals, a certificate of honor and the Holt Cup which was awarded for the best county display in the world.

Perhaps the opinion of the general public at that time, as well as that of the reader hereof, may be expressed in the words of a German farmer from Iowa who attended the Panhandle Fair in Amarillo in 1913. Hale County had been awarded first place in irrigated districts and sweepstakes over all displays. The Secretary of Plainview's Chamber of Commerce, O. M. Unger, noticed the farmer leaning on his elbow scrutinizing Hale County's display. Approaching him in conversation, Mr. Unger informed him that Hale County had also raised a large number of fine thoroughbred hogs.

"I don't doubt dat," commented the German. Waving his hand toward the exhibits,—"From de looks o' dese ribbons, I tink you must be all hogs in Hale County."

At the advent of the World War, experimentation ceased and farming became more settled, and was limited to the growing of staple crops and those best adapted to the country.

High Power Production

The ten year period from 1918 to 1928 may be classed as an era of high power production. The manufacturers of high power machinery had perfected their inventions made primarily for the development of the vast domain in Western Canada. Having supplied that market, they were seeking a new outlet for an increased output, and turned to the farming district of the prairies of West Texas. The high prices of farm products, the shortage of man power on the farms during the war, and high price of farm labor immediately following all helped to speed the coming of the tractor and paved the way for the wave of high-power farming that swept the country.

The tractor first made its appearance in Hale County in 1918 and in the year following it came into general use. The same year the first harvester-combine was brought into the county when three McCormick-Deering combines were introduced. With this machine which cuts the wheat, threshes it and pours the grain into a truck ready for market as it moves through the field, the old method that entailed so many laborers and much time and work rapidly gave way to the new.

At the present time there are from six to eight hundred harvester-combines in use in the county. More than fifty per cent of all farming and probably eighty per cent of the wheat grown in Hale County is done by tractor. There is scarcely any limit to the amount of acreage a capable man can handle by tractor if he has the means to finance it.

The years following 1928 have been a reaction to the era of high power farming. The cycle turned downward when men realized that the machine had usurped their jobs.

Irrigation

The outstanding achievement of the period of experimentation was the discovery and development of irrigation.

During the year 1910, members of the Plainview Chamber of Commerce became interested in the successful irrigation experiments that were made in the region around Portales, New Mexico, and a committee of men were sent to Portales to make investigation. The business men, led by J. O. Wyckoff, President of the organization, then entered into a contract with J. H. Slaton to drill a test well on his farm a few miles west of Plainview, Mr. Slaton agreeing to purchase the well in case the experiment proved successful.

The experiment caused much excitement and enthusiasm ran high when the actual drilling of the well started. The first strata of water was reached at 20 feet, which tested 125 gallons of water per minute. A second strata was found at 79 feet. The well was drilled to a depth of 130 feet in order to insure water in sufficient quantity for irrigation, and at that depth tested 1700 gallons per minute.

The bringing in of the Slaton well was an important page in Hale County's history. To J. O. Wyckoff is due much of the credit for the success of the experiment. With unwavering faith and enthusiasm he watched the progress of the work from the spudding in of the well until the final test was made, although practically every one else had despaired of finding water sufficent for irrigation and clamored for abandonment of the project. Mr. Wyckoff proposed to finance the scheme with his own personal funds rather than to see it fail.

A great jubilee and water carnival celebrating the discovery of the great under-ground water supply was held, which lasted two days. Much publicity was given the success of the experiment and a vast crowd of people from a distance was in attendance. The strength of the well was tested and was

WHEAT GROWING, HARVESTING WITH COMBINE,
IRRIGATING ALFALFA, COTTON

AGRICULTURAL DEVELOPMENT 49

estimated at 1700 gallons per minute, this being the capacity of the pump and not the well.

Mr. Slaton was most happy to take the well off the hands of the committee. The bringing in of this well was followed by a wave of enthusiasm, and during 1911 irrigation wells were drilled on the farms of E. H. Perry, Robert Alley, P. B. Snyder, R. P. Smyth, E. Graham, E. Dowden, and Klingman & Hall.

The following year, (1912) Dr. Frederick Pearson, of New York, visited Hale County and became interested in irrigation. Through the efforts of M. D. Henderson, Dr. Pearson organized a syndicate known as the Pearson Syndicate and purchased 60,000 acres of scattered tracts of choice land in the Plainview vicinity and began developing it. The Texas Land and Development Company was organized in October, 1912, with Mr. Henderson as manager, to act as agent for the syndicate in the development and sale of the farms.

Dr. Pearson launched a plan to put down four hundred irrigation wells on the farms and to build improvements in the way of houses, barns, etc. for the purpose of selling off the tracts in farms of 80, 160 and 320 acres each fully equipped and ready for occupancy. During the year 1913 some eighty-five deep wells for irrigation were drilled and equipped with pumping plants. This great project was brought to a close by the death of Dr. Pearson on May 7, 1915, with the sinking of the ill-fated Lusitania by German submarine. But it started the development of the country with almost limitless possibilities by proving the vast water supply underlying the plains available for irrigation.

Without doubt the greatest blow the development of Hale County ever received was the sinking of the Lusitania by the German U-Boat. The great program that Dr. Pearson had outlined for the development of natural resources and the building of railroads and establishing the necessary markets was halted at his passing. Nevertheless 127 irrigation wells had been completed and many of the farms fully improved. The farms that remained unsold at the close of the sales program have been successfully farmed by tenants under the supervision of the Company and have been the means of furnishing homes and livelihood for many hundreds of families during the twenty odd years of its existence. The Company has been under the management of Captain Winfield Holbrook since 1919.

By 1918, thirty-three wells had been drilled in addition to those of the syndicate, making a total of 160 in the Plainview vicinity. Few wells were drilled during the next ten years. A few years of favorable rainfall were followed by abnormally high prices during the war. The advent of high-power farming resulted in large-scale farming and advance of dry land prices, and irrigation farming was eclipsed for a time. The severe drouth of 1934-35 demonstrated the value of irrigation, when the severest drouth in the history of the country scourged the plains. Irrigation wells were operated day and night to produce alfalfa and other feed crops to relieve the starving herds of cattle and livestock. Since 1930, certainty of income by irrigation and security from crop failure in years of drouth again brought irrigation to the front. It has opened up a new agricultural world in comparison to dry farming. Instead of a few drouth-resisting crops, the farmer may grow alfalfa, truck, fruit trees and a variety of other special crops.

The average yield of alfalfa under irrigation is 3-$\frac{1}{3}$ tons per acre; Row crops 3000 lbs. threshed grain; cotton $\frac{2}{3}$ of a bale, wheat 30 bus., oats 55 bus. and barley 35 bus. per acre. Each well irrigates on an average of 95 acres. There are 503 irrigation wells in Hale County according to a recent survey, and 1200 in the irrigation district.

The Cotton Industry

King Cotton, now one of the leading industries in Hale County, was until after the turn of the century a stranger in a strange land and took many slights and rebuffs before he was finally welcomed.

Although a few scattered experiments were made even as far back as the first settler who grew a few stalks of cotton in his garden, the Petersburg community was probably the first to grow cotton in harvestable quantity. In 1900 J. T. Phillips and Henry A. White planted cotton near Petersburg. Mr. White planted cotton the following year and the season being favorable, he made a bumper crop, all of which he was able

AGRICULTURAL DEVELOPMENT 51

to harvest before it was damaged by frost and it made the highest grade. There was no gin in the county at that time and the cotton was ginned in Floyd County.

John Pendley is said to have built the first gin in Plainview in 1903 on the lot where the Campbell building now stands, at the northeast corner of the Court House Square. This was a one-stand gin, operated by T. J. Garner, and was run but a short time.

The second gin in Plainview was built in 1905 by L. A. Knight and H. E. Hume. The plant was located on the south side of Sixth Street between Baltimore and Columbia Streets, and was a complete Continental system—a two-stand gin, a Thomas press with a steam engine. Little cotton was grown in 1905 and the owners were greatly disappointed with the venture.

In 1906 Knight and Hume sold the gin to J. N. Jordan. Mr. Jordan was an experienced cotton grower and he saw that cotton could be grown successfully in Hale County. To stimulate interest in the cotton industry, he had circulars printed which he distributed advertising Hale County and vicinity as a cotton country. Then he purchased a car load of cotton seed which he freighted from Childress to Plainview with wagons, and sold the seed to individuals in order to get them started in cotton production. In 1906 the plant ginned 730 bales at Plainview. All the cotton ginned and purchased in Hale County in 1905 and 1906 was freighted by wagon to Canyon which was the nearest railroad terminal. The freight rate from Plainview to Canyon at that time was $2.00 per bale.

In 1907 the people were convinced as to the possibility of cotton growing when several fields produced more than a bale to the acre. Plainview then being the nearest railroad terminus, all the cotton produced in Hale, Floyd, Crosby, Lubbock, Swisher and Briscoe Counties was sold in Plainview, which totaled 4000 bales in 1907. Carter Mercantile Company in Lubbock freighted 50 bales to Plainview by ox wagon. Mr. Jordan continued to operate the gin until it was destroyed by fire in November, 1908.

After the Jordan gin burned, there was no other gin erected in Plainview until 1911, when Charles Malone established a plant immediately north of the present Texas Utilities plant.

This gin was moved to Crosbyton in 1914. Ginning records show that 1400 bales were ginned in Hale County in 1911, 317 bales in 1912 and only 16 bales in 1913.

There was a decided sentiment among the people that the cotton industry would bring in the negro, and at that time the population of the county was one hundred per cent American born white people who were determined to keep it so. For this same reason the early cotton growing in Lubbock County, started as an experiment in 1900 by S. S. Rush, ended in disaster when the cowboys forced him to plow up his field. That the negro followed the cotton was not questioned, and they were filled with resentment at the possibility of the colored race encroaching upon the cowboys' territory. In 1901, when the experiment was repeated, the cowboys drove a herd of cattle into Mr. Rush's field to graze upon the growing cotton. Not to be beaten, the farmer planted again in 1902 and succeeded in harvesting sixteen bales, which he freighted to Abilene to be ginned, a distance of 165 miles.

For several years following 1913, little interest was taken in growing cotton. At the close of the war renewed interest was taken in this commodity due to the high price of cotton and also an influx of farmers from East Texas who were familiar with cotton-growing and who recognized the advantage of climatic conditions which prevented the existence of the boll weevil, the great enemy of the cotton industry.

The West Texas Cotton Oil Mill was built in Plainview in 1926. Here four separate products are made from the cotton seeds: ie., crude cotton-seed oil, cotton-seed cake, cotton-seed hulls and linters.

The crude oil is shipped to refineries at Dallas, Cincinnati, New York and New Orleans, principally to packers, Proctor and Gamble being the largest buyers. The cotton-seed cake and also the cotton-seed hulls are consumed in the local trade territory and are used by dairymen and feeders of cattle, sheep and hogs. The linters, a low grade of cotton lint, moves to Chicago, Philadelphia and Nitro, Virginia, for the manufacture of various products.

The seeds of the cotton were for many years considered a waste product and were brushed aside and burned. Today they form the base for many useful by-products and have be-

AGRICULTURAL DEVELOPMENT

come the most remunerative part of the cotton industry.

The Plainview Cotton Compress was built in 1924 by J. W. Murchison. The size of the bale is reduced 75 per cent by compression, thus reducing the shipping expense. The plant has a capacity of 40,000 bales.

There are fifteen gins in Hale County at the present time,—five in Plainview, two each in Hale Center, Petersburg, Abernathy and Cotton Center and one each at Halfway and County Line.

The Wheat Industry

Wheat, as a major industry, has justly earned for the Panhandle Region the title, "The Bread Bowl of the Southwest." Hale County is fortunate in that it lies at a dividing point between the north and south plains where the wheat belt overlaps the cotton-producing area.

In the early days numerous experiments were made in wheat growing, but the first to be grown in harvestable quantity was sown by Sterling P. Strong in 1892 on his home section one mile east of Plainview. 275 bushels were threshed from a field of twenty acres. As there was no market for the grain, no appreciable amount was grown in Hale County until after the coming of the railroad, on January 1, 1907.

The first car of wheat to be shipped from Plainview by rail was grown in 1904 by J. V. Leatherwood, near Old Emma in Crosby County. For lack of marketing facilities this was held for three years awaiting the coming of the railroad, then freighted by wagon a distance of sixty-five miles to the terminus.

Farmers from wheat-growing regions of the north came to the county in the boom that followed the coming of the Santa Fe Railroad and they took the lead in the industry. In 1909 Hale County's total production of wheat was 16,578 bushels. In the decade that followed the acreage was gradually increased until 1919 when the output totaled 926,167 bushels. The old method of wheat-growing and harvesting was used entirely. The planting was done by hand or by horsepower, the ripened grain cut with a binder, shocked, stacked and threshed with a threshing machine operated by a steam engine, which burned coal. The coal was shipped by rail from Colorado, which added to the expense and decreased the profits from the harvest.

In 1919 the harvester-combines were introduced into Hale County. The old regime gave place to the new almost entirely during the next decade, and the 1929 census showed a production of 2,761,671 bushels.

The wheat industry has contributed much to Hale County. It has raised the standards of living of the people and promoted culture and education. The receipts from the harvest coming to the producers in lump sums of sometimes several thousand dollars makes it possible to pay debts, build new homes and farm improvements, buy farm implements, and automobiles and send the children to college, which is not usually done when the same amount of money comes in in small amounts. The modern method of production entails no hardship upon the farmer's family. It contributes to a higher class of citizenship in that it does not attract the illiterate class and uses no child labor.

The wheat industry furnishes a basis for dairy, poultry and livestock industries and for balanced farming.

Milling Industry

The milling industry was started in Plainview in 1907 when the Harvest Queen Mills, then a pioneer flour mill, was built by Jones Bros. from Indiana. This was a small frame structure with little storage capacity or warehouse space. There was little wheat available at that time, and the Jones Brothers later sold the mill to George K. Neher. Mr. Neher was an inexperienced miller and he soon became discouraged.

In 1910 the Harvest Queen Mills was sold to Albert G. Hinn. Mr. Hinn was joined soon afterwards by his father, the late Charles Hinn who had had more than forty years experience in the milling business in Wisconsin and realized the possibilities for the future of the mill at Plainview. Messrs. Hinn improved and added to the original mill and continued to operate it for many years. This mill was destroyed by fire in January, 1926.

Immediately following the fire loss, Mr. Hinn erected a new fire-proof day-light mill having approximately 600 barrel daily capacity. Its concrete grain bins have a storage capacity of one million bushels. The new mill was completed and began operating in October, 1926.

Poultry

The South Plains Poultry Association was organized in December, 1911, and originated the West Texas Poultry Show, which was held annually until 1924. 300 thoroughbred birds were entered at the first Poultry Show, 500 at the second, and the maximum number exhibited at one time was 1900 in 1922. J. C. Goodwin, E. B. Miller and W. J. Klinger served as Secretary-Treasurer during the existence of this organization which did much to promote the raising of pure-bred poultry in Hale County.

The Southwestern Turkey Improvement Association was organized in 1934 and started the Southwestern Dressed Turkey Show in 1935, which is held annually, for the purpose of introducing farm dressed turkeys. The climate of the plains being peculiarly adapted to turkey growing, the Association has not only greatly improved the grade of turkeys but cooperates in the marketing. Some four car loads of dressed turkeys are shipped from Hale County each year. The Plains Cooperative Creamery started an exclusive Turkey Hatchery in 1936, with a 7,500 capacity and hatched 10,000 poults. In 1937 both the capacity and output were doubled. This is said to be the first and only exclusive Turkey Hatchery in Texas. The Plains Cooperative handles dressed turkeys for its members. Demonstrations by the County Agent in breeding, feeding and caring for turkeys have done much to educate the farmers in growing poults out for the market as prime birds.

County Agricultural Agent

The office of County Agent was established in Hale County April 1, 1916. Raleigh F. Hare was appointed agent and served both Hale and Floyd Counties until 1918, after which the county was without an agent for five years. The following persons have served as County Agent of Hale County: E. W. Thomas (1923-1925), Paul Huey (1925-1927), R. M. Milhollin (1927-1930), Roy B. Davis (1930-1932), W. W. Evans (1932-1936) and C. B. Martin (1936-   ).

One of the principal activities of the County Agent has been the promotion and improvement of the Dairy industry, the latest feature being the organization in 1937 of the Central Plains Dairy Herd Improvement Association involving Swisher and Hale Counties. An extensive program in trench silo construction, teaching farmers to properly conserve their feed, was conducted to stimulate the dairy industry. As a result of these demonstrations, 90 trench silos were dug and filled in 1936 for the purpose of conserving surplus feed crops that are produced in abundance in good years to feed the dairy herds during the years of crop shortage. It is estimated that dairy development will be increased from 25 to 30 per cent by use of the trench silo.

Demonstrations in the feeding of hogs, lambs, and beef cattle have taught the farmers how to feed livestock in a commercial way. To encourage this type of farming, an Annual Fat Stock Show was organized in 1936, held for the second time in 1937. After this show closes, the fat cattle and lambs are shipped to Kansas City for the purpose of educating the Club boys and adult feeders as to the quality of livestock the market demands.

The conservation of soil, water and feed are revolutionizing the development of agriculture at the present time. Demonstrations in running contour lines and terracing have proven very effective. The Agricultural Adjustment Program has aided materially in this development.

The main objective of the County Agent is to encourage the farmer to plan a well balanced livestock farm program, ie., to first produce his living at home, plant a variety of crops,—cotton, wheat and grain sorghums, and market them through dairy cattle, poultry, or feeding some class of livestock for the market. Many have found this plan advantageous.

Topography

Hale County is situated in the center of the Llano Estacado or Staked Plains and is in the center of the northern tier of counties of the territory known as the South Plains.

The county is 30 miles wide from east to west and about 34 miles from north to south, having an area of 1,036 square

LIVE STOCK AND POULTRY

AGRICULTURAL DEVELOPMENT

miles or 663,040 acres, of which 98 per cent is smooth tillable land. Its surface is free from breaks and is apparently a level plain. It slopes gently to the southeast, the altitude ranging from 3250 to 3600 feet.

It is crossed by the Runningwater Draw which heads in Quay County, New Mexico, traverses the plains and merges into Blanco Canyon where it becomes known as the White River. Runningwater Draw enters Hale County near its northwest corner, passes through Plainview and passes into Floyd County near the center of the county line. This Draw is a running stream until it reaches a point some 15 miles northwest of Plainview where it enters a subterranean channel and flows intermittently for some twenty miles. The Double Mountain Fork of the Brazos crosses the southwest corner of the county and the Crawfish Draw which heads in Hale County crosses the south part of the county. Both of these are dry creek beds. Runningwater Draw is a dry creek bed at Plainview except after heavy rains to the northwest, when it overflows its banks, sometimes having the appearance of a great river, which disappears in a few days.

BUREAU OF CENSUS, WASHINGTON, POPULATION OF HALE COUNTY, TEXAS
From 1890 to 1930

	1930	1920	1910	1900	1890
Hale County	20,189	10,104	7,566	1,680	721
Population per Square Mile	19.5	9.8	7.3	1.6	—
Town of Plainview	8,834	3,989	2,829		
Town of Hale Center	1,007				
Town of Petersburg	548				
Town of Abernathy, in Hale Co.	743				
Town of Abernathy, (in Lubbock Co.)	115				
Classification of Population					
Native White	19,658	9,980	7,408	1,660	706
Foreign Born White	94	117	153	16	12
Mexican	113	—	—	—	—
Negroes	320	7	5	3	3
Urban Population	8,834	3,989	2,829	—	—
Rural Population	11,355	6,115	4,737	1,680	721
Number of Families in Hale County	4,677	2,176	1,600	326	133
Home Owners	2,095	1,148	946	271	—
Tenants	2,490	945	627	39	—
Tenure unknown	92	83	27	16	—

DEPARTMENT OF COMMERCE, BUREAU OF THE CENSUS, WASHINGTON,
SPECIFIED CROPS FOR HALE COUNTY, TEXAS
CENSUSES OF AGRICULTURE, 1910 TO 1935
(Data not available where figures are not shown)

ITEM	1934	1929	1924	1919	1909
Crops					
Corn for grain:					
Acres................	158	2,081	1,227	3,363	5,757
Bushels..............	803	25,407	19,876	55,667	49,205
Wheat, Total:					
Acres................	189,648	214,706	68,765	57,954	2,826
Bushels..............	2,167,809	2,761,671	1,220,559	926,167	16,578
Oats, Threshed:					
Acres................	489	450	4,130	5,477	941
Bushels..............	7,090	10,951	81,796	252,393	8,835
Oats Cut and Fed Unthreshed:					
Acres................	71	294	2,245		
Barley Threshed:					
Acres................	2,428	507	987	426	—
Bushels..............	25,920	5,548	13,655	17,263	—
Grain Sorghum (for grain):					
Acres................	2,962	19,474	39,934	99,732	14,329
Bushels..............	24,368	236,383	774,207	1,965,774	123,514
All Hay and Sorghums for Forage:					
Acres................	51,578	79,239	33,840	37,640	28,570
Tons.................	17,558	74,768	62,033	59,553	23,242
Sweet and Grain Sorghums Cut for silage, hay and Forage:					
Acres................	49,547	76,540	29,007	30,996	—
Tons.................	13,602	70,059		50,385	
Cotton, Lint:					
Acres................	63,196	64,882	91,939	6,630	98
Bales................	6,582	16,741	28,563	2,079	15
Irish Potatoes (All Varieties):					
Acres................	247	10	8	4	6
Bushels..............	14,646	490	332	257	188
Sweet Potatoes and Yams:					
Acres................	1	5	6	15	7
Bushels..............	97	341	645	1,874	244
	(1935)				
Apples:					
Trees Not of Bearing Age...	144	750	488	3,155 }	45,095
Trees of Bearing Age.......	1,078	3,544	5,943	23,882 }	
Bushels..............	779	4,741	6,696	11,898	165
Peaches:					
Trees Not of Bearing Age...	316	1,929 }	3,657 }	1,971 }	13,756
Trees of Bearing Age.......	4,395	4,977 }		11,582 }	
Bushels..............	3,588	4,883	2,111	1,277	—
Plums and Prunes:					
Trees not of Bearing Age...		1,240 }	1,944 }	1,100 }	6,439
Trees of Bearing Age.......		2,704 }		3,624 }	
Bushels..............		1,571		401	
Grapes:					
Vines not of Bearing Age...	468	3,816 }	8,162 }	1,936 }	12,418
Vines of Bearing Age.......	6,299	6,389 }		8,984 }	
Pounds...............	40,234	40,454		31,656	4,300

AVERAGE YEARLY PRICES OF FARM PRODUCTS AT PLAINVIEW, TEXAS
1922-1936

Year	Wheat	Cotton	Barley	Oats	Ear Corn	Alfalfa	Sorghum		Grains
	Bu.	Lb.	Bu.	Bu.	cwt.	Ton	Heads Ton	Threshed, cwt.	Bundles
1922	$1.08	$0.06	$0.52	$ .45	$ .38½	$15.27	12.00	$1.35	$0.04
1923	0.85½	0.28½	0.61	.49	0.67	18.57	19.45	1.52	0.042
1924	1.04	.22	.62	.52	.66	18.13	17.20	1.49	.05
1925	1.55	.19	.75	.50	1.00	18.63	19.60	1.73	.04¼
1926	1.18	.086	.57	.46	.62	14.30	8.50	1.30	.02¼
1927	1.20	.21	.58	.43	.83	15.90	11.75	.97	.03
1928	1.14	.18	.60	.45	.75	16.85	13.85	.98	.03½
1929	.83	.099	.84	.56	.78	18.65	16.20	1.03	.02¾
1930	.69	.08	.40	.32	.90	17.00	17.00	1.10	.04
1931	.29	.046	.21	.20	.29	9.50	4.49	.33	.01-¾
1932	.29	.052	.14	.12	.15	6.75	2.80	.23	.009
1933	.75	.089	.47	.28	.50	11.00	8.00	.65	.02½
1934	.68	.12	.37	.34	.52	17.50	23.50	2.25	.06½
1935	.80	.106	.40	.31	.52	11.35	9.95	.73	.03½
1936	1.01	.11½	.44	.31	.99	11.38	17.00	1.55	.04
Average 15 years	$0.826	$0.13	$0.50	0.38	0.646	$14.71	13.42	$1.147	$.04

DEPARTMENT OF COMMERCE
BUREAU OF CENSUS, WASHINGTON
SPECIFIED ITEMS OF FARM DATA AND LIVESTOCK FOR HALE COUNTY, TEXAS
CENSUSES OF AGRICULTURE, 1910 TO 1935
(Data not available where figures are not shown)

Item	1935	1930	1925	1920	1910
Farm Data					
Number of Farms	1,859	1,729	1,293	1,031	731
Full Owners	586	535	451	352	387
Part Owners	235	265	114	249	101
Managers	8	23	7	15	10
Tenants	1,030	906	721	415	233
All Land in Farms	591,102	595,056	398,024	581,713	379,679
Value of Land and Buildings	$18,259,086	$29,420,156	$17,704,230	$25,930,722	$9,706,085
Live Stock					
Horses and colts of all ages: Number	5,279	6,113	5,792	7,528	4,549
Mules and mule colts of all ages: Number	2,225	3,316	3,807	2,743	2,197
Cattle and Calves of all ages: Number	16,607	20,677	12,055	25,833	14,716
Sheep and Lambs of all ages: Number	18,997	22,336	5,659	17,611	4,128
Swine of all ages: Number	6,457	9,395	6,897	14,175	9,142
Goats and kids: Number	No report	125	2	59	42
Chickens: Number	No report	123,866	105,398	101,712	39,479

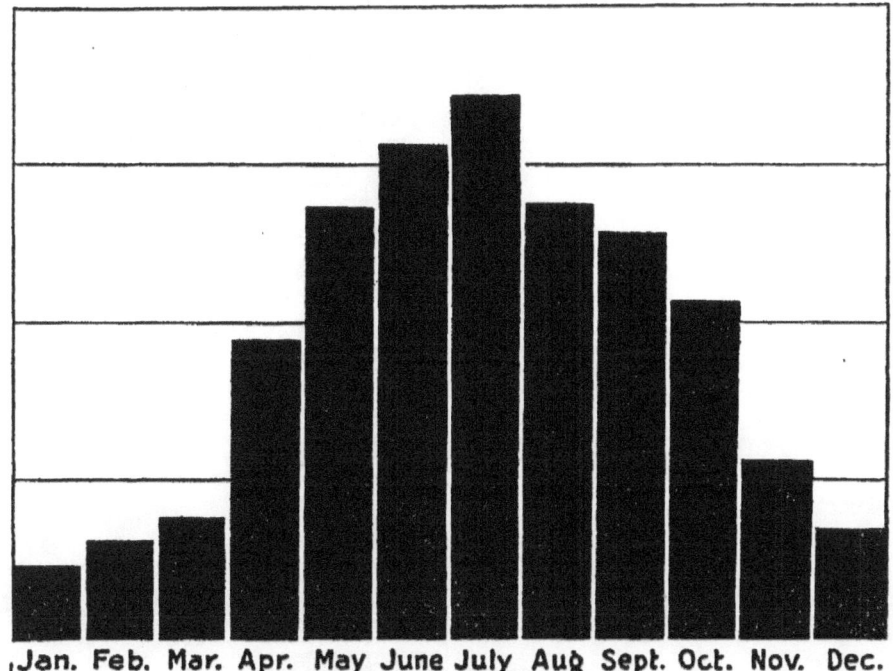

Average Monthly Precipitation Over Period of 42 Years (1894-1936)

Jan.	Feb.	Mar.	Apr.	May	June	July	Aug.	Sept.	Oct.	Nov.	Dec.
.44	.65	.75	1.90	2.63	3.15	3.45	2.64	2.52	2.14	1.10	.68

Yearly Average 22.05

Climate

The following statistics are shown by W. J. Klinger, Official Observer, Government Weather Station at Plainview:

Mean Annual Temperature.................59° Fah.
Mean Summer Temperature..............72.9° Fah.
Mean Winter Temperature...............47.6° Fah.

Average Date of First Frost..........November 25th
Average Date of Last Frost.............April 13th
Average Length of Growing Season..........211 days

Mean Annual Rainfall ....22.05 inches
Average Annual Snowfall................10.5 inches

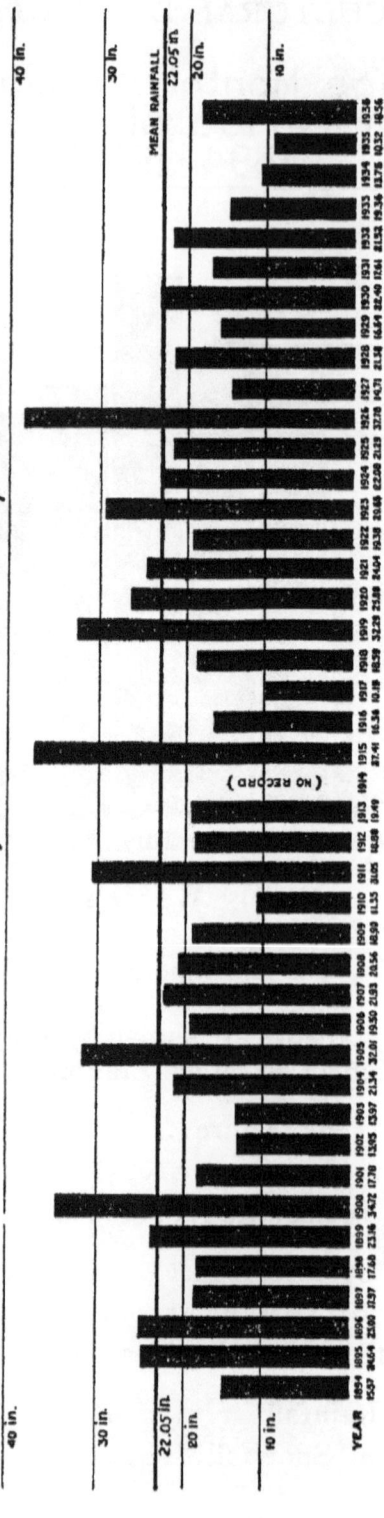

Cycle Index Showing Annual Rainfall For Forty Two Years

CHAPTER V

TRANSPORTATION

Early Modes

The earliest known method of transportation in the vicinity of Hale County is recorded in Casteneda's account of the Journey of Coronado. When the Spanish explorers crossed the Llano Estacado in 1541, they found the native Indians following the buffalo on foot and using dog trains with Moorish packsaddles to transport their belongings.

The first horses to be brought into what is now the State of Texas were the Spanish ponies of Coronado and his men. These animals no doubt were a spectacle even more amazing to the "Querchoes" Indians than was the colorful grandeur of Spanish nobility that invaded the solitude of the prairies. Just when the Spanish horses came into general use among the Indians of the Plains is not known, but in time the horse became the Comanches' greatest asset and gave them a power hitherto unknown over less warring nations and races. When the United States cavalry crossed Hale County in the early seventies, the redskins scuttled before them on fleet Indian ponies.

The horse and saddle reigned supreme during the years of the cattle industry which began on the Plains in the late seventies. Wagon trains drawn by oxen first transported the ranch supplies from a railroad terminal in Kansas to the ranches of the Texas Panhandle. This mode of transporting freight and supplies—by oxen, mules or horses—was used entirely until the coming of the railroads. Supplies were freighted from Colorado City from 1881 until 1888 and afterward from Amarillo.

The covered wagon or "prairie schooner" was the principal means of travel used by all early settlers and homeseekers. The old "Mackenzie Trail," traveled by General Mackenzie's troops first in 1871, was for many years the only road across the plains. History records that this road had been used by the Indians and Mexicans for many years prior to that time. Its deep ruts probably first cut by the wheels of a Mexican cartera were plainly visible when Mackenzie first followed it into New Mexico in quest of the Comanches. Early settlers of Hale County followed this trail westward in search of a location. It was a landmark to the cattlemen who herded the cattle on the prairies, and even when the ground was covered deep in snow, the deep ruts made indentures on the snow's surface by which the traveler was able to find his way.

A few of the early settlers brought two-wheeled carts, buckboards, or canvas-top hacks. The cart was used for light utility conveyance which was a little more practical than the horse and saddle with saddle bags, or the side-saddle, for every plainswoman owned a side-saddle. The lumber wagon with split-bottom chairs for seats was not an uncommon mode of travel for local use. The top buggy, rubber tired,—the aristocrat of the early modes of conveyance,—was in use at the turn of the century.

There were no trails across the prairies in the early days, or even fences to follow, and traveling was done entirely by direction. The sun served as a guide by day and the moon and stars by night, and it was the custom of the settlers to keep a light in the window or hang a lantern on the windmill tower on dark or stormy nights to guide to shelter any traveler who might be out or lost on the prairies.

No attempt was made to build or improve the roads prior to 1900. When the ruts became too deep, a new track was soon made by driving outside the old one. The roads were naturally in good condition except when heavy rains filled up the lakes and made them impassable, in which case the driver unhitched his horses, mounted one and led the others and went his way, leaving the wagons standing protected only by a wagon-sheet until his return.

A stage line was opened from Amarillo to Estacado via Plainview soon after the railroad came to Amarillo. A one-seated buckboard was first used, but this was soon displaced by a Concord stagecoach with two seats which faced each other and with a driver's seat at the top. This was drawn by wild little mules which raced from one stage stand to another. Stage stands were arranged about twenty miles apart where a fresh team was kept waiting.

Every town had its livery stable, and the "wagon yard" where travelers might leave their covered wagons and livestock to be cared for, or make camp if they wished, was an accomodation to be found in the larger towns.

Railroads

In 1887 Amarillo became the terminal of a branch line of the Panhandle & Pecos Valley Lines of the Santa Fe, which consisted then of 543 miles of road from Woodward, Okla. to Pecos, Texas. On January 1, 1902, Mr. Avery Turner moved to Amarillo and became Vice President and General Manager of the Pecos Valley Lines. His duties also included those of Chief Engineer, Land and Tax Commissioner, Claim Agent and Superintendent. He traveled over the Staked Plains and Panhandle with horse and buggy making careful study of both the land and its prospect and possibilities for development sufficient to justify the building of a railroad. On June 1, 1903, Mr. Turner made a trip to Plainview to inspect the country with this purpose in mind. The following is a copy of his notes made on this trip: (Courtesy Mrs. Avery Turner)

"NOTES MADE BY AVERY TURNER WHILE MAKING TRIP TO PLAINVIEW, JUNE 1ST, 1903

"Left Canyon City 7:15 A.M. by stage. First 7 miles rolling and little rough. Crossing of Tierra Blanca Creek will take 75 ft. bridge, pile, 1% grades to get out of brakes on the plain with 3 or 4 small bridges. Probably cheapest plan is one and one-half miles East of town for junction, no rock, sandy soil.

"After getting on top, land is level, except for Happy draw and 3 lakes and the North Tulia Creek to Tulia, town 35 miles. Tulia County seat, 350 people.

"Then cross Tulia Creek and South Tulle, then level to Plainview, except 3 lakes.

"Plainview is County-seat, 700 people, 2,500 in County. Good trading point.

"Only one big pasture on line. T-Anchor, 256 sections just South of Canyon. Will soon be broken up. Run through it for 9 miles. Balance owned in small ranches, average 3 sections. Very few over 4 sections, none over 7 sections. Can often count 20 homes in sight. Land is better than on P. V. Black soil, yets holds water well, grow any crop. The kaffir is never a failure. Ultimately be best hog country, cattle all graded fine now.

"Favored by shallow water, 60 ft. is deepest; about 50 ft. at Tulia and 30 ft. to 40 ft. at Plainview.

"Each home has bunch of thrifty trees and many good orchards; all have reservoir and grow vegetables, good houses. Big pastures lay 20 miles West, line cuts center between them and Palo Duro.

"Line from Plainview to Lubbock is grass roots, proposition running water draw at Plainview; only bridge. Same soil, shallow water and small pastures till you get near Lubbock. Far as would go at present till cross line built.

"Swisher County has inhabitants 1,500
Hale County has inhabitants 2,500
Lubbock County has inhabitants 1,800

                                         5,800

"Briscoe, Floyd, Crosby are all good counties on East of line. It would serve a population of 10,000 people to start and develop well. People are bound to get a line and will aid one and get it. Grading and bridging very cheap. R/W given. Good class of settlers.

"Production will be cattle and hogs and fruit and vegetables. No fuel in country, small grains grow, corn, but too cool for reliability. May be best to leave Tulia on left.

"In grading, best to use graders and cut ditches each side and grade two feet above ground to drain well. Sod rots and track goes down.

"Grading 5,000 per mile, bridging 400 ft.

TRANSPORTATION

```
"$ 60,000.00  Grading
   2,500.00  Bridge
  95,000.00  Rail
  42,000.00  Fastenings
  42,000.00  Laying
 105,000.00  Ties
   7,500.00  Water
   7,500.00  Depot
   5,000.00  Supervision
————————
$366,500.00  Total"
```

Although Mr. Turner earnestly desired to extend the railroad farther south, he believed that the time was not yet ripe.

So eager were the citizens of Hale County to secure a railroad that for several years they kept up a constant effort to secure a contract for the building of a railroad in any direction from Plainview. On July 6, 1903, a group of citizens met in the office of Judge L. S. Kinder and formed a company called "The Amarillo, Plainview and Southern Railway Company. The Board of Directors elected were J. H. Slaton, R. P. Smyth, J. N. Donohoo, L. A. Knight, Dr. L. Lee Dye, Dr. J. H. Wayland, W. E. Dyer, Chas. McCormack and L. S. Kinder.

The Company formed was chartered for $75,000 and it was required that 5 per cent of this amount must be paid in before a charter would be granted. Members of the committee stated that it took all the money in Plainview to raise the 5 per cent, but the money was raised, nevertheless.

Three years later the directors of this company entered into a contract with a promoter, C. B. Pasch, of Amarillo, who then interested Major E. C. Gordon, of Alabama, who secured the cooperation of the Caldwells, of Tennessee. Through these men the Talmages, of Chicago, and Major Stallings became interested, and their efforts culminated in a contract with the Santa Fe in 1906.

The bonus that was paid to the Santa Fe was $75,000, which at that time was considered a very large sum. Although much of the lands in Hale County had been granted to Railroad Companies for building railroads in East Texas, the law which allowed sixteen sections of land as a bonus for each mile of railroad built was repealed in 1882, and there remained no lands in the public domain to promote the building of roads in West Texas.

The principal consideration of the bonus was the options which the people gave the Railroad Company in land, appraising it at a very low price per acre, enabling the Company to sell the land after the road had been built for as much as or perhaps twice the price.

The time limit when the Railroad must reach Plainview in order to secure the bonus of $75,000 was 12 o'clock noon on January 1, 1907. This requirement was met within a few hours of the dead line and the coming of the railroad was celebrated on December 31, 1906.

An account of the opening of the Plainview Line is given in a letter from Mr. A. E. Meyer, Auditor of the Panhandle and Santa Fe Railroad Company, to the author, dated March 9, 1934, as follows:

"The Plainview line was officially opened on February 18, 1907. Prior to that date, however, some freight and passenger traffic was handled as a matter of accommodation to the public. Below is a list of the station agents at Plainview together with the respective periods of service in that capacity:

"J. Newt Cole	1- 1-07 to	11-15-08
John Kendrick	11-15-08 to	1-15-10
C H Hinton	1-15-10 to	5-23-10
R McGee	5-23-10 to	2-15-12
W J Klinger	2-15-12 to	5- 1-13
R F Bayless	5- 1-13 to	7-20-15
John Lucas	7-20-15 to	date

"I have been unable, thus far, to ascertain the names of the crew that brought the first regular train into your city, however it is understood that the late Mr. Avery Turner, who was at that time Vice President and General Manager, arrived in Plainview on a special train on December 28, 1906 and had as his guests Mrs. Turner, Miss Cobb (now Mrs. Henry Harding), Mr. L. T. Lester and Mr. Lester's son and daughter. I believe Mr. Lester was then a banker at Canyon and he only recently passed away. Mr. B. R. Clark was the conductor of that train and Mr. Harry Gardner was the engineer. Mr. Clark is now a Justice of the Peace here and Mr. Gardner is sales manager for Walter Irvin, Inc., dealers in Ford automobiles in Amarillo.

"I am further told that Mr. K. I. Reid was the conductor of a train carrying passengers which followed the special on the date referred to, but I am unable to ascertain the names of the other members of the train and engine crew."

(SIGNED) "A. E. MEYER."

The opening of the Plainview Line was a day of rejoicing never to be forgotten by the citizens of Hale County and the South Plains. It was celebrated with a great jubilee and all day gathering. The coming of the Santa Fe marked the opening of a vast area of land to agricultural pursuit which until that time had been only a grazing range, for centuries for the buffalo and in recent years for cattle. The railroad brought many families into the country to build homes and develop industry.

In the summer of 1909, the Santa Fe Railroad Company extended the Plainview Line to Lubbock, bringing railroad facilities to Hale Center and founding the town of Abernathy.

The citizens of Hale County continued to work unceasingly in an effort to get other railroads to build into the county in order to provide more direct connections with state, interstate and world markets. The Fort Worth and Denver Railroad finally rewarded their efforts and built into Plainview on a branch line from Childress to Dimmitt in 1928. A bonus equal to that paid to the Santa Fe was given the Fort Worth and Denver railroad. A branch line from South Plains to Lubbock brought railroad facilities to Petersburg in the fall of 1928. The coming of the Denver Railway was celebrated in Plainview on November 20, 1928, with a banquet at the City Auditorium given by the Chamber of Commerce, at which one thousand out-of-town guests were honored at a Wild Duck Dinner. The coming of this road was an occasion of great rejoicing, and the business men of Plainview expressed their appreciation by taking advantage of the hunting season to furnish the ducks for the dinner. D. P. Everett is the agent of this road at Plainview, and J. M. Erwin at Petersburg.

Motor Transportation

Almost simultaneously with the coming of the first Railroad was the advent of the automobile. At the time the first cars were brought to Hale County they were still in the stage of experimentation and were but crude forerunners of the improved models of the present time. No one knew how to adjust the machines or to diagnose the trouble when anything went wrong and many times the early travelers were forced to walk home leaving the car behind or to be pulled in by a team of mules.

The noise of the early automobiles made them a menace to livestock and many frightened horses were badly torn by barbed wire fences in their frantic efforts to escape. A law was passed compelling a driver to bring his automobile or motor vehicle to a standstill at the signal of a person riding or driving a horse and to remain stationary until such animal had passed. During the year 1907 a state law was enacted fixing the speed limit at eighteen miles per hour on highways and eight miles per hour in city streets. Every automobile was required to "have attached thereto a bell or other appliance for giving notice of approach which when rung or operated could be heard a distance of three hundred feet."

The early models were run by chain drive, had but one or two cylinders, were hand cranked, and had no windshields or doors, nevertheless, they were the "Pride of the Plains," and many homeseekers who came by train had their first ride in an automobile when real estate agents in Plainview whisked them from the depot to lands far out where they purchased farms, little dreaming they were buying so far from town.

The first automobile sales agency in Hale County was established in 1909, when E. E. Winn and Otus Reeves opened the Ford agency. The total number of sales during the first year was ten cars. In the next few years other agencies were secured. R. A. McWhorter and L. A. Knight sold the Buick car and started Knight's Garage. In the early days of the industry, many cars of various makes were brought into the country and tried out which are no longer built. It was not until the year following the close of the world war that the automobile came into general use. Credit corporations speeded

TRANSPORTATION

up the sales by making it possible to pay for them on the installment plan, for prior to that time cars were sold only for spot cash, though in a few instances cars were sold on open account.

The automobile once ridiculed as a "rich man's plaything" is now considered a necessity to every farmer, business man, and resident of the county. A network of paved highways and improved roads have made even the most outlying farms easily accessible to railroad centers. Trucks can reach any farm in the area and the small truck and "pickup" have become an indispensable aid to the farmers for marketing facilities. During the years that followed "the depression," which began in 1931, the trucking industry has sprung up and motor freighting has become a major industry. It reaches not only agriculture, but every form of business requiring transportation of merchandise.

Motor transportation has found its place not only in the commerce of the community but the social life as well. Urban advantages unknown a quarter of a century ago to the farmer twenty miles from town are his today. The motor car has made it possible for any citizen of Hale County to enjoy the same social advantages, attend the same plays and entertainments that were possible formerly only for people living in town. The school bus transporting from 25 to 40 children at a time has made possible the consolidation of rural schools with all the resulting advantages not available in small rural schools.

In the thirty years since the coming of the railroad and the automobile, amazing progress has been made in the development of the vast natural resources of the land and water of Hale County. From the time when the dog trains dragged their wearisome burdens across the plains until the coming of the prairie schooner, the virgin sod remained unbroken, and the riches that the Spanish Gold Hunters failed to see lay hidden until transportation made their development possible.

CHAPTER VI

HISTORY OF EDUCATION

The First School

The first school in Hale County was a private school taught at Old Epworth in 1886-1887 by Miss Allie Freeman. After personally superintending the education of his children for three years, Mr. Graves secured through a teachers' agency a private tutor for his daughters, Miss Freeman, who came from the east and made her home with them. Several families who moved into the community in 1885 and 1886 were desirous of school advantages for their children, so an arrangement was made by which they shared the expense of the teacher and Mr. Graves allowed them the use of one room in his home for a community school room.

The children who attended this first school were as follows: Amy, Helen and Lottie Graves, Eda and Porter Jones, Clara, Arthur and Frank Adams, Bettie Lester, Dillie, Bert and Lillian Shepley, Bud, Sally and Lee Baker, Dan, Albert and Will Allen and Wilbur and Minnie Harkey.

Miss Florence Gill was employed as a private tutor by Mr. Graves in 1887 and spent three years in the Graves home. She also taught music and expression. The teachers arranged for a circulating library and books were sent from the east which supplied the pupils with first class literature. The children in this school were given the same training and cultural advantages available in more thickly populated communities in the wholesome atmosphere of early western life.

The Sod School House

Soon after Z. T. Maxwell and E. L. Lowe settled on their homesteads, now a part of the townsite of Plainview, a number of other families moved into the vicinity. The need of a school to educate their children was soon felt. No public school fund was available, either to erect a school house or to pay a teacher, and the county was not yet organized. The responsibility rested entirely upon the individuals, so the heads of families set about the task of meeting the requirement.

A lot on which to build a school house was donated by Mr. and Mrs. Hugh McClelland. The building of the school house was not a staggering proposition to the settlers, since they all lived in dugouts. A day was set apart in the summer of 1887 on which to erect the building and every man in the community was on hand to do his part. Judge J. M. Carter with several helpers was sent to the canyons a distance of forty miles to get a ridge pole and rails for the roof. Workers were divided into groups and each group was assigned a definite task. Col. R. P. Smyth engineered one shift which plowed the sod into strips from a portion of the Maxwell land now included in the city park. Another group cut the strips of sod into bricks twenty inches in length, loaded them into wagons and rushed them to the building site. Other workmen dug a hole in the ground 20 by 30 feet, four feet deep. The walls were built four feet above the ground by laying the sod bricks in a wall eighteen inches thick. One window on each side supplied light and a door was placed in the end, facing the east. Before the sun went down the school house was completed with the exception of the roof. The party returned with the ridgepole several days later and all turned out to finish the work. The long pole was laid from end to end of the building and short poles placed from the ridgepole to the side walls and cedar brush was placed over them. This they covered with a layer of sod with the grass outside and the school house was complete. The pleasure of neighborly association and cooperation made light the work of the building and no one felt it a burden. Lumber to make the seats was freighted from Colorado City a distance of 160 miles and was paid for through subscription. Hammer and saws quickly transformed the rude planks into seats,— crude though they were—from which dangled the little feet of Plainview's first school children.

Miss Maggie Camp, of Snider, Texas, was employed as the first teacher. Her salary was paid by subscription and she boarded around among the patrons. There were no text books available and the children studied from miscellaneous school books which their parents happened to possess. Mrs. Kate Cannon was employed as teacher in 1888, and rode to school each day with horse and sidesaddle from her "home-on-the-range" six miles from Plainview. Pupils living long distances from town came to school riding horseback or in two-wheeled carts or buckboards. Ferd Faulkner was employed as a second teacher during the year.

Among the pupils who attended the first school, in 1887, at Plainview in the little sod school house were as follows: Fannie, Walter, Harry, Earnest, "Plug" and "Tat" (twins) Griffin, Mattie Lowe, Mont and Tom Carter, Hubert Parker, Billy, Oscar, Ed, Bob, Betty and Mary Bryan, Charlie and Will McClelland, Cicero and Stella Pendley, Will, Sallie and Sam Maxwell, Ada, Anna, Hubert and Willis Harlin.

Public Free Schools Established

The first public free schools were established in Hale County in the summer of 1889, at which time two school districts were created. District No. 1 contained two schools,—Plainview and Mapes,—and District No. 2 had one school,—Epworth. The community of Mapes was then called the "Missouri Settlement," since most of the people in that vicinity came from Missouri. Miss Alice Rosser opened the school at Mapes in a brush arbor during the summer before the school house was built.

The scholastics in Hale County in 1889 numbered 108, being 37 in Plainview, 24 at Mapes and 37 at Epworth. The sum of $420.00 was apportioned from the Public School Fund and the sum of $1,323.52 was apportioned from the County Treasury, making a total of $1,744.44, or $16.15 per scholastic, to be expended for school purposes in Hale County during the year 1889-1890.

The sum of $675.00 was set aside to build a school house at Plainview and a contract was entered into with the Masonic Lodge of Plainview who paid for the labor and material to build a second floor to the school house to be used as a Masonic Hall. Thomas G. Nance, Pastor of the First Christian Church, was given the contract to erect the building, which was placed on the present site of the Lamar School.

HISTORY OF EDUCATION 75

The Llano Estacado Institute

The name of the Plainview School was changed to The Llano Estacado Institute in 1895 under the supervision of O. C. Mulkey and the curriculum was made to include academic work. The first graduating class of The Llano Estacado Institute was the class of 1897. At that time Alfred T. Howell Jr., John Humphrey and Samuel R. Merrill graduated with fitting ceremonies on May 17, 1897.

Plainview High School

On March 12, 1902, the Plainview Independent School District was organized. The Llano Estacado Institute was changed to Plainview High School, and the grade school was later named Lamar. The class of 1904 was the first graduating class of the Plainview High School.

The following persons have served as Superintendent of Plainview Independent Schools: E. C. Nelson (1908-1910), W. H. Grim (1910-1911), Miss Ellen Robinson (1911-1913), B. M. Harrison (1913-1915), A. G. Harrison (1915-1916), J. W. Campbell (1916-1917), W. P. Webb (1917-1919), W. E. Patty (1919-1926), Geo. W. Page (1926-1927), W. P. Fulton (1928), Lee Clark (1928-1931) and Chas. E. Davis (1931-1936), O. J. Laas (1937).

The following persons have served as Principal: S. W. Meharg (1902-1908), T. O. Price (1906), Miss Ellen Robinson (1908-1911), A. L. Green (1911-1912), W. H. Warren, (1912-1913) E. J. Woodward (1913-1914), H. P. Webb (1914-1917), R. A. Burgess (1917-1920), R. B. Sparks (1920-1927) and O. J. Laas (1927-1936).

Public Schools of Hale County

Plainview School was established in 1889. The first trustees were J. M. Carter, Z. T. Maxwell and John Pendley. D. C. Lowe and Miss Lizzie Butts were the first teachers. The Plainview Independent School District now contains seven schools, ie. High School, Junior High, Lamar, Central, Highland, Seth Ward and Booker T. Washington (colored). 72 teachers are employed in the district. The scholastic enrollment is 2074.

Mapes School was established in 1889. The first trustees were J. M. Carter, Z. T. Maxwell and John Pendley. Miss Alice Rosser was the first teacher. The name of the school was changed in 1890 to Fairview, and two years later was changed to Prairieview.

Prairieview School, formerly known as Mapes, and also Fairview, was named Prairieview in 1892. This school has the distinction of being the oldest school in Hale County. It employs two teachers.

Epworth School was established in 1889. The first trustees were L. A. White, A. E. Adams and G. D. Allen. B. A. Berry was the first teacher. This school was absorbed by the Hale Center School in 1893.

Liberty School was established in 1891. The first trustees were J. M. Snider, S. T. Pepper and C. H. Gilbert. B. L. Spencer was the first teacher. This school now employs four teachers.

Runningwater School was established in 1891. The first trustees were Dennis Rice, T. C. Overhuls and J. V. Matlock. Miss Mamie Valade was the first teacher. Runningwater became an Independent School District in 1924. It now employs four teachers.

Union School was established in 1892. The first trustee was G. F. Formway. John B. Shelton was the first teacher. This school was discontinued after a few years.

Hale City School was established in 1892. The first trustees were Jesse J. B. McCullar, L. B. Lovelace and W. P. Blake. C. F. Kerr was the first teacher. This school was absorbed by the Hale Center School in 1893 and the school house was moved to Hale Center.

Progress School was established in 1892. The first trustees were W. C. Hood, W. J. Patrick and O. E. Ballard. Fannie Barber was the first teacher. This school was changed to Pearce in 1896.

Pearce School was established in 1896. The first trustees were A. L. Maupin, M. T. Cocke and W. H. Pearce. Leslie Maupin was the first teacher. This school was discontinued in 1903.

Ivey School was established in 1892. The first trustees were J. M. Snider and J. N. Donohoo. T. L. Vanvacter was the first teacher. This school was consolidated with Lakeview Independent School District in 1919.

Center Plains School was established in 1892. The first trustees were W. S. Boliver, P. S. Green and O. T. Talley. George L. Mayfield was the first teacher. This school was absorbed by Norfleet School in 1908. It was re-established as Center Plains in 1910. In 1937 the district was divided and the south part added to Cotton Center District. The north side remains Center Plains but they transfer their students to Hale Center by bus.

Helm School was established in 1892. The first trustees were I. J. Helm and J. M. Harkey. This school went into Hale Center District in 1906 and was absorbed by Hooper School in 1908. The first teacher of this school was Minnie M. Starkey.

White School was established in 1892. The first trustees were J. M. Snider and J. N. Donohoo. F. V. Neil was the first teacher. This school was discontinued in 1897. It was re-established in 1914 with J. T. Terrell and L. A. Martin as trustees, and taught by Eleanor Price. This school was absorbed by Bellview in 1917.

Hale Center School was established in 1893, through the consolidation of the Epworth and Hale City Schools. The first trustees were B. A. Hudgins, L. T. Lester and C. H. Harlan. George L. Mayfield was the first teacher. School opened in this school on January 1, 1894. Hale Center became an Independent School District in 1917. It has two school buildings, and employs fifteen teachers.

McWhorter School was established in 1896. Ida L. Oliver was the first teacher. The school house burned in 1921. The new school house was located two miles east of the old one and the name was changed to Science Hill.

Happy Union School was established in 1897. The first trustees were J. V. Neal, M. T. Cocke and A. L. Maupin. Lillie Leonard was the first teacher. This school employs one teacher.

Petersburg School was established in 1900 and consolidated with Allman School in Floyd County. In 1901 a school was opened at Petersburg, with J. M. Braselton as its first teacher. Petersburg Independent School District was organized in

1920. It has two schools and employs twelve teachers.

Westside School was established in 1901. The first trustee was T. A. Douthitt. Della Triplett was the first teacher. The district was consolidated with a school in Lamb County the first year and the first school was taught at Westside in 1902. This school now employs three teachers.

Southeast School was established in 1902. The first trustees were T. J. Tilson, W. B. Sheffy and Mr. Dodson. James R. DeLay taught during the first year. This school was not named but was located in a rented house sixteen miles southeast of Plainview, hence it was designated as Southeast. It was moved to another residence two miles distant the next year and was taught by Charlie Parker. During the year a school house was built and the school was named Bellview, Col. T. J. Tilson naming the school in honor of John Bell, an early settler in the community.

Bellview School was moved in 1904 from its location a half mile distant to the present site. Its trustees were Col. T. J. Tilson, John Bell and Mr. Dodson. Anna Cannon was the first teacher. Bellview became an Independent School District in 1918 and absorbed the White School. It employs two teachers.

Midway School was established in 1904. The first trustees were M. F. Mechner, W. B. Sheffy and J. M. Maddox. L. W. Sloneker was the first teacher. This school consolidated with the Snyder School in 1922.

Ellen School was established in 1905, and was named for the Ellen Post Office. The first trustee was John J. Simpson. Minnie Lee was the first teacher. This school employs two teachers.

Locust Grove School was established in 1904. The first trustees were W. S. Boliver, P. S. Green and O. T. Tally. Della Triplett was the first teacher. This school was absorbed by Norfleet School in 1908.

Star School was established in 1906. The first trustee was John Read. J. W. Ware was the first teacher. This school consolidated with Lakeview Independent School in 1919.

Snyder School was established in 1908. The first trustee was P. B. Snyder. Myra Cosby was the first teacher. This school was established in the Mennonite Colony and for several years employed only Mennonite teachers. The school was

HISTORY OF EDUCATION

named for P. B. Snyder, pastor of the Mennonite Church. Snyder School became an Independent School District in 1922 and absorbed the Midway School. It employs two teachers.

Norfleet School was established in 1908. The first trustees were R. S. Wagoner, J. W. Cunningham and J. W. Boggus. A. E. Matlock was the first teacher. This school absorbed the Locust Grove and Center Plains Schools when established. It was absorbed by the Cotton Center Independent School District in 1925.

Bartonsite School was established in 1908. The first trustees were J. J. Barton, J. P. Carr and E. Harlan. B. W. Wilkins was the first teacher. This school was absorbed by the Cotton Center Independent School District in 1925.

Hooper School was established in 1908. The first trustees were I. J. Helm, J. C. Hooper and F. W. Struve. Jennie King was the first teacher. This school absorbed the Helm School in 1908. It employs two teachers.

Halfway School was established in 1908. The first trustees were R. L. Hooper, J. W. Dye, B. B. Huguley. Miss Clora Sanderson was the first teacher. It employs two teachers. Halfway is now an Independent School District.

Strip School was established in 1909. The first trustees were J. B. Jones, P. L. Wimberly and J. C. Atwood. Audra Thompson was the first teacher. This school was discontinued in 1912.

East Mound School was established in 1909. The first trustees were W. B. Martine and W. B. Seamans. Lula Howell was the first teacher. This school now employs two teachers.

Holechre School was established in 1909. The first trustees were M. S. Hudson and M. P. Rahlzahn. Nell Holland was the first teacher. This school became the Stoneback school in 1912.

Abernathy School was established in 1910. The first trustees were J. I. Powell, V. Stambaugh and J. C. Atwood. Beulah Wilson was the first teacher. A school was taught in Abernathy in a private residence in 1909-10, by Mrs. Ola Legg, this school being financed by Dr. M. C. Overton, a real estate agent who founded the town of Abernathy. Mrs. Legg succeeded Miss Wilson in 1911 and taught continuously until 1922 when she was elected to the office of County Superintendent of Schools. Abernathy became an Independent School District in 1917. It absorbed the County Line and Eagle Springs Schools in 1936. Employs 15 teachers.

Mayfield School was established in 1911. The first trustees were G. W. Brown, R. S. Wagoner and L. H. Triplett. Nell Holland was the first teacher. The school was named in honor of George L. Mayfield, who at that time was County Judge and ex officio County Superintendent of Schools. This school employs two teachers. The school house burned in February, 1937.

Iowa Avenue School was established in 1910. The first teacher was Kate Cooper. This school employs two teachers.

Mount Vernon School was established in 1912. The first trustees were J. M. Brazele, K. D. Thomas and Tom Abney. O. J. Tyler was the first teacher. This school employs one teacher.

Stoneback School was established in 1912. The school was named in honor of Mr. and Mrs. Stoneback of that community. The first trustees were C. B. Rees, and H. B. Meester. Florence Mash was the first teacher. In 1937 the entire student body was taken to Hale Center by bus.

Woodrow School was established in 1913. It was named in honor of Woodrow Wilson, then President of the United States. M. D. Leach was the first trustee and Vera Holland was the first teacher. This school was absorbed by the Liberty School in 1921.

Lakeview School was established in 1914. The first trustees were J. B. Jones, Elbert Overton and G. C. Pierce. A. H. Tedford was the first teacher. Lakeview became an Independent School District in 1919 and absorbed the Star and Ivey Schools. This school employs four teachers.

Valleyview School was established in 1914. The first trustees were M. C. Cornelius and E. D. Matlock. The first teacher was Lou Ida Hatchett. The pupils in this district are transported to Olton School in Lamb County by bus. This change in the school was made about 1931.

Anchor School was established in 1916. The first trustee was E. A. Shackleford and Alma Rash was the first teacher. This school was consolidated with the Cotton Center Independent School District in 1925.

Sunshine School was established in 1916. The first trustees were C. W. Boyd, G. W. Struve and W. F. Beard. The first teacher was Gladys Thomas. This school employs one teacher.

Reed School was established in 1918. The first trustees were A. H. Reed, J. H. Brown and C. H. Buckingham. The first teacher was Hazel Crouch. Since 1937 the student body is sent by bus to Abernathy.

Wilson School was established in 1918. The first trustees were J. W. Waddill, W. C. Sewell and T. J. Vines. The first teacher was Vera Stambaugh. This school employs one teacher.

Stansell School was established in 1920. The first trustee was W. C. Stansell and the first teacher was Anna Foster. This school was named for W. C. Stansell. Since 1937 the student body is sent by bus to Plainview.

Clements School was established in 1921. The first trustees were E. R. Springer, W. B. Smith and C. A. McSpadden. The first teacher was Eristiena Lane. This school was named in honor of Charles Clements, who at that time was County Judge and Ex Officio County Superintendent of Schools. The school employs two teachers.

Cousins School was established in 1917. The first trustees were R. M. Fortenberry, I. E. Botts and J. H. Drake. The first teacher was Ethel Thomas. This school was named in honor of R. B. Cousins, at that time President of West Texas State Teacher College at Canyon, who was active in promoting educational interests in Hale County. In 1937 Cousins School bought a bus and is now sending their entire student body to Plainview.

Science Hill School was established in 1921 after the McWhorter school house burned. The school was named by C. D. Hughes in memory of a school of that name in Kentucky. The first trustee was C. D. Hughes and the first teacher was Helen Evans. An election in 1937 effected the division of this district and the consolidation of the south side with Abernathy School and the north side with Cotton Center School.

Cotton Center School was established as an Independent School District in 1925 as a result of the consolidation of Anchor, Bartonsite and Norfleet schools. It is situated in the center of a cotton-growing community, hence its name. The first trustees were E. A. Shackelford, F. M. McKnight and

C. J. Sturdivant. G. A. Lowery was the first Superintendent of this school. Nine teachers are employed at Cotton Center.

Eagle Springs School was established in 1925. The school was named for Eagle Springs. The first trustees were A. N. Johnson, C. I. Rhodes and H. M. Morehead. The first teacher was Vera Truett. This school consolidated with Abernathy in 1936.

Lakeside School was established in 1931. The first trustees were E. C. Curtis, J. F. Lassiter, J. F. McDonough, Ernest Miller, J. C. Fuller and J. C. Howard. Carrie Frazier and Evelyn Shankle were the first teachers. This district was established with territory withdrawn from the north side of Petersburg District. The school employs one teacher.

The following persons taught in the public free schools of Hale County prior to 1900:

D. C. Lowe, Lizzie Butts, Alice Rosser, B. A. Berry, Charles Scott, B. L. Spencer, Mamie Valade, Fannie Barber, T. L. Van Vacter, F. V. Neil, George L. Mayfield, C. F. Kerr, Minnie M. Starkey, R. B. C. Howell, Mattie Williams, O. C. Mulkey, Mrs. J. I. Mulkey, Eugenia Welter, John B. Shelton, Ida L. Oliver, M. N. Parks, W. O. Morton, Mrs. L. G. Wilson, W. A. Smith, J. G. Williams, C. I. Browder, John B. Whaley, Jamie Browder, Willie Sowder, Mattie Williams, Olive Beasley, Nora Eddy, Althea Winn, T. W. Waddill, Isabella Howell, Amy Graves, Lottie Graves, T. G. Ross, Lula Beasley, Sally Savage, Alice Bradford, J. M. Blake, Ione Burch, J. W. Moore, Mary Bryan, A. Ernsberger, Carrie Ernsberger, Pearl Estes, Ruth Estes, Daisy Hooper, Lillie Leonard, Leslie Maupin, W. C. Mathes, S. R. Merrill, E. Spooner, L. L. Cooper, Ruth Maggard, W. J. Williams, B. McCartie, C. V. Young, G. L. Bradford, Ola Huguley, S. S. Sloneker, J. J. Stamps.

Central Plains College
and Conservatory of Music

Central Plains College and Conservatory of Music was the first Junior College to be built in Plainview. It opened on September 18, 1907, and operated for three years. This school was founded by the Holiness Church with the intention of making it a denominational school to be known as Central Plains Holiness College. Mr. Ferd Faulkner donated twenty-

HISTORY OF EDUCATION

five acres of land for a campus and also made other large contributions to make the founding of the school possible. A Board of Trustees was elected, composed of Ferd Faulkner, S. S. Sloneker, Ben Sebastian, A. J. McCrary and R. T. Miller.

Dr. L. L. Gladney, who then occupied the chair of Philosophy and Divinity in a college in Meridian, Mississippi, was offered the presidency. Dr. Gladney met with the Trustees in Plainview in February, 1907, at which time he recommended that the school be made non-sectarian and interdenominational, since the population of the country was too small to make the maintenance of a denominational school practicable. This plan was accepted and the school was named Central Plains College and Conservatory of Music.

Fifty acres were put into a campus and a three story administration building of cement blocks was erected. Two dormitories were also built. School opened in a partially finished building with an enrollment of 68 students, 159 enrolling during the first year. The school was operated along the lines of Meridian Male College and its sister, Meridian Female College, of Meridian, Mississippi, a co-educational school with military training for both boys and girls. Capt. W. W. Cherry was head of the Military Department. The school carried the student from the primary grade to A. B. degree.

After three years of school work, the Holiness Church found the burden of sponsoring the College too great, and proffered it to the Methodist Church at the District Conference held at Lockney June 16, 1910. The Methodists accepted the responsibility and the school was turned over, free of debt, to the Plainview District Conference.

Seth Ward College

The name of the school was at once changed from Central Plains College and Conservatory of Music to Seth Ward College, named in honor of Bishop Seth Ward. Dr. L. L. Gladney was retained as president of the school during the school year 1910-1911. In 1911 W. M. Pearce became president, and later N. B. Johnson held that position, with J. E. Willis, Dean. The Board of Trustees of Seth Ward College were as follows: L. M. Faulkner, R. A. Long, J. W. Wayland,

W. H. Terry, E. H. Perry, O. P. Kiker, W. A. Nash, J. N. Donohoo, M. S. Leveridge, D. E. Ansley, G. W. Shearer, W. C. Mathes, W. M. Lane, D. B. Doak, J. F. Owens, E. E. Robinson, E. P. Thompson, T. F. Gilliland and C. N. N. Ferguson.

For five years the Seth Ward College prospered under Methodist administration, and Wayland and Seth Ward Colleges vied with each other in friendly rivalry. Inter-collegiate athletics and debates contributed to the social life of Plainview.

Early in 1916, the Boys Dormitory burned. Before the building could be replaced, the administration building caught fire on March 26, 1916, and burned to the ground, the Girls Dormitory also burning at the same time. The school term was finished in the Methodist Church of Plainview, but the loss was so great that Seth Ward College was never rebuilt, and the school was discontinued. On August 30, 1932, 100 former faculty members and ex-students of Seth Ward College met together for a reunion of old acquaintances and to commemorate the memory of Old Seth Ward College. This is now an annual event.

Wayland Baptist College

Wayland Baptist College was founded primarily through the efforts of Dr. J. H. Wayland. Such an institution on the plains of West Texas had been for many years the dream of this pioneer physician who came to Plainview in 1891 and practiced medicine when the country was in the early pioneer stage. Among the people who lived in the dugouts scattered over the prairie he found many people of culture and refinement and a great many of the settlers were people of University degrees. He realized that the boys and girls reared on the plains would not have the educational advantages that their parents had had unless schools were built to make it possible.

After cherishing the idea for many years, even to the drawing of the plans for the College in his spare hours, Dr. Wayland finally interested the Staked Plains Baptist Association in the project at its meeting in 1906. No definite action was taken, however, until 1907, when Dr. B. M. Carroll, of Waco, became interested in the proposition and committees were appointed and work began. The school was organized

HISTORY OF EDUCATION

in 1909 by the Staked Plains Baptist Association. The charter first called for the name "Wayland Literary and Technological Institute," but this was later changed to Wayland Baptist College.

Plans for the building were drawn and perfected by Architect J. C. Goodwin according to Dr. Wayland's sketches. Work was begun on the construction of the administration building in April, 1909. S. A. Baugess was employed to superintend the building. Mr. Baugess resigned after the foundation was laid and Kenneth H. Cox superintended the construction until the building was erected.

Dr. Wayland's original gift to the school was 25 acres of ground for a campus and $10,000, which was later increased to 30 acres for a campus and $100,000. Dr. I. E. Gates, who became the first president of the school, initiated and managed an advertising campaign for Wayland Baptist College and funds for the building were raised principally through donations.

Wayland Baptist College was formally opened for administration on September 27, 1910, in Matador Hall, before the administration building was ready for occupancy. 62 students were enrolled on the opening day, 225 enrolling during the first session. The curriculum was complete, including grammar school grades as well as Academic and Junior College work,—also music and art. The grammar grades were discontinued in a few years.

In 1913 Wayland Baptist College was correlated with the Baptist Convention of Texas and admitted into the system of schools fostered by the Baptists of Texas to carry on the denominational work in the Panhandle. The school was recognized as a standard Junior College in 1917, and in 1926 was admitted into membership in the American Association of Junior Colleges, making its credits acceptable in any College or University without an entrance examination.

The administration building is a three-story fireproof structure of reinforced concrete and brick. The third floor is used for a Boys Dormitory. Matador Hall, a Girls Dormitory, is a two-story brick veneer structure, made possible through donations made by the First Baptist Church of Matador, Texas, hence its name, Matador Hall. The Lindsay Nunn Gymnasium was a gift of Mr. and Mrs. Lindsay Nunn, of Amarillo. It has a seating capacity of approximately 600. The Lindsay Nunn Library, valued at $3,000, is also a gift of Mr. and Mrs. Lindsay Nunn. The Laboratory equipment was the gift of Dr. and Mrs. E. B. Atwood.

The first Trustees of Wayland College were as follows: T. D. Webb, President, W. B. Joiner, Secretary, J. G. Hamilton, Treasurer, L. G. Wilson, Rev. G. I. Britain, B. F. Dixon, Thornton Jones, J. H. Wayland, R. J. Goode, Rev. J. W. Winn, W. A. Donaldson, W. W. Nelson and T. N. Carmack.

The following persons have served as President of the school: Dr. I. E. Gates (1910-1916), O. L. Hailey (1916-1917), R. E. L. Farmer (1917-1919), Dr. E. B. Atwood (1919-1923), and G. W. McDonald (1923-).

Deans of the college have been: R. E. Bell, W. H. Wray, J. P. Reynolds, E. C. Nelson, J. C. Stephens, W. P. Clements, J. E. Willis, A. F. Winston, B. H. Warren and Dr. Z. T. Huff.

In 1935 Wayland Baptist College completed a quarter of a century of administration as an educational institution. The high standard of her work, her reputation for religious training and for the development of good citizens and lasting character are widely known. The school has fulfilled the objective and the dream of its founder.

Business Colleges

The first Business College in Hale County was opened in Plainview in August, 1910, by Aldrah Braden Edwards, in the Odd Fellows Hall, then located in the Wayland Building at Fifth and Broadway. Wayland Baptist College, which opened on September 27th of that year, had advertised a Commercial Department. An arrangement was therefore made by the officials of Wayland College with Mr. Edwards to teach the Wayland Commercial students. Twenty-three students were enrolled, 17 boys and 6 girls. In October Mr. Edwards abandoned the project. The College moved the student body to the unfinished College building and M. Buford was employed as instructor. Mr. Buford resigned two months later, and no teacher was secured until the fall of 1911.

M. S. Hoover opened the Wayland Commercial School in

September, 1911, with an enrollment of some 20 students. A number of students graduated from this department in the spring of 1912, however, the city of Plainview at that time had not sufficient business to give them employment. The boom which followed the coming of the railroad had died down and no firm in the town had sufficient volume of business to employ a stenographer full time. Those who found employment did so by doing public stenography or part time work, which enabled two or three to handle the work of all the business firms. Mr. Hoover resigned at Wayland College in the summer of 1912 and operated a Business College at Seth Ward College in 1912-1913.

J. E. Watson took charge of the Wayland Business College in November, 1912, and conducted it until May 18, 1918. He then opened the Watson's Business College in the McLaughlin Building and operated it until July 25, 1925, when he sold the school to Roy J. Lippert.

Roy J. Lippert changed the name of the school to Lippert's Business College, which he continues to operate, now located in the Viegel Building.

J. E. Watson opened the Plainview Business College and Watson's School of Correspondence in January, 1927, which he continues to operate.

Plainview Chautauqua

The Annual Chautauqua was an educational feature held in Plainview for one week each summer for fifteen consecutive years. It was inaugurated under the auspices of the Plainview Commercial Club, of which Judge J. E. Lancaster was President and James R. DeLay was Secretary. The first Chautauqua was held from August 26th to September 1st inclusive, 1907. This seven days program furnished the people with wholesome entertainment, recreation, education and amusement. Many speakers of renown were included in its programs as well as many rare musical concerts and educational features. The Annual Chautauqua was discontinued in 1922.

The Public Library

The Public Library in Plainview was established through the united efforts of the Women's Clubs. A formal opening of the Library was held at the City Hall on June 25, 1913. The Clubs were represented at the opening by the following members who served as hostesses: The Civic League, Mrs. Mary V. Dye; The Browning Club, Mrs. D. H. Collier; The Travel Study Club, Mrs. L. T. Mayhugh and The As You Like It Club, Mrs. J. J. Bromley.

One hundred books were placed on the newly made shelves and donations of books and cash were made by various citizens on the day of the opening. For a time the Library occupied the room in the City Hall now used by the Fire Department. It was then moved to the Campbell Building, and later returned to the City Hall. When the City Auditorium was erected in 1922, a permanent location was secured for the Library in that building.

The Library at first was kept open two afternoons each week, members of the various clubs taking turns serving as librarians. Miss Edna Mayhugh was the first paid librarian. The librarian's salary during the first four months was a personal gift from Mrs. Florence N. Catto. Other librarians have been Mrs. W. E. Armstrong, Mrs. Mary V. Dye and Mrs. L. P. Davis.

For a number of years the Library was supported entirely by the Women's Clubs. Later an appropriation was made by the Board of City Development and was supplemented by the School Board. Members of the Women's Clubs continue to serve on the Library Board, and to them is due much credit for the administration of the Public Library.

Home Demonstration Work

The Home Demonstration Work was organized in Hale County by the A. & M. College Extension Service in June, 1924, after the Commissioners Court, on application from the rural communities, had voted an appropriation to assist with the work. Miss Leila E. Dye was sent to Plainview as the first Home Demonstration Agent.

During the first year there were organized in sixteen communities 8 Girls Clubs and 14 Women's Clubs, making a total of 22 organizations. The work covers demonstrations in three main projects: (1) Home Food Supply, which includes production, preservation and storage of foods, (2) Home Improvements, both interior and exterior, and (3) Clothing, which includes selection of material, making of garments, planning wardrobe and budget of clothing for entire family; also a productive project, usually poultry, gardening or dairying.

During the financial crisis of the early thirties, the Home Demonstration Work was a vital factor in enabling rural people to "Live at Home." The art of home-canning and preservation of fruits, vegetables and meats was developed in Hale County as never before known. A total value of $33,759.57 was placed upon the work done in these clubs in 1935.

The following persons have served as Home Demonstration Agents in Hale County: Miss Leila E. Dye (1924-1925), Miss Gladys Short (1925-1926), Miss Opal L. Wood (1927-1929), Mrs. Julia E. Kelly (1929-1936) and Miss Chloie Huffaker (1936-   ).

CHAPTER VII

NEWSPAPERS

The newspapers of Hale County have played an important part in the history and development of the country. They have been a vital factor in the life of the community, keeping the people in touch with the affairs of the community and informed in regard to affairs of the state and nation. They have given graciously of their spaces in publicity to all religious, social and civic activities and have been a constructive force in the furtherance of every worthy cause. As an advertising medium and press agent, they have heralded to the world information regarding the growth and development of the country and attracted worthwhile homeseekers. As a medium of education they are hand in hand with the schools and rank with transportation in development and progress. Hale County owes much gratitude to her newspapers for the part they have played in the progress of half a century.

The Hale County Hesperian was the first newspaper in Hale County. This was established by D. B. Hill and John Davidson in Plainview in October, 1889. Mr. Hill immediately disposed of his interest to Mr. Davidson, who soon afterwards sold to a Mr. Cates. Mr. Cates traded the newspaper to J. M. Shafer in June, 1891, who changed the name of the paper.

The Hale County Herald was the new name Mr. Shafer gave to the paper first known as the Hesperian, a name derived from the Greek word "Hesperia," meaning western lands. J. W. Johnson, for many years a member of the grocery firm of Hatchell and Johnson in Plainview, claimed the honor of being the first subscriber to the Hale County Herald. J. M. Shafer was owner and publisher of the Herald until 1911, his son, Tom Shafer, acting as managing editor from 1904 to 1911.

Mr. Shafer sold the Herald to B. O. Brown in 1911. E. B. Miller purchased one-half interest in the paper in 1912 and a year later became sole owner. He then sold one-half interest to H. S. Hilburn. The Herald became a semi-weekly paper and beginning January 1, 1913, was published as a daily paper for a period of six months, when the name was changed to The Plainview Herald. During the following year it was published as a tri-weekly and then was changed back to a semi-weekly paper.

On March 4, 1929, the Herald Publishing Company was incorporated and bought the Plainview News. Since that date the Plainview Evening Herald has been published daily and the Plainview News has been published weekly. The Herald Publishing Company owns its own building, an up-to-date brick structure, and continues to publish the Herald on the old site used by Mr. Shafer. H. S. Hilburn is editor, E. B. Miller Advertising Manager and E. Q. Perry Business Manager.

The Texan Press was founded in Plainview by J. Winford Hunt on August 30, 1890, who edited and published the newspaper until 1892, when it was consolidated with the Lubbock Leader, a paper founded by Leslie Maupin on July 1, 1891, both papers being published at Estacado to serve Lubbock and Hale Counties.

The Texas Press-Leader resulted from the consolidation of the Texan Press and Lubbock Leader, and partnership of J. Winford Hunt and Leslie Maupin, who edited and pub-

The Plainview News was edited and published by C. M. Shuffler. Mr. Shuffler then changed the name to the Plainview News.

The Plainview News was edited and published by C. M. Shuffler and son from May 23, 1906, until September 6, 1907, when they sold the News to J. C. Edwards and W. A. Parker. Edwards and Parker conducted the business until it was purchased by Jesse M. Adams on June 15, 1911. Mr. Adams edited the paper from that date until 1925. On January 1, 1925, Mr. Adams started on a trip around the world, writing travel-stories for the Plainview News, leaving his son-in-law, E. Q. Perry, to edit the paper during his absence. Illness overtook him during his sojourn in India, from which he could not entirely recover. He suffered a relapse while visiting the Holylands and death overtook him at Toulon, France, on May 10, 1925. Mr. Perry continued to edit the Plainview News after Mr. Adams' death until March 2, 1929, when the Plainview News and the Plainview Herald consolidated and a corporation known as the Herald-News Publishing Company Inc. continued publishing the Plainview News as an official weekly paper for Hale County.

The Community Weekly was established in Plainview in 1930 by R. S. Norman, who moved the plant from Hermleigh, Texas. A stock company was organized and the Community Publishing Company was incorporated under charter granted July 12, 1930, with the following stockholders: R. B. Mitchell, Pres., L. S. Kennedy Vice Pres., O. C. Burgess, Sec.-Treas., W. A. Nash, Ed Day, J. E. Rigler, J. C. Boyd, Frank Triplett and Frank Simonton. The purpose of the paper being to sponsor community interests, associated communities were organized. The first communities associated and their editors were: Liberty—Mrs. B. T. Wells; Cousins—Mrs. Ott Grantham; Runningwater—Mrs. John Eakin; Providence—Mrs. F. M. Kennedy; Seth Ward—Mrs. R. H. Germany; Prairieview—Mrs. L. A. Hoyle; Stansell—D. C. Kimball, and Olton—A. L. Dennis. The Community Weekly consolidated with the Beavers Printing Company on November 28, 1930. Milton Beavers then became manager and served in that capacity until March 8, 1936, when Mrs. R. S. Norman took over active management. Mr. Norman was editor of the paper from date of establishment on June 12, 1930, until his death on December 15, 1935. Mrs. Norman is now manager and editor.

The Hale Center American was established in 1922 by H. T. Merritt, who brought the plant from Merkel, Texas. J. C. Hurst purchased the plant in February, 1929, and Fred Wortham edited the paper from that date until October of that year. Mr. Hurst then edited his own paper until 1933. R. J. Dison edited it from 1933 to 1935, when he was succeeded by Vic Lamb. The Hale Center American and the Abernathy Review were consolidated in 1930, at which time Mr. Hurst installed the linotype, and since that time both papers have been printed at the plant in Hale Center. Prior to 1930 both the papers were hand set and turned by hand. Vic Lamb is now editor of the Hale Center American.

The Abernathy Review was established in 1922 by S. J. Redman, who sold the paper to W. A. Richter in 1924. Mr. Richter published the paper until 1925. J. J. Riley later purchased it, edited it for a short time and resold it to Mr. Redman, who sold it to Stockton Henry, of Lubbock. In 1927 J. C. Hurst purchased the Abernathy Review and edited and published it for several years. The paper was consolidated with the Hale Center American in 1930 and both papers are now printed in Hale Center. Vic Lamb edited the paper until 1935. Buford Davenport is the present editor.

The Petersburg Journal was established at Petersburg on January 27, 1927, by E. R. Gibson, who has edited and published the paper continuously since that date.

Other newspapers were established in Hale County which served the community for a time and were discontinued.

The Texan Press was established at Plainview on August 30, 1890, by J. Winford Hunt. This paper, published at Estacado, consolidated with the Lubbock-Leader, and became the Texas Press-Leader in 1892.

The Texas Press-Leader was published in Plainview from 1892 until 1906, when it was sold to Rev. C. M. Shuffler and son Ralph, who changed the name to The Plainview News.

The Plainviewan was a single-sheet published daily for a while in Plainview in 1913 by a Mr. Hopkins, who will be remembered by his self-styled pseudonym, "Rearin'-to-go Hopkins."

The Epworth Chronicle, owned by Manley Cox, of Estacado, was edited and published by J. Winford Hunt, at Epworth in 1892. The paper was discontinued when Epworth and Hale City went together in 1893 and started Hale Center.

The Hale City Globe was established at Hale City in 1891. It was edited and published by W. P. Blake until 1892 when the plant was moved to Hale Center. A few months later Mr. Blake discontinued the paper and moved his equipment elsewhere.

The Hale Center Live Wire was an early newspaper published at Hale Center, edited by I. S. Boulier.

The Hale Center Messenger was edited and published in 1903 and 1904 by J. E. Wimberly.

The Hale Center News, established by a Mr. McAdams,

was printed in Lockney and was published during 1927 and 1928.

The Petersburg News was established in 1911 by a Mr. Watrous. This was sold to O. E. Brashear in 1911.

The Petersburg Tribune, successor to the Petersburg News, was edited and published by O. E. Brashear in 1911.

The Petersburg Star, published at Lockney, was edited by Miss Alma Jo Livingston in 1926.

The Two-County News was established at Abernathy in 1909 by Ed Hardin, serving Hale and Lubbock Counties. This paper was discontinued in 1911.

The Abernathy Breeze was established about 1915 by Robert E. Downey, who edited and published it for several years and discontinued it.

HALE COUNTY NEWSPAPERS 1937

Plainview Evening Herald (daily)..........Plainview
Plainview News (weekly)..................Plainview
Community Weekly (weekly)...............Plainview
Hale Center American (weekly)..........Hale Center
Petersburg Journal (weekly).............Petersburg
Abernathy Review (weekly)................Abernathy

CHAPTER VIII

LEGAL AND JUDICIAL HISTORY

Judicial Districts

The 34th Judicial District was fixed by an Act of the 18th Legislature approved and effective March 27, 1883, at which time the judicial districts of the state were reorganized. 22 counties, including Hale County and counties west, east and south were placed in the 34th District. Hale County was attached to Baylor County for judicial and land purposes and all legal and land matters were transacted at Seymour.

The 31st Judicial District was reorganized by an Act of the 18th Legislature approved Apr. 9, 1883, and effective September 1, 1884, reorganizing the judicial districts of the state. Hale County, together with 29 counties north were placed in this district, and Hale County was attached to Donley County for Judicial purposes and legal business was then transacted at Clarendon.

The 32nd Judicial District was reorganized out of the 32nd, 33rd, 35th, 39th and 42nd Districts by an Act of the 20th Legislature approved March 31, 1887. Hale County, together with 24 other counties to the west, east and south were placed in 32nd District. Hale County was attached to Crosby County for Judicial Purposes, that county having organized in 1886, and all legal and land matters were transacted at Estacado.

The 47th Judicial District was created by an Act of the 21st Legislature approved Feb. 18, 1889, by reorganizing the 31st, 32nd and 39th districts. The 47th district was composed of 16 counties of the Panhandle Plains, including Hale County. Court then convened in Hale County, on the first Mondays in April and October. The unorganized counties of Bailey, Lamb and Swisher were attached to Hale County for Judicial purposes. Judge W. B. Plemons, of Amarillo, was appointed first District Judge and L. G. Wilson, of Plainview, was appointed District Attorney.

The 50th Judicial District was created by an Act of the 22nd Legislature approved March 13, 1891, reorganizing the 32nd and 39th Districts. Hale County, together with 13 counties to the east, west and south, were placed in the 50th District.

The 64th Judicial District was created by an Act of the 29th Legislature approved February 8, 1905, by dividing the 47th and 50th Districts. 11 counties, including Hale, were placed in the 64th District. This district was reduced in 1929 to Floyd, Briscoe, Castro, Hale, Swisher, Bailey and Lamb Counties. The following Attorneys have served as officers of the 64th Judicial District: District Judge; L. S. Kinder (1905-1914), R. C. Joiner (1914-1926), Charles Clements (1926-1934), R. C. Joiner (1934-1936), and C. D. Russell (1936 until the present time). District Attorney: Reuben M. Ellerd (1905-1906), C. S. Williams (1907-1908), L. C. Penry (1908-1912), George L. Mayfield (1912-1916), A. C. Hatchell (1916-1920), Charles Clements (1920-1926), Meade F. Griffin (1926-1934) and Charles H. Dean (1934 until the present time).

Court of Civil Appeals

The Court of Appeals was organized by an Act of the 15th Legislature approved May 6, 1876, to be held in the Supreme Court Building at Austin. All appeals from District Courts were made returnable at Austin.

The State of Texas was divided into five Supreme Judicial Districts by an Act of the 23rd Legislature approved May 13, 1893, and a Court of Civil Appeals was established in each of the five districts. 84 counties, including Hale County, were then placed in the Second Supreme Judicial District, and appeals were made returnable at Fort Worth.

The Supreme Judicial Districts were reorganized by the 32nd Legislature by an Act approved March 11, 1911, at which time the Seventh and Eighth Districts were created. The Seventh Supreme Judicial District was composed of the following counties: Dallam, Sherman, Hansford, Ochiltree, Lipscomb, Hartley, Moore, Hutchinson, Roberts, Hemphill, Oldham, Potter, Carson, Gray, Wheeler, Deaf Smith, Randall,

LEGAL AND JUDICIAL HISTORY 97

Armstrong, Donley, Collingsworth, Parmer, Castro, Swisher, Briscoe, Hall, Childress, Bailey, Hale, Floyd, Motley, Lamb, Cottle, Foard, Hardeman, Wilbarger, Crosby, Lubbock, Hockley, Cochran, Yoakum, Terry, Linn, Garza, Dickens, Kent, King, Fisher, Dawson and Scurry. These counties, with the exception of Fisher, Dawson and Scurry, comprise the Seventh District at the present time.

Judge H. C. Randolph, of Plainview, was appointed to the office of Justice of the Court of Civil Appeals of the Seventh District and served until his death on April 19, 1932. Judge A. B. Martin, of Plainview, succeeded Judge Randolph in that office and served until March, 1937, when he resigned to accept the appointment by Governor Jas. V. Allred to the Supreme Court Commission.

The District Court

The first session of the District Court in Hale County was held at Plainview January 7, 1889. There being present Attorneys L. G. Wilson, Joe E. Rosson and E. B. Covington, E. B. Covington was elected special judge to hold the court. The only business transacted at that time was the appointing of a jury for the spring term.

The first Grand Jury was as follows: J. W. Smylie, Foreman, T. C. Overhuls, John Bell, T. W. Parker, C. F. Graham, J. M. Martin, J. W. Johnson, Hugh McClelland, R. A. Phillips Sr., A. N. Jones, T. E. Smith, W. B. Ford. The first indictments by the first grand-jury were for the following causes:

1. Theft of a cow
2. Giving away liquor on election day
3. Theft of a steer
4. Assault to murder
5. Receiving and concealing stolen property.

The first Petit Jurors called were as follows: D. L. Shepley, W. H. Portwood, F. M. Parks, J. E. Cannon, F. M. Bradford, Z. T. Maxwell, T. B. Leverett, Thomas Miller, A. H. Henson, C. H. Harlan, H. M. Burch, P. F. Bryan, C. J. Mapes, J. H. Leach, F. M. Bradford, Wm. Pendley, L. A. White, D. W. Owens, W. B. Duncan, L. T. Lester and J. W. Cox.

The first case tried in the District Court was a civil suit which was tried April 2, 1889. The second case was tried on November 4, 1889.

Locating the County Seat

At the time Hale County was organized, most of the settlers lived in the country near Plainview so Plainview was chosen countyseat. Five years later Hale Center was established through consolidation of Epworth and Hale City. An election was called for September 9, 1893 to decide whether the countyseat should be located at Plainview or moved to Hale Center. The result of the election was 192 votes for Plainview and 166 for Hale Center.

Prohibition

At the first session of the Commissioners Court a special election was called to be held September 15, 1888, to decide whether intoxicating liquors should be sold in Hale County. Prohibition carried by majority vote. A second election for prohibition was held on March 2, 1889, which resulted in a unanimous vote for prohibition,—18 to 0. An election for Local Option was held on March 18, 1911, at which time prohibition carried in Hale County 593 to 133.

During the war, the need of protecting the military camps from the influence of liquor aided the cause of prohibition. An Amendment to the State Constitution, Sec. 20, Art. 16, was submitted to the Legislature in an election on May 24, 1919, in which Hale County voted 543 for prohibition and 205 against. In the meantime the National Prohibition Amendment had been submitted and ratified by the State Legislature on Feb. 28, 1918.

The attitude of Hale County toward prohibition is further reflected in the vote in the national election on Nov. 6, 1928. Herbert Hoover was said to be "bone dry" and Al Smith, the democratic nominee, was supposed to be "wet." Hale County's vote in the Presidential election was 2,143 for Herbert Hoover and 1,099 for Al Smith. This was the first and only time in history that Hale County voted Republican.

On August 26, 1933, an election for the Repeal of the 18th Amendment resulted in 859 votes for repeal and 560 against. Hale County voted in the same election 933 votes against the legalization of 3.2 beer in Hale County and 592 for legalization. On the Repeal of State Wide Prohibition on August 24, 1935, Hale County voted 1,284 against repeal and 568 for repeal.

For the first time in history, and without the consent of the voters of the county, beer was (supposedly) legally sold in Hale County, after the repeal of the 18th Amendment, but on January 16, 1936, the sale of beer was stopped in Hale County on an interpretation of Texas Liquor Control Act from Attorney General W. M. McCraw. An election was held on February 8, 1936, to determine whether 3.2 beer should be sold in Hale County, which resulted in 1,548 votes against and 1,025 for the sale of beer.

Woman's Suffrage

The question of Woman's Suffrage, or the ratification of the 19th Amendment to the Constitution of the United States was submitted to the voters of Hale County in a special election on May 24, 1919. Hale County's vote was 388 for and 181 against ratification. The 19th Amendment which gave to the women the right to vote was proclaimed effective by the Secretary of State on August 26, 1920.

Women in Office

The first woman to hold a public office in Hale County was Mrs. Ola Legg, who was elected to the office of County Superintendent of Schools in 1922. Other women who have held office in Hale County are Mrs. Maggie Magee and Mrs. Pat Connelly who held the office of County Treasurer, Miss M. Della Ansley, District Clerk and Miss Inez Ott, County Clerk. Mrs. Emma Grigsby Meharg of Plainview was the first woman in Texas to hold the office of Secretary of State, receiving the appointment from the first woman governor of Texas, Mrs. Miriam A. Ferguson. Mrs. Meharg also had the honor of being the first woman in Texas to organize the State Legislature, which duty she performed in January, 1927.

Early Lawyers of Hale County

The first lawyer in Hale County was L. G. Wilson, who came to Plainview May 1, 1888. He was born in Missouri, and graduated in law from the University of that state in 1886. He was married to Frances Snyder November 1, 1889. Mr. Wilson was active in the organization of Hale County and became its first County Attorney, which office he resigned to accept the appointment of District Attorney in the 47th Judicial District in 1889. He is now retired from the practice of law.

Judge L. S. Kinder came to Plainview in September, 1888. He was a kinsman of Mr. Wilson, their mothers being sisters. Born in Cape Cod County, Missouri, on November 9, 1865, he was educated in Missouri and graduated in law at the State University of Missouri in February, 1888. He served as Deputy County Clerk of Hale County in 1889 and was appointed County Attorney upon Mr. Wilson's resignation. He was elected District Attorney of the 50th Judicial District in 1892 and served as Judge of the 64th District for ten years. His experience and length of service earned for him the name of dean of the legal profession on the Central Plains. He married Mary L. Rhodes at Plainview on December 24, 1890, theirs being the second marriage license issued in Hale County. He died June 2, 1931.

Joe E. Rosson was born at St. Charles, Ark. January 12, 1868. He received his B. L. degree from Cumberland University at Lebanon, Tenn. in 1887. Mr. Rosson located at Estacado and was married to Beatrice Melton in 1888. He moved to Plainview in 1897 and acquired an extensive practice in civil law. He died in Plainview February 12, 1900.

Col. R. P. Smyth was born at Austin, Texas, where he received his education and graduated from the Texas Military Institute in 1887. He joined the Texas National Guards immediately following his graduation, was made Captain in the State Militia November 25, 1879, and became Colonel of the 2nd Reg. Inf. T.N.G. October 22, 1886. He moved to Estacado in March, 1887, where he was occupied as a surveyor, and moved to Plainview in 1888. He was married on July 21, 1892 to Miss Florence Tucker of Ft. Worth, who died in April 1894. Colonel Smyth began the practice of law in Hale County in September, 1893, having studied law under Fred Chandler and Major McGregor, who commanded Lee's Lighthorse Artillery during the Civil War. He was made Brigadier General of Texas Volunteer Guard on Jan. 26, 1893. During his service in the Spanish American War, he was Colonel of the 3rd Regiment U. S. Volunteer Infantry (Texas) commis-

LEGAL AND JUDICIAL HISTORY

sioned May 14, 1898. He practiced law in Hale County until 1907, after which he devoted his time to surveying.

Judge H. C. Randolph was born at Austin, Texas, September 22, 1861. His father at that time was State Treasurer. He (H. C.) was the nineteenth student to enroll at the State University, where he graduated in law in 1885 in the first graduating class. He came to Plainview in 1901 and entered into a partnership with Col. R. P. Smyth in the law firm of Randolph and Smyth. Some years later he practiced with his son Peyton B. Randolph in the firm of Randolph and Randolph. He was later appointed to the Commission of Appeals at Austin, which he served for some time. He was appointed to the office of Associate Justice of the Court of Civil Appeals in the 7th District, which office he held for a number of years, until his death April 19, 1932.

Attorneys Wilson, Kinder, Smyth and Randolph were for many years active in every phase of the country's development and were aggressive leaders in the movement to secure a railroad in Hale County.

Roster of Attorneys

The following lawyers have practiced at the bar in Hale County during the fifty years ending 1937:

L. G. Wilson, L. S. Kinder, R. P. Smyth, Joe E. Rosson, H. C. Randolph, Thurman Kinder, O. F. Wayland, Burn Wilson, Reuben M. Ellerd, L. C. Penry, J. E. Lancaster, E. Graham, C. S. Williams, L. W. Dalton, C. D. Russell, W. C. Mathes, George L. Mayfield, R. C. Joiner, W. B. Lewis, T. D. Webb, Fred C. Pearce, Peyton B. Randolph, A. M. Martin, Otus Trulove, Y. W. Holmes, L. R. Pearson, Charles Clements, A. C. Hatchell, Gamaliel Graham, L. D. Griffin, M. J. Baird, Meade F. Griffin, B. H. Oxford, Royce Oxford, Edwin McMath, W. W. Kirk, Frank Day, Joe Sharp, Burke Mathes, C. H. Curl, J. W. Paulk, Harold M. LaFont, R. V. Tudor, Maple Wilson, Lucian Morehead, W. Z. Graham, C. H. Dean, Ernest Tibbet.

Bar Association

The Hale County Bar Association was organized in 1924, with the following charter members and officers: Meade F.

Griffin, President, Frank Day Secretary, M. J. Baird, Charles Clements, E. Graham, L. D. Griffin, R. C. Joiner, L. S. Kinder, W. W. Kirk, A. B. Martin, George L. Mayfield, Royce Oxford, P. B. Randolph, C. D. Russell and C. S. Williams.

In 1935 Peyton B. Randolph was elected President and Harold LaFont Secretary.

County Officers

Following is a list of the persons who have served as County Officers from the organization of the County down to the present time:

COUNTY JUDGES

1888 —F. M. Lester*	1916-20—Charles Clements
1888-92—J. C. Burch	1920-22—L. D. Griffin
1892-96—J. M. Snider	1922-26—Meade F. Griffin
1896-00—H. M. Austin	1926-28—Geo. L. Mayfield
1900-06—W. C. Mathes	1928-32—E. C. Abernathy
1906-12—Geo. L. Mayfield	1932 —Harold M. LaFont
1912-16—W. B. Lewis	

*Officers were elected on Aug. 20, 1888, to serve until a regular election could be held in November, 1888.

COUNTY CLERKS

1888-90—E. L. Lowe	1910-16—B. H. Towery
1890-92—Sterling P. Strong	1916-32—Jo W. Wayland
1892-06—W. B. Martine	1932-36—Dudley H. Stovall
1906-10—J. W. Campbell	1936 —Inez Ott

COUNTY TREASURERS

1888-90—C. W. Marsalis	1898-00—J. T. Williams
1890-92—A. Vince	1900-04—R. Holland
1892-94—C. W. Marsalis	1904-18—John G. Hamilton
1894-96—W. B. Knight	1918-24—J. M. Johnson
1896-98—R. Holland	1924-36—Mrs. Maggie McGee
	1936- —Mrs. Pat Connelly

COUNTY SHERIFFS

1888-90—R. A. Ford	1912-16—J. C. Hooper
1890-94—L. A. Knight	1916-22—J. C. Terry
1894-06—R. E. Burch	1922-28—Sam Faith
1906-08—John Y. Ligon	1928-34—N. B. Burkett
1908-12—G. A. London	1934 —J. K. Hooper

LEGAL AND JUDICIAL HISTORY

COUNTY ATTORNEYS

1888-* —L. G. Wilson	1910-16—Charles Clements
1890-92—L. S. Kinder	1916-20—L. D. Griffin
1892-94—M. R. Baker	1920-22—M. J. Baird
1894-96—O. C. Mulkey	1922-26—Frank R. Day
1896-00—A. T. Howell	1926-32—Royce Oxford
1900-04—Geo. L. Mayfield	1932-34**—Joe Sharp
1904-06—R. P. Smyth	1935 —Vincent Tudor
1906-10—E. Graham	

*L. G. Wilson resigned and L. S. Kinder was appointed to fill the vacancy.

**Joe Sharp resigned and Vincent Tudor was appointed to fill the vacancy.

COUNTY SURVEYORS

1888 —G. H. Chipman	1902-06—W. J. Williams
1888-90—W. E. Jones	1906-08—N. K. Smith
1890-94—L. A. White	1908-10—R. P. Smyth
1894-96—W. E. Porterfield	1910-14—Thos. P. Whitis
1896-98—N. K. Smith	1914-18—L. O. Shropshire
1898-00—W. E. Porterfield	1918-24—R. P. Smyth
1900-02—N. K. Smith	1924 —W. J. Williams

COUNTY TAX ASSESSORS

1888-94—J. H. Bryan	1906-12—S. J. Frye
1894-96—J. W. Smylie	1912-16—J. N. Jordan
1896-00—J. B. Leach	1916-32—W. H. Murphy
1900-02—Levi Schick	1932- —W. C. Malone
1902-06—J. P. Lattimore	

COUNTY SUPERINTENDENT OF SCHOOLS

1922—Mrs. Ola Legg

COUNTY TAX COLLECTOR

1920-28—B. H. Towery	1932* —W. C. Malone
1928-32—J. M. Johnson	

* The office of Tax Collector was combined with the office of Tax Assessor in 1932. Prior to 1920, when the office of Tax Collector was established, it was combined with the office of Sheriff.

County Commissioners

1888, John Pendley, J. W. Cooper, G. W. Baker, R. W. O'Keefe

1888, A. J. Welter, R. L. Stringfellow, A. E. Adams, J. N. Morrison
1890, S. T. Pepper, R. L. Stringfellow, F. M. Lester, J. C. Chapman
1892, S. T. Pepper, W. C. Hood, B. A. Hudgins, W. L. McGehee
1894, Harry Brown, J. L. Blake, B. A. Hudgins, S. T. Cooper
1896, J. P. Lattimore, W. H. Ragland, M. E. Merrill, A. J. Whitney
1898, J. P. Lattimore, W. H. Ragland, W. L. Harrington, J. V. Matlock
1900, J. D. Mitchell, M. T. Cocke, Chas. Strite, J. W. Ray
1902, J. T. Williams, J. W. Smylie, M. E. Merrill, J. W. Ray
1904, J. T. Williams, J. W. Smylie, M. E. Merrill, J. W. Ray
1906, J. T. Williams, J. H. Reed, M. E. Merrill, W. R. Elrod
1908, E. Dowden, Wm. Britt, T. W. Smith, Geo. J. Boswell
1910, J. T. Williams, Wm. Britt, Robert F. Alley, G. L. Phillips
1912, W. J. Espy, J. W. Roberson, W. N. Claxton, G. L. Phillips
1914, W. J. Espy, J. W. Roberson, W. N. Claxton, G. L. Phillips
1916, W. J. Espy, J. W. Roberson, W. N. Claxton, M. C. Cornelius
1918, L. W. Sloneker, E. B. Shankle, W. N. Claxton, M. C. Cornelius
1920, G. Marshall Phelps, E. B. Shankle, J. H. Hooker, H. R. Tarwater
1922, W. J. Espy, E. B. Shankle, J. H. Hooker, H. R. Tarwater
1924, W. J. Espy, N. M. Sell, J. H. Hooker, H. R. Tarwater
1926, G. W. Whitfield, N. M. Sell, J. H. Hooker, J. A. Finney
1928, G. W. Whitfield, C. W. Terry, Carroll Bird, J. A. Finney
1930, G. W. Whitfield, C. W. Terry, Carroll Bird, J. A. Finney
1932, G. W. Whitfield, H. H. Roberson, Carroll Bird, J. E. Shropshire
1934, H. L. Gunter, H. H. Roberson, L. M. Rankin, J. E. Shropshire

LEGAL AND JUDICIAL HISTORY 105

1936, H. L. Gunter, R. A. Daugherty, L. M. Rankin, J. E. Shropshire

Justices of the Peace

1890, A. L. Conkling, F. M. Bradford, F. M. Lester, J. T. Chapman
1892, W. J. Beasley, Z. H. Peter, F. M. Lester, Fred Christian
1894, W. J. Beasley, Z. H. Peter, F. M. Lester, Fred Christian, W. M. Chandler
1896, W. J. Beasley, M. T. Cocke, J. T. Hill, T. L. Van Vacter
1898, W. J. Beasley, Ed M. White, F. M. Lester, H. A. Isbell, J. A. Syfrett
1900, W. J. Beasley, W. E. Mickey, B. A. Hudgins
1902, W. E. Armstrong, J. W. Smylie, W. H. Baker
1904, W. E. Armstrong, B. A. Hudgins, A. S. J. Martin
1906, W. E. Armstrong, Charley Benson, A. S. J. Martin
1908, W. E. Armstrong, Warren Smithee, J. W. Anderson, Bob Lemond, J. A. Taylor
1910, W. E. Armstrong, A. S. J. Martin, W. D. Anderson, J. W. Taylor, J. M. Anderson
1912, S. J. Frye, T. C. Masterson, J. W. Taylor, B. F. Tufford, W. D. Anderson
1914, S. J. Frye, A. E. Bailey, T. C. Masterson, J. W. Taylor, L. D. Griffin
1916, Earl C. Keck, J. W. McDaniel, Roger Mayhugh, T. J. Fletcher, T. C. Masterson
1918, E. A. Young, Roy Bailey, G. R. Scott
1920, J. W. McDaniels, G. R. Scott, N. C. Hix, S. J. T. Yowell, E. A. Young
1922, E. A. Young, J. W. McDaniel, W. L. Towsen, M. J. Miesenheimer
1924, J. P. Siler, J. W. McDaniel, Will Towsen, Ed Kiser
1926, J. P. Siler, J. W. McDaniel, W. L. Towsen
1928, J. P. Siler, J. W. McDaniel, W. L. Towsen, J. J. Merrill
1930, J. P. Siler, J. W. McDaniel, W. G. Sears, J. J. Merrill
1932, J. P. Siler, W. R. Tisdell, W. G. Sears
1934, J. P. Siler, J. W. McDaniel, R. E. Terry, B. F. Taylor
1936, J. P. Siler, J. W. McDaniel, R. E. Terry, B. F. Taylor

CHAPTER IX

FINANCIAL HISTORY

Banks

There were no Banks in Hale County prior to 1900. No great amount of cash was kept ready for use by the early settlers, and those who made trips to distant trading points to purchase supplies usually had sold some cattle, or perhaps hauled wagon loads of buffalo bones gathered up enroute to cover the cost of their purchases. The merchants in Hale County sold to every one on credit and the bills were paid when the cattle were marketed.

The First National Bank of Plainview was the first bank established in Hale County. This Bank was organized in June, 1900, by L. A. Knight and J. H. Slaton. It was chartered June 30, 1900, with a capital stock of $50,000. Knight and Slaton were at that time partners in the cattle business and felt the need of a financial center in their own territory. Having marketed a large number of cattle, they were in position to finance the venture, and four-fifths of the stock was owned by Knight and Slaton. L. A. Knight was the first president, J. H. Slaton Vice President and W. A. Todd, who had been trained in a Bank in Scotland, became the first cashier. The bank at first was housed in a small wooden building which stood where the First National Bank Building now stands, on the corner of Sixth and Broadway. The little frame building was removed in 1909 and a two-story brick building known as the First National Bank Building was erected. The bank moved into the new building in 1909.

In 1910 L. A. Knight sold his interest in the First National Bank. W. C. Mathes was elected President and J. H. Slaton Vice President, and Cashier. Guy Jacob was employed as Assistant Cashier. A short time later, J. H. Slaton became President of the Bank and served in that capacity until 1919.

The First National Bank purchased and absorbed the Citizens National Bank of Plainview on September 29, 1919. The following officers were elected at the time of merger: E. C. Lamb President, R. A. Underwood Vice President, J. C. Anderson Cashier and J. H. Slaton Chairman of the Board. A few years later E. C. Lamb resigned as President and Dr. C. C. Gidney became President, R. A. Underwood Vice President (active) and J. G. Dougherty Cashier. The First National Bank merged with the Plainview National Bank on October 20, 1930.

The Plainview Bank and Trust Company was chartered October 15, 1906, with a capital stock of $50,000. The first Board of Directors was composed of the following: L. T. Lester, Jas. B. Posey, J. B. Hall, J. B. Oswald, E. Graham, J. O. Oswald and S. S. Sloneker, with Jas. B. Posey President. This Bank merged with the Citizens State Bank in May, 1908, and a charter was issued for the Citizens National Bank.

The Citizens State Bank of Plainview was organized in Plainview in January, 1906. A charter was granted February 9, 1906, and the Bank was opened for business February 10, 1906, with a capital stock of $75,000. The following persons were selected as directors: J. L. Vaughn, J. N. Donohoo, R. C. Ware, Dr. J. H. Wayland, J. E. Lancaster, Q. D. Hoyle and E. B. Hughes. The directors then elected the following officers: J. L. Vaughn, President, J. N. Donohoo Vice President (Active) R. C. Ware Vice President, and E. B. Hughes Cashier.

The Bank was first housed in an old frame building at the southwest corner of the Court House square. In the spring of 1907 it was moved into the J. H. Wayland building on the corner of what is now Fifth and Broadway and remained there until the spring of 1911 when it was moved into the corner of the Hotel Ware at Sixth and Broadway. In May, 1908, the Citizens State Bank was merged with the Plainview Bank and Trust Company and the charter was surrendered and the two became the Citizens National Bank.

The Citizens National Bank of Plainview was granted a charter on March 26, 1908, with a capital stock of $100,000. The directors of the new organization were as follows: J. L. Vaughn, J. N. Donohoo, R. C. Ware, Dr. J. H. Wayland, J. E. Lancaster, Homer Pack, James B. Posey, Wayne Paxton and E. B. Hughes. The officers then elected were: J. N. Donohoo President, James B. Posey Vice President, (active) J. L. Vaughn Vice President, R. C. Ware Vice President, E. B. Hughes Cashier and W. A. Todd Assistant Cashier.

In 1914, at the January stockholders meeting, the following directors were elected: J. N. Donohoo, R. C. Ware, Wayne Paxton, W. W. Underwood, R. A. Underwood, John Buntin and E. B. Hughes. They in turn elected the following officers: J. N. Donohoo Chairman of the Board, E. B. Hughes President, R. C. Ware Vice President, W. W. Underwood Vice President (active), R. A. Underwood Cashier and Harold Y. Hughes Assistant Cashier. These officers served continuously until September 29, 1919, at which time the Citizens National Bank sold their interest to and same was merged with the First National Bank of Plainview.

The Third National Bank of Plainview was organized by L. A. Knight. This Bank was chartered on June 29, 1910, with a capital stock of $100,000, and was located in the Ansley Building on the corner of Sixth and Ash Streets. It was afterwards moved to the brick building one block west, across the street east of the First National Bank. The first Board of directors were as follows: L. A. Knight, L. G. Wilson, H. M. Burch, J. E. Lancaster and R. W. O'Keefe. The first officers were: J. E. Lancaster President, L. A. Knight Vice President, L. G. Wilson Vice President, H. M. Burch Cashier and H. C. Von Struve Assistant Cashier. In 1914 Judge Lancaster resigned as President and L. A. Knight became President at that time and served in that capacity until his death on July 7, 1924. Judge L. S. Kinder was then elected President of the Bank.

The Plainview National Bank came into existence on August 1, 1928, when the name of the Third National Bank was changed to Plainview National Bank. The Bank was moved at that time to the Skaggs Building on the corner of Seventh and Broadway. Judge L. S. Kinder continued to serve as President of the Bank until his death on June 2, 1931, and J. D. Steakley was Vice President (active). This bank purchased and absorbed the Security State Bank on August 20, 1930, and merged with the First National Bank on October 20, 1930.

FINANCIAL HISTORY

The bank closed on September 16, 1931, at which time a receiver was appointed.

The Guaranty State Bank of Plainview was chartered September 9, 1919, with a capital stock of $50,000. The first Board of Directors was composed of the following. L. Paul Barker, Rube S. Beard, John B. Pope Jr., France Baker and Cline D. Hensley. R. S. Beard was elected President and C. D. Hensley Cashier. This Bank opened in the Ellerd Building where the Skaggs Building now stands, on the Corner of Seventh and Broadway, and operated at that place until the new Guaranty State Bank Building was erected, and the name was changed to the Security State Bank.

The Security State Bank came into being by changing the name of the Guaranty State Bank to Security State Bank on May 17, 1927. The following directors were elected at that time: J. C. Terry, C. G. Goodman, Lester James, Roy Irick, and E. H. Bawden. The Security State Bank was sold to the Plainview National Bank on August 20, 1930.

The Plainview State Bank was chartered Jan. 16, 1932, and opened in the location of the old Plainview National Bank in the Skaggs Building, with a capital stock of $50,000. The date of opening was February 1, 1932. The first Board of directors was composed of the following persons: Archie S. Underwood, J. W. Murchison, Dan Royal, J. C. Wilson and George R. Evans. The first officers elected were: Dan Royal President, John W. Murchison Vice President, George H. Shriber Cashier. This Bank was changed to the City National Bank on February 19, 1934.

The City National Bank of Plainview was chartered February 19, 1934, with a capital stock of $100,000, and opened with a surplus of $10,000. The directors were as follows: A. S. Underwood, J. W. Murchison, George H. Shriber, and Harold Hamilton. The following officers were elected: J. W. Murchison, President, George H. Shriber Vice President and Cashier, and Harold Hamilton Assistant Cashier.

The Hale County State Bank in Plainview was chartered June 1, 1934, with a capital stock of $25,000 and the bank opened with a surplus of $25,000. A formal opening was held on the night of June 6, 1934, at which time $16,000 was deposited. The first Board of Directors was composed of the following persons: John K. Crews, Frank Eiring, Harry Willett, R. F. Moore and B. F. Simpson. The first officers were: John K. Crews President, Frank Eiring Vice President (active), Harry Willett, Vice President, and E. M. Rice Cashier. These men came from Matador where they had recently sold a Bank which they had operated with the same stockholders. The only Plainview stockholders were Guy Jacob and Herbert Dysart. This Bank was opened in the location of the old First National Bank on the corner of Sixth and Broadway. In December, 1935, R. A. Jefferies succeeded Frank Eiring as Vice President and Mr. Jefferies and R. A. Bowers succeeded Frank Eiring and B. F. Simpson as members of the Board of Directors.

The First State Bank of Hale Center was chartered February 23, 1907, with a capital stock of $10,000. The first Board of directors were as follows: J. R. P. Sewell, J. H. Reed, J. C. Frye, W. L. Harrington, M. J. Ewalt and R. W. Lemond. The first officers were: J. R. P. Sewell President, R. W. Lemond Vice President, J. K. Malone Cashier. Later M. J. Ewalt became President with Joe Lee Ferguson Vice President and N. W. McCleskey Cashier. Later on Robert F. Alley became President, Nick Alley Vice President and Claude Gentry Cashier. Nelson Perdue then became Cashier and held the position for several years. The Bank was changed to a National Bank in 1935.

The First National Bank of Hale Center was established on May 21, 1925, when the First State Bank of Hale Center was changed to a National Bank. It was chartered on May 20, 1925, with a capital stock of $25,000. The present officers are: Robert F. Alley President, Nick Alley Vice President and Al H. Lemond Cashier. This Bank has the distinction of being the oldest bank in Hale County.

First State Bank of Abernathy was chartered on November 12, 1909, with a capital stock of $10,000. It was later raised to 25,000. The first Board of Directors was composed of the following: C. A. Burrus, W. H. Ragland, S. R. Merrill, W. A. Shelton and M. C. Overton. Dr. M. C. Overton was the first President and Claude C. Burrus was cashier. The Bank was housed in the first brick building to be erected in Abernathy.

Dr. Overton resigned soon after the Bank was organized and was succeeded by S. R. Merrill who served as President until his death in June, 1933. L. A. Harral succeeded Mr. Merrill as President and Mr. Burrus was succeeded as cashier by C. G. Goodman. N. C. Hix followed Mr. Goodman, and on the resignation of Mr. Goodman A. B. Reid became cashier. The present officers of this Bank are as follows: L. A. Harral, President, N. C. Hix Vice President, A. B. Reid Cashier, Ercell Givens and Lee Roy Waters Assistant Cashiers. The Board of Directors are: Louisa E. Merrill, L. A. Harral, Leonard Harral, A. B. Reid and N. C. Hix.

The Guaranty State Bank of Petersburg was chartered on May 24, 1921, with a capital stock of $15,000. It was opened for business June 12, 1921, with the following officers: E. B. Shankle President, R. A. Jefferies Vice President and Cashier. These two, together with M. J. Gregory, Chas. Schuler and Roy Bailey constituted the Board of Directors. In April, 1925, the Bank withdrew from the Guaranty Fund and the name was changed to the First State Bank of Petersburg.

The First State Bank of Petersburg dates from April, 1925, when the name of the Guaranty State Bank was changed to First State Bank. Mr. Shankle resigned as President in April, 1932, and Tom Davis was elected President, R. A. Jefferies Vice President and Cashier. Mr. Jefferies served as Cashier of the Bank from the organization of the Guaranty State Bank until 1936, when he resigned and moved to Plainview to become associated with the Hale County State Bank. Miss Katy Dell Germany became Assistant Cashier in January, 1928. Mr. John Hughes succeeded Mr. Jefferies as Cashier in December, 1935.

Plainview Building and Loan Association was organized October 21, 1921, and a charter was granted November 3, 1921, with a capital stock of $500,000. The capital stock was afterwards increased to $1,500,000. The charter members were as follows: C. T. Field, W. E. Risser, C. D. Russell, Dr. C. C. Gidney, Dr. J. C. Anderson, J. H. Slaton, D. Hefflefinger, E. H. Perry, O. Z. Gulledge, E. P. Gulledge, E. Harlan, C. D. Wofford, W. J. Klinger, E. H. Humphreys, P. J. Wooldridge, C. F. Vincent, Claude Powers, L. S. Kinder, Meade F. Griffin and L. A. Knight.

On November 15, 1921, the following Board of Directors was elected: Dr. C. C. Gidney, L. A. Knight, Claude Power, P. J. Wooldridge, W. E. Risser, C. D. Russell, Dennis Hefflefinger, E. H. Perry and E. H. Humphreys. The first officers were as follows: C. D. Russell President, Dr. C. C. Gidney First Vice President, L. A. Knight Second Vice President, E. H. Perry Secretary-Manager, D. Hefflefinger, Treasurer; Kinder, Russell & Griffin Attorneys. E. H. Perry was Secretary-Manager until January, 1926, when he resigned. C. B. Harder served for a short time and A. E. Boyd served in that office until December, 1931, at which time Lester James was elected Secretary-Manager, which office he still holds.

Dividends from 10% to 11.9% were paid from the end of the first year to 1930. A great many homes were built during the active period of this institution, giving work to large numbers of workmen and paying good dividends to the investor. This loan Company has been a big factor in the general upbuilding of the town and community.

The Home Building & Loan Association of Plainview, Texas, was organized December 13, 1935, obtaining a charter from the State of Texas on January 1, 1936. The following officers and directors were elected: C. D. Russell, President, Bradley M. Sims First Vice President, D. Hefflefinger, Treasurer, Lester W. James Secretary-Manager, L. R. Bain, A. E. Boyd, E. M. Osborne, E. Q. Perry, which officers and directors are still serving. The Association has an authorized capital of $500,000 with a paid in capital of $67,000.

The purpose of the Association is to assist the people in homeownership through financing the buying, improving, building or refinancing of their homes, and to encourage thrift by offering a safe, convenient plan of investment. The Association paid a 4% dividend to its stockholders in 1936, being its first year of operation.

On May 14, 1936, it became a member of the Federal Home Loan Bank System, and on August 3, 1936, obtained "Insurance of Shares" through membership in the Federal Savings & Loan Insurance Corporation, thus giving its stockholders additional security of investment. The Association is an approved representative of The National Housing Administration, and in addition to its regular plan of loans is offering the facilities of the F. H. A. loans.

The Federal Land Bank and the Joint Stock Land Bank of Dallas were big factors in financing farm loans, which enabled the farmers to place improvements on new farms or additional improvements on old farms, and the development of agriculture in Hale County was greatly enhanced through farm loans.

The building of homes and improvements of city property and erection of business buildings made possible by the various home building associations and loan companies was most active between 1925 and 1930, the height of the building boom reaching its peak in 1928 and 1929. 206 residences were built in Plainview in 1928. New construction in 1929 is shown in the following table:

	Approximate value
165 Residences	$502,850
Business Buildings	495,000
Additions to Buildings	77,150
Paving	35,000
Utilities	15,000
Total new construction for 1929	$1,125,000

The high wave of prosperity and the prospect for even greater prosperity were so great that many people were swept beyond the point of conservatism and many citizens built homes and other buildings so heavily encumbered that they were unable to hold their property when the tide of prosperity suddenly subsided and many people were thrown out of employment. Great losses were sustained through reverses and unsafe investments during the early years of the world-wide depression, which was the most severe in history. While Plainview was without a bank, business firms and citizens transacted business through the Banks at Amarillo, Lubbock and nearby towns. The situation became paralyzing to business generally when the National Bank Moratorium was declared by the President on March 6, 1933. To enable the stores to operate, a clearance was held for one hour each day in the office of the Retail Merchants Association under guard of the County Sheriff with moneys brought from the Bank to make change for currency. The depression, which began in 1929, reached its lowest ebb in 1930 and 1931. In 1933 business began to improve gradually when the Governmental program of relief became effective, releasing large sums of money for wheat and cotton reduction. Conditions have improved gradually and real estate values have increased probably 60% over the low ebb.

The Retail Merchants Association was organized in Plainview April 1, 1914, by Frank Bone and C. W. Sewell, with 25 merchants as members. C. W. Sewell was the first president and Frank Bone was the first secretary. Mr. Bone resigned two weeks later and George T. Perdue became secretary. Several months later Mr. Perdue resigned and Mrs. W. L. Braddy became secretary and held that position until 1918 when the Association disbanded during the war. E. H. Humphreys succeeded Mr. Sewell as president. The retail Merchants Association was again organized in Plainview, Sept. 1, 1922, with W. E. Boyd, President, C. E. Carter, Paul Barker, Maury McGlasson, C. C. Stubbs, Fred Brown and W. K. Harp as directors, and 59 members in the organization. Mrs. Adella S. Drew was made Secretary at that time and has served in that capacity since then.

CHAPTER X

MEDICAL HISTORY

The early physicians of Hale County practiced under vastly different circumstances than do those of today. Each doctor was required to meet any emergency that might arise in his practice at any time or place and under any circumstance. His territory covered hundreds of miles over the unbroken prairie which he traveled with horse and buggy, keeping his directions by the sun by day and the stars by night, sleeping on the ground, and often facing severe storms and blizzards. Having no hospitals or trained nurses, his patients were often brought into his own home to be cared for by his wife. At all times he labored under handicap of lack of medical supplies and facilities.

Prior to the coming of the first physician, persons who had acquired some degree of knowledge through experience in caring for the sick were pressed into service. Horatio Graves was often called upon to set a broken bone or render assistance to the injured or ill in the Epworth community and Mrs. Hugh McClelland (Aunt Prudy, she was called) was often called upon in time of sickness. Mrs. J. M. Shafer, wife of the editor of the Herald, and others often rendered neighborly assistance to those who were ill.

Although Texas had enjoyed but half a century of independence from Mexico, much progress had been made in the betterment of health conditions. In order to protect the public from illegal practitioners, a law was passed requiring that each physician register his license in the county in which he wished to practice and to file his diploma.

Early Physicians

Dr. James A. Atkins was the first physician to practice in Hale County. He was born in Minehead, Somersetshire, England, January 21, 1851. He graduated from the Kentucky School of Medicine at Louisville, Kentucky, in 1889, and began the practice of medicine in Plainview July 10, 1890. He established and operated the first drug store in Plainview, at what is now the corner of Fifth and Broadway, and was the only practicing physician in Hale County and surrounding plains until April, 1891. He died at Plainview August 20, 1891.

Dr. J. H. Wayland was the second physician to practice in Hale County. He was born in Randolph County, Missouri, April 22, 1863, and graduated in medicine from the Kentucky School of Medicine in 1886. He came to Hale County April 20, 1891, and established and operated the second drug store in Plainview. He was for many years an active member of the Baptist Church and is the founder of Wayland Baptist College at Plainview. He retired from active practice in 1920 and now operates the Wayland Hotel.

Dr. L. Lee Dye was born in Russell County, Virginia, October 19, 1854. He graduated in medicine from the Medical Department of the University of Tennessee. He practiced first at Fall Branch, Tenn., and moved to Plainview in October, 1891. He owned and operated the third drug store in the county. Three generations of Dr. Dye's family have practiced medicine in Hale County. His son, E. Lee Dye, a graduate of the Medical School in Fort Worth, practiced in Hale County first in 1915. Everett Lee Dye Jr. graduated in medicine at Baylor University. Dr. Mary Ramsdell Dye, wife of Dr. Everett Lee Dye Jr., is a graduate of Baylor University, and has practiced in Plainview since 1933. She is the second woman to practice medicine in Hale County, Dr. Mary Henry being the first.

Dr. L. C. Wayland, a graduate of the Kentucky School of Medicine, began his practice in Plainview in 1903. Dr. Wayland practiced for two years in Lubbock, where he owned and operated the first drug store in Lubbock. He has practiced in Plainview continuously since that time and has the distinction of having practiced the longest number of years in Hale County of any of the doctors.

Dr. E. F. McClendon, born in Trinity County, Texas, was a graduate of medical school in St. Louis, Mo., College of Physicians and Surgeons, in 1890. He served in the army during the Spanish-American War in Cuba and Porto Rico. He practiced in Plainview continuously from 1909 until his death on June 25, 1937.

Dr. S. J. Underwood, born in White County, Tenn., graduated in medicine from the University at Fort Worth in 1899. He has practiced at Hale Center since 1909. Dr. Underwood has been prominent in civic development, and helped to organize the Panhandle Plains Dairy Show. He was for ten years a director of West Texas Chamber of Commerce, and is a breeder of Registered Jersey Cattle.

Drs. J. C. Anderson and C. C. Gidney, who formed a partnership in 1894 at Granger, Texas, came to Plainview in 1910. They continued the partnership until 1926, when Dr. Anderson accepted an appointment to the office of State Health Officer and moved to Austin. Dr. Gidney died at Plainview August 24, 1933.

Dr. R. B. Longmire, born at Hickory, Miss., graduated in medicine at Tulane University at New Orleans. He came to Plainview in 1910, and moved to Hale Center where he has practiced continuously since that time.

Dr. E. M. Legg, Abernathy's first physician, was a graduate of Baylor University. He came to Abernathy in 1909. His son, Eugene Pinson Legg, graduated in medicine in 1936. Dr. E. M. Legg died at Abernathy March 6, 1915.

Dr. J. F. Owens, born at Brownwood, Georgia, was a graduate of the Medical School at Atlanta, Ga., graduating in 1890. He served as president of the Georgia State Medical Society. He came to Plainview May 1, 1909, and practiced until his death on Apr. 8, 1925.

Dr. O. H. Judkins began his practice of medicine in Plainview in January, 1908. He moved to Corpus Christi in 1913, and later to San Antonio. He studied in Vienna, London and Paris.

Dr. W. H. Flamm graduated in medicine at Creighton Medical School in Omaha, Nebr., May 5, 1908. He began the practice of medicine in Plainview in 1909, and moved to Amarillo in 1915. Since that time he has studied in nearly all large clinics in United States and Europe and his practice is now limited to general surgery.

Dr. A. H. Lindsay graduated from Memphis Hospital Medical College in 1895. He moved to Plainview in 1909 where he practiced medicine until 1920. He was City Alderman in Plainview in 1910. He died in Amarillo March 26, 1934.

Dr. E. O. Nichols graduated in medicine from the Tulane University at New Orleans in 1909. He came to Plainview in 1912 and bought an interest in the Plainview Sanitarium, where he has practiced surgery continuously since that time, with the exception of a period of time when he was in army service during the war.

Other Plainview physicians who served during the World War are Drs. J. V. Guyton, L. W. Dawson, and Don P. Jones.

Dr. W. N. Lemmon, who practiced in Plainview from 1930 to 1932, served as a Medical Missionary to the Philippine Islands from 1909 to 1925, and organized the Sallie Long-Reed Memorial Hospital at Loag Illocos Norte, Luzon, in 1910. He founded the Mary Chiles Hospital in Manila in 1911, which he served as chief surgeon until 1925, and also launched the Masonic Crippled Children's Hospital, now a part of the Mary Johnson Methodist Hospital in Manila. He is now on the staff of the Epworth Methodist Hospital in Liberal, Kansas.

Roster of Medical Doctors
(their native states, and date of Registration in Hale County.)

James A. Atkins (England) 1890, J. H. Wayland (Missouri) 1891, L. Lee Dye (Virginia) 1891, L. B. Lovelace 1891, C. G. Austin 1891, Edgar M. Harp 1893, Charles A. Baldwin 1899, J. F. Shones 1900, Frazier Bridges (Mississippi) 1900, John Norris Jr. 1901, W. N. Wardlaw (Texas) 1902 (died 1930), L. C. Wayland (Missouri) 1903, Phillip H. Chilton 1903, John A. Jones 1903, Joseph Ponder 1904, A. B. Parr 1904, A. T. Edwards 1904, Isaac E. Smith 1904, J. B. Whitehead 1905.

G. W. Carter (Kentucky) 1906, James Norval Stoops 1906, J. C. Hudson 1907, I. W. Jenkins 1907, J. D. Hanby 1907, J. F. Hendricks (Alabama) 1908, G. M. Abney (Texas) 1908, Jas. F. Duncan (Alabama) 1908, F. B. Crutcher (Texas) 1908, W. H. Flamm (Nebraska) 1908.

A. H. Lindsay (North Carolina) 1909, R. W. Sanders (West Virginia) 1909, L. G. Oxford (Texas) 1909, J. A. Witt (Texas) 1909, Ernest A. Hendricks (Alabama) 1909, Roy Philson Stoops 1909, C. J. Clifton (Illinois) 1909, W. A. Winn (Louisiana) 1909, E. M. Legg (Tennessee) 1909, E. F.

MEDICAL HISTORY

McClendon (Texas) 1909, S. J. Underwood (Tennessee) 1909, J. F. Owens (Georgia) 1909,

James Pickett (Alabama) 1910 (Died May 19, 1923), C. C. Gidney (North Carolina) 1910 (Died Aug. 24, 1933), J. C. Anderson (Arkansas) 1910, R. B. Longmire (Mississippi) 1910, E. A. Woldert (Texas) 1911, W. D. Akers (Virginia) 1911, J. A. Green (Georgia) 1911, E. O. Nichols (Texas) 1912, J. V. Guyton (Alabama) 1912, Ralph S. Farris (Nebraska) 1912, Silas Ballard (Tennessee) 1912, P. M. Waltrip (Kentucky) 1913, Forest O. Phillips (Iowa) 1913, W. C. Judd (Nebraska) 1914, H. E. Stolp (Illinois) 1914,

N. E. Greer (Arkansas) 1915, V. M. Longmire (Texas) 1915, R. C. Hannah (Alabama) 1915, R. A. Miller 1915, L. V. Dawson (Missouri) 1915, J. P. Lattimore (Texas) 1915, E. Lee Dye 1915, Robert L. Ramsdell 1916, T. H. P. Duncan 1916, J. L. Guest (Texas) 1917, W. A. Bates (Maine) 1917, J. Bennett McBride (Texas) 1917, I. E. Smith (Kentucky) 1917, Walter Theron Travis (Kentucky) 1918, G. W. Lassater (Tennessee) 1918, Robert F. Harp.

J. J. Breaker 1920, Wm. J. Findlay (Missouri) 1920, C. A. Cantrell (Texas) 1920 (Died Aug. 1930), Don P. Jones (Illinois) 1920, O. L. Thweatt (Alabama) 1921, A. L. Lincecum (Texas) 1921, J. P. Carrington (Texas) 1921, W. E. McMordie (Texas) 1921, Michael Abraham Shadid (Syria) 1922, Claude Walcott 1923, James R. McClain (Mississippi) 1924, W. E. Redford (Kentucky) 1925 (Died July 18, 1936), Harry S. Price (Louisiana) 1925, M. A. Cooper (Texas) 1926,

McKinley Howell (Mississippi) 1927, J. Harvey Hansen (Iowa) 1927, Bendo Allen Prestege (Texas) 1927, N. J. Hamilton (Kentucky) 1927, W. T. Givins (Texas) 1927 (Died Dec. 12, 1934), D. D. Smith (Texas) 1928, Chas. Archibald Meader, Alopathic, (Missouri) 1928, W. H. Girdner (Texas) 1928, A. D. Ellsworth (Minnesota) 1929, Rufus A. Roberts (Texas) 1929, Bascomb Lanier Chipley (S. Carolina) 1929, Ted Ghent Estes (Texas) 1929,

Wm. N. Lemmon (Missouri) 1930, Wm. D. Rea (Kentucky) 1930, Mary Mitchell Henry (Texas) 1930, C. D. Henry (Texas) 1930, Elbert L. Spence (Tennessee) 1930, J. H. Guthrie (Tennessee), P. H. Mitchell (Alabama) 1931,

Everett Lee Dye Jr. (Texas) 1932, Mary Ramsdell Dye (Texas) 1933, J. S. Rinehart (Indiana) 1933, Grover C. Hall (Missouri) 1934, R. G. Spann (Oklahoma) 1936, Robert H. Mitchell (Texas) 1936 and P. C. Anders (Alabama) 1936.

Roster of Osteopathic Doctors

With date of Registration in Hale County.

Joseph Merrill 1901, Lewis N. Pennock 1909, (Died Oct. 22, 1920), Daisy Pennock 1910, Norman B. Mayhugh 1913 (Died May 14, 1933), Joseph L. Houseworth 1914, K. J. Clements 1918, D. D. Howe 1922, W. H. Bellew 1923, Lloyd Newberg McAnally 1925, Wendell S. Warner 1929, Jas. G. Dickie 1931, Walter J. Williams 1934, John Rudolph Miller 1934 and John Marion Bubone 1934.

Roster of Dentists

With date of Registration in Hale County.

Alpheus Dyer (not registered) 1883, F. H. Burns 1890, C. W. Jones 1897, J. D. Hagood 1897, O. E. Dickinson 1902, S. B. Tadlock 1903, A. L. Hawkins 1907, Nathan C. Letcher 1908, C. L. Barnes 1910, C. D. Wofford 1910, Geo. J. Williams 1913, Isaac Wilson Hicks 1914, J. T. Hamilton 1914, W. W. Sands 1915, O. I. Cook 1915, Marion Sims 1915, James W. Russey 1916, W. J. Lloyd 1916, William T. Edwards 1917, J. A. Ferguson 1917, P. B. Bernt 1918, Flavius A. Greene 1919, J. C. Holcaugh 1920, Donald K. Ratliffe 1925, E. B. Griffin 1927, J. E. Wood 1928, Edwin H. Kirchoff 1928, Francis W. Wehrhein 1928, H. T. Green Jr. 1929, Herbert E. Waterman 1929, David C. Rougeau 1930, Leon Marion Jows 1930, Grover C. Turner 1935, W. B. Stevenson 1934, Y. Pinkney Taylor 1937 and D. O. Hollingsworth.

Medical Society

The Hale-Swisher-Floyd-Lubbock County Medical Society was organized in Plainview on March 18, 1904, with the following officers and charter members: Doctors H. D. Barnes, Tulia, President, R. C. Andrews, Floydada, Secretary, W. N. Wardlaw, Plainview, Treasurer, J. A. Jones, Runningwater, R. D. Reynolds, Lubbock, A. B. Parr, Tulia, L. Lee Dye, and L. C. Wayland, Plainview.

Hale County Medical Society was organized at the office

of Dr. H. D. Barnes, in Tulia, Acting Counselor for the Third Panhandle District on Dec. 6, 1909. Dr. J. F. Owens, of Plainview was elected President. On February 6, 1912, Swisher County was annexed to Hale County and Briscoe was attached to Floyd and Motley Counties. On April 12, 1921, the name was changed to Hale-Floyd-Briscoe-Swisher County Medical Society, by which name it is still known.

Physicians who have served as President of the Medical Society since 1904 are: Doctors H. D. Barnes, W. H. Freeman, R. C. Andrews, J. F. Owens, J. F. Duncan, L. C. Wayland, A. H. Lindsay, W. H. Flamm, Jas. Pickett, E. F. McClendon, C. C. Gidney, E. O. Nichols, J. L. Guest, N. E. Greer, S. J. Underwood, V. Andrews, Don P. Jones, L. V. Smith, J. E. Crawford, C. I. Holt, C. D. Henry, E. Lee Dye, A. D. Ellsworth, J. D. Simpson, Mary R. Dye and C. L. Jackson.

Plainview Sanitarium

The first hospital in Hale County was a private hospital established by Dr. J. V. Guyton in 1912, with his wife, Mrs. Mary V. Guyton, a graduate of St. Joseph Hospital, in charge. This was started in a residence.

The Plainview Sanitarium was established in 1913. Dr. Guyton formed a partnership with Dr. E. O. Nichols and together they built a hospital of twelve rooms, which they named the Plainview Sanitarium. In 1915 Dr. Nichols purchased Dr. Guyton's half interest. Two years later he sold one-half interest to Dr. J. L. Guest, at which time the Sanitarium was enlarged to thirty-five rooms. Drs. Nichols and Guest continued this partnership until 1928 when Dr. Nichols purchased Dr. Guest's interest and enlarged the hospital to fifty rooms. Plainview Sanitarium was chartered for a Nurses' School in 1918, Miss Lord being the first graduate, in 1920. Misses Irene Brown and Susie Fullingim were the graduates in 1921.

The Plainview Sanitarium and Clinic is now operated by Dr. E. O. Nichols and is open to all physicians. The Staff is composed of the following physicians and nurses: Drs. E. O. Nichols, Grover C. Hall, J. H. Hansen, Rufus A. Roberts, R. H. Mitchell, D. O. Hollingsworth D.D.S., Susie C. Riggs R.N. and Delia C. Kellar R.N.

County Health Nurse

The office of County Health Nurse was established in Hale County in January, 1926, at which time Miss Margaret Hooper was appointed to that office. Miss Hooper was succeeded on January 1, 1926, by Miss Nell Ayres. Miss Ayres served as County Health Nurse until September 15, 1931, when the office was discontinued for economic reasons.

An Old Fashioned Prescription
MAKE ME LAUGH

(This poem was written and dedicated by the late Dr. J. F. Owens to his daughter, Cristelle Owens Miller, who in turn dedicates it in memory of her father to the members of his profession in Hale County.)

When you would that something
  For me you could do
That would help me along
  And keep my heart true,
Don't feed me on statistics
  And political chaff,
But search for my mirth-strings,
  And pull till I laugh.

When I'm blue and despondent,
  And life seems so dreary,
Make me laugh till the effort
  Of fun-making grows weary;
It will raise me up quickly
  From the depth of despair;
Just tug at my mirth-strings,
  Till a grin is found there.

Make me laugh at myself,—
  Make me laugh, if you scold;
Make me laugh all the time;
  It is worth more than gold.
When I'm laughing I'm happy;
  When I'm laughing I'm good;
If you knew how it helps me,
  You'd make me laugh if you could.

CHAPTER XI

Religious History

The Religious History of Hale County began with the coming of the first settler in 1883. Rev. Horatio Graves started a Sunday School in his home and preached the Gospel to those who came together. The Graves home, which stood one and one-half miles southwest of the present site of Hale Center, soon became a religious center for the scattered settlers and the cowboys from the large ranches who rode many miles on horseback to attend "meeting" and to visit the settlers.

The only organized church on the Staked Plains at that time was the Quaker, or Friends Church at Estacado, in Crosby County, of which Rev. Anson Cox was pastor. A few years later a Union Sunday School was organized in the Epworth Schoolhouse one-half mile from the Graves home. Circuit riders made occasional visits to the frontier and missionaries of all denominations visited the Epworth community, traveling, as was their custom, on horseback with Bible and other belongings tucked away in the old saddlebags. All visiting ministers were made welcome and were invited to preach at the Epworth Schoolhouse, regardless of creed. Mr. Graves filled the pulpit when no visiting minister was available.

All denominations worshipped together even after the earlier churches were organized, the minister from each denomination usually preaching one Sunday a month and each serving several other congregations. Usually the pastor of a church partially supported himself and family by raising cattle or farming, or other gainful occupation.

The first Sunday School in Plainview was a Union Sunday School organized by E. L. Lowe in 1887 in the home of E. L. Lowe where it continued to meet until the little sod school house was erected.

The First Methodist Episcopal Church South was organized in Plainview in the sod school house in October, 1888, by Rev. J. H. Stegall, a circuit rider from the Snyder District, and Rev. Thomas G. Duncan. There were five charter members, ie., E. L. Lowe, Mrs. M. A. Lowe, Judge and Mrs. J. C. Burch and Mrs. J. H. Bryan. Misses Mary Bryan and Mattie Lowe were the first two members admitted into the church after organization.

Prior to 1888, no Methodist Minister had ever been sent to any charge on the plains above the Caprock. The Journal of the Northwest Texas Conference of 1888 showed Estacado as a Mission with Rev. John B. Hawkins as missionary to all the vast territory on the plains. Rev. Hawkins, Rev. Thomas G. Duncan and Rev. W. B. Ford made occasional visits to Plainview, though the great distance that must be traveled forbade their preaching at one place more often than once in from three to five months. In those occasional visits the missionaries fanned the spark of religious fervor that burned in the hearts of the settlers who well knew the hardships the circuit riders endured in a life in the saddle out on the trackless prairie in all kinds of weather, and ministers of the Gospel were afforded the warmest hospitality and cooperation.

Rev. Thomas G. Duncan became the first pastor of the Plainview church, which appeared on the Conference records the following year as "Plainview Mission," taking the place of "Estacado Mission." Rev. R. M. Morris became the pastor in 1889 and during his pastorate the first church building was erected. This was a small box structure, ceiled inside with plank flooring, erected by the cooperation of the worshippers with lumber freighted from Amarillo a distance of ninety miles. A two-room parsonage was built on the corner of what is now Seventh and Beech Streets, with the church immediately south of it. In 1892 the Plainview Circuit reported to Conference a membership of 225, and in 1898 it was designated as "Plainview Station."

The little church building was sold in 1897 to the First Christian Church, and a larger building was erected. For many years the tall spire of the Methodist Church directed the people to the church that for many years was the pride of Plainview. A new brick church was erected in 1909, at which time the old church was sold to the Presbyterian Church U. S. The new church, built during the pastorate of Rev. Thos. S. Barcus, on the corner of Seventh and Baltimore

Streets, was dedicated Sept. 4, 1910. An Educational Annex was built in 1934 during the administration of Rev. G. W. Bailey.

The following persons have served as pastor since the organization: Thomas G. Duncan (1888-1889), R. M. Morris (1889-1891), B. F. Jackson (1891-1895), J. T. Bloodworth (1895-1897), T. F. Robeson, supply, (1897), H. L. Munger (1898-1899), Ben Hardy (1899-1901), J. H. Walker (1901-1903), S. E. Houk (1903-1904), C. M. Shuffler (1905-1907), T. S. Barcus (1907-1909), C. N. N. Ferguson (1909-1912), S. A. Barnes (1912-1915), J. W. Story (1915-1917), E. E. Robinson (1917-1920), J. W. Israel (1920-1921), O. P. Clark, (1921-1923), L. N. Lipscomb (1923-1927), C. L. Cartwright (1927-1929), D. B. Doak (1929-1931), W. G. Bailey (1931-1934), and C. R. Hooton (1934 until the present time).

The Hale Center Methodist Episcopal Church South was organized in July, 1889, by Rev. R. M. Morris, then pastor of the Methodist Church in Plainview. There were three charter members,—Mrs. L. T. Lester, Mrs. A. M. Jones and Mrs. A. N. Jones. Services were held in the Epworth School House two miles southwest of the present site of Hale Center. The first church building was erected in 1901. This building burned in 1909, and a new church was built in 1911. The first full-time pastor was called in 1917. Prior to that time the pastors divided their time with other congregations.

Pastors since 1917 were as follows: W. L. Lightfoot, G. H. Bryant, G. T. Palmer, J. B. McReynolds, Ed R. Wallace, W. H. Terry, J. P. Patterson, O. M. Anderson and R. S. Watkins.

The Lakeview Methodist Church South was organized by R. M. Morris, of Plainview, in March, 1893, at the old Ivey School House in the Strip Community. This was the third Methodist Church to be organized in Hale County.

The First Methodist Church of Petersburg was organized in August, 1911, by Rev. W. H. Carr. The charter members were: Mrs. M. E. Black, W. T. Holt, Mrs. Chapman, Miss Ida James and Mrs. George T. Thorpe. The church building was erected in 1929.

The following persons have served as pastors: W. H. Carr, S. J. Upton, T. C. Willet, W. B. Wilkins, J. W. Brown, L. H.

Davis, Rev. Blevins, Preston Florence, W. H. Strong, M. P. Hines, J. E. Payne, J. E. Kerby, J. W. Price, Cecil Matthews, F. O. Garner and C. O. Coppage.

The First Methodist Episcopal Church of Plainview (called "Northern" Methodist) was organized in 1910. The membership of this church was composed for the most part of Methodists from the Northern states who could not adjust themselves to the church of their choice being designated as "South." A wooden bungalow church was built on the corner of Ninth and Columbia Streets and was dedicated June 26, 1910. Rev. C. E. Hastings was the first and only pastor of this church. In 1914 the church disbanded and the building was sold to the Church of Christ.

The Methodist Church of Abernathy was organized in 1910. The church worshipped at the school house until 1925 when a church building was erected. Ministers who have served as pastors at Abernathy are as follows: J. P. Caloway, D. C. Ross, B. Y. Dickinson, J. W. Brown, S. J. Upton, J. G. Howell, L. H. Davis, R. F. Dunn, J. F. Michael, J. A. Wheeler, H. W. Barnett, O. B. Herring and Ed A. Tharp.

Other Methodist Churches have been organized in Hale County in the following communities: Snyder, Bellview, Liberty, Halfway, Runningwater, Valleyview.

The Presbyterian Church U. S. (South) was organized in Plainview by Rev. W. P. Dickey in 1888. The charter members of this church were Messrs. and Mesdames J. M. Carter, C. L. Carter and J. W. Smylie. Mrs. C. L. Carter and six children and two children of Mr. and Mrs. J. W. Smylie were baptized at the organization. Services were held in the little Methodist Church alternately with other denominations. Rev. J. D. Tidball became the first pastor and preached to the congregation once a month. Mr. Tidball moved away after a short pastorate and no other pastor was secured. This organization was afterwards formally dissolved by the Dallas Presbytery.

The Cumberland Presbyterian Church of Plainview was organized in Plainview on August 13, 1903, by Rev. J. T. Franklin and Rev. A. L. Carter, with twenty-six charter members. Ruling Elders were Geo. L. Mayfield, W. P. Alexander and J. J. Park, with F. L. Mitchell as deacon. Rev. Josiah Phillips and Rev. Louis Grafton served as pastors of this

RELIGIOUS HISTORY

church. Rev. Grafton was withdrawn by the Mission Board on June 1, 1905.

The First Presbyterian Church U. S. A. was organized in Plainview in 1904 by Dr. Henry Little upon application signed by seven persons who became charter members, ie., Col. R. P. Smyth, J. M. Carter, Mr. and Mrs. W. E. Armstrong, Mrs. W. A. Todd, Mrs. J. F. Smyer and Mrs. George Boswell. Rev. H. C. Rimmer was sent out by the Mission Board and served as pastor for a short time when he was withdrawn by the Board. Since plans were under way in the General Assembly to unite the Cumberland Presbyterian Church and the Presbyterian Church U. S. A., no other pastor was sent and the congregation was advised to worship with the Cumberland Church until decision was made. The union of the two churches was effected in the General Assemblies of these churches at a joint meeting in Decatur, Illinois, in May, 1906.

Rev. W. A. Erwin was appointed as Missionary and was sent to Plainview to unite the two churches. Upon his arrival he first purchased a lot upon which to build a church, which is the present location of the church, on the corner of Eighth and Baltimore Streets. In 1907 Rev. J. H. Abney was sent by Mr. Erwin with instruction to unite the congregations and set them to work. Mr. Abney's first action was to buy a second lot adjoining the one Mr. Erwin had purchased.

The congregations of the U. S. A. and Cumberland churches assembled in the Knights of Pythias Hall in Plainview on August 14, 1907, and were united in the Presbyterian Church U. S. A. by Rev. J. H. Abney. The membership at the time of uniting of the congregations, was composed of the following:

Col. R. P. Smyth, Mrs. W. A. Todd, Mrs. J. H. Abney, Mrs. E. B. Hughes, Miss Effie Casey, Mrs. Mary Best, C. E. McClelland, Mrs. W. Bain, Mrs. E. Graham, Mr. and Mrs. S. W. Meharg, Mr. and Mrs. W. T. Waddill, Mrs. W. B. Knight, Mrs. E. P. Norwood and George L. Mayfield, (all of whom were present at the union of the church,) and Mrs. Alice Johnson, Miss Mamie Johnson, Miss Fronie Johnson, J. C. Goodwin, Mrs. W. R. Simmons, Mr. and Mrs. Lee Mitchell, Anna Lee Mitchell, Mrs. J. M. Broom, Mr. and Mrs. J. W. Smylie, Miss Alice Smylie and Miss Mary Smylie.

Upon Mr. Abney's arrival, the two churches had been inactive for some time, but he found an active and earnest Ladies Aid Society whose members were so confident that they would soon have a Presbyterian Church that even before his coming they had purchased the pews for a church at a cost of four hundred dollars, giving a note for the purchase price. The money was raised by serving luncheons and banquets and the note was paid in full. The pews were stored in Mrs. Todd's barn for two years before the church could be built. In 1908 a little gray church of cement blocks was erected on the lot that Reverend Erwin had purchased on his first visit. The first service held in the church was the Christmas tree in 1908. In 1916 the little gray church was removed and a brick church was built during the pastorate of Rev. T. B. Haynie, and a manse was also erected during the pastorate of Sterling Park, on the lot which Mr. Abney purchased.

The following persons have served as pastor of the Presbyterian Church U. S. A.: H. C. Rimmer, J. H. Abney, W. A. Posey, Sterling Park, T. B. Haynie, Gordon Lang, H. E. Bullock, John W. White, L. Burney Shell, N. F. Grafton and Fred S. Rogers.

The Presbyterian Church U. S. was organized for the second time in Plainview on February 24, 1910, by Rev. Leonard Gill, on application of prospective members. The following were charter members:

Mr. and Mrs. W. E. Armstrong, Mr. and Mrs. H. V. Tull, Mr. and Mrs. George S. Fairriss, Mr. and Mrs. E. L. Kerr, Mr. and Mrs. R. A. Barrow, Miss Ruby Barrow and J. F. Smyer.

The congregation purchased the wooden building of the Methodist Church when their new brick church was finished. The following persons served as pastor: Rev. John P. Kidd (1910-1911) and Rev. J. F. Foxworth (1912-1913).

On dismissal from the Presbytery at their request, the members of the congregation united in a body with the First Presbyterian Church U. S. A. on July 6, 1913. The church building was sold to the Presbyterian Church at Runningwater and moved to that place.

The Runningwater Presbyterian Church U. S. A. was organized in the Runningwater School House in 1907 by Rev. J. H. Abney, who served the church as pastor, preaching at

Runningwater alternately with the Methodist Minister. The following persons were charter members: Mr. and Mrs. J. W. Ray, Miss Lillie Ray, Mr. and Mrs. Lee Duvall, Miss Lillie Ship, Mrs. A. M. Anderson, Mable Anderson, Mrs. John Hobbs, Mr. and Mrs. J. V. Matlock, Charles Knight, Mr. and Mrs. W. D. Knight, Mrs. George Boswell, Mrs. Drake, Mrs. Epps, Mrs. Bagley, Mable Matlock and John Ship. In June, 1913, the building erected by the Methodist Church in 1897 was purchased from the Presbyterian Church U.S. and moved to Runningwater. This building, which has been used alternately by the various denominations, still stands at Runningwater and has the distinction of being the oldest religious edifice in Hale County.

The Petersburg Cumberland Presbyterian Church was organized on September 7, 1911, by Rev. J. L. Elliott. The church building was erected in 1920. The charter members were as follows: Mrs. M. J. Saxon, W. B. Saxon, L. B. Saxon, Dovie M. Saxon, Ella D. Saxon, Mr. and Mrs. I. Z. Smith, Florence Smith, Mrs. M. C. Smith, S. T. Smith, Mrs. M. J. Porter and J. H. Howell:

The following ministers have served as pastor: J. L. Elliott, W. H. Stephens, L. H. Davis, B. L. Baits, O. A. Mealor, L. B. Crawford, S. A. Berrie, C. C. Bolding, W. O. Parr, A. W. Yell, B. W. Phillips, G. P. Humphries, G. O. Dean, R. Q. Dyess and W. H. Cheatham.

The Hale Center Cumberland Presbyterian Church was organized about 1904. This church had sixty members and for a number of years was very active. R. W. Lemond was clerk. A church building was erected several years later. This church has not been dissolved and still owns a church building, but through the years most of the members have moved away and it has been inactive for some years.

Rev. J. H. Abney served as Sunday School Missionary during 1907 and 1908 and during that time he organized Sunday Schools in most of the rural communities,—Union Sunday Schools, in which all denominations joined. As the years passed, churches were organized by other denominations in these communities, a number of which grew out of the Sunday Schools organized by Rev. Abney while serving as Sunday School Missionary.

The First Christian Church of Plainview was organized September 9, 1889, by Rev. Thomas G. Nance in the little sod school house. Services were held in the sod school house and in 1897 the church purchased the little Methodist Church when the Methodists built the church which now stands at Runningwater. Later this church divided into two organizations which were then called the "Progressive" and "Non-Progressive" Christian Churches. The "Progressive" church then met in the school house and the other division retained the building, but later that organization disbanded and the church building was sold. On May 29, 1909, the First Christian Church was incorporated and a new brick church was erected during the pastorate of Rev. Jewell Howard, which church was dedicated July 3, 1910.

The Charter members of this church were as follows: S. T. Pepper, Lizzie Pepper, Stella Pendley, Isaac McMormack, Mrs. E. J. Beard and Messrs. and Mesdames John Pendley, Hugh McClelland, J. P. Lattimore, Bud Oldham, Duncan, M. L. Bryant, L. A. White, W. P. Boyd, and H. C. Miller, Mrs. Fannie Pendley, Mrs. R. A. Ford and Mrs. J. M. Shafer.

The following ministers have served this church as pastor: Thomas G. Nance, Mit Bandy, Dallas Smith, Gerald Smith, Arnold, Jewell Howard, L. L. Gladney, J. O. Haegemeyer, Swift, H. A. Highsmith, G. W. Davis, H. B. Johnson, R. S. Norman, Wright, Leslie G. Smith, W. K. Dickinson, E. W. Wheatley, R. O. Beaman and W. P. Jennings.

The Church of Christ was organized in Plainview in the fall of 1909, by J. D. Burleson, of Lockney, in the old wooden Court House. The congregation first met in the Court House, then in the Odd Fellows Hall in the Wayland building, and afterward in the new Court House. In 1914 they purchased the wooden church erected by the First Methodist Church U. S. A. on the corner of Ninth and Columbia Streets, which building was later replaced by a brick church building.

The charter members of this church were as follows: Messrs. and Mesdames R. M. Peace, J. W. Westcoat, H. L. Sprott and Jeff Pipkin, Mrs. W. B. Lewis, Miss Minnie Westcoat, J. H. Holland and John Peace.

The First Church of Christ in Petersburg was organized by C. W. Smith, founder of the little town of Barwise. The charter members were Messrs. and Mesdames Ed M. White, Henry White, and Will Mickey, Mrs. A. S. J. Martin and Mrs. Tom Black. A church building was erected in 1908.

The Plainview Missionary Baptist Church was organized on November 23, 1890, in the school house in Plainview, by Drs. John S. Stamps and I. B. Kimbrough. Drs. Stamps and Kimbrough were both missionaries and had come to Plainview in search of a field of service. Dr. Stamps had organized the Baptist Church at Amarillo a few weeks prior to this, and a few weeks later Dr. Kimbrough organized the first Baptist Church in Floyd County.

The early history of the Baptist Church in Plainview has numerous interesting and romantic features. The first of these was introduced by Rev. Stamps, who, when he left Virginia, brought with him the Articles of Faith of the "Old Mill Creek Church in Virginia." This manuscript had been in the Stamps family and had been handed down from generation to generation since the days when Virginia was under the English law which termed all Baptists as "heretics" and did not allow "heretics" to preach, and it is well known that Patrick Henry once defended several Baptist preachers in the courts of Richmond, Virginia, who were charged with "preaching the Gospel of the Son of God." At the organization of the Baptist Church in Plainview, Dr. Stamps related the history of this creed which he stated was the identical manuscript which his ancestor had used in the Old Mill Creek Church. The old mill was the watermill on the creek and was built of great hewn logs, and was two stories high. The officers could not hear the minister preaching in the top of the mill while it was running, so the Baptists brought their grists to mill and while the miller was grinding the grist, they went into the top of the building to hold services. It was a dear thing to be reared in that church and Rev. Stamps adhering to the faith of his fathers, introduced into the Plainview Baptist Church these Articles of Faith, which were read and adopted article by article.

Dr. I. B. Kimbrough became the first pastor of the church. He attended a Baptist Convention at Fort Worth soon after organizing the Plainview church, and in giving a report of his missionary work on the frontier, he told them of the newly organized church and made this statement: "If every person here today would give one dollar, it would be enough to pay for the material to build the church in Plainview." A large contribution was made at the convention which was supplemented by funds donated by other Baptist churches where Dr. Kimbrough preached. When Dr. Kimbrough returned to Plainview he carried in his pocket the money to build the first Baptist church home in Plainview,—the amount of $2,700. The members of the church hauled the lumber from Amarillo with their wagons and contributed their services in erecting the building, the cash all being used to pay for lumber. Members of the church filled their wagons with buffalo bones picked up over the prairie as they drove to Amarillo for lumber and sold them there. From the proceeds of the sale of buffalo bones at $20 per ton, they purchased seats for the church, and a part of the money was secured in this way to pay for the large church bell, which was welded according to specifications of the local church, by a firm in Cincinnati. The old church bell was used for many years, and placed inside the new brick church as a relic. In 1937 the old church bell was again put into use and its chimes may now be heard each Sabbath day.

The Staked Plains Baptist Association, which was organized soon after the organization of the local church, covered a vast territory. As described in the Minutes, it was "bounded on the north by the Fort Worth and Denver Railroad; on the south by the T. & P. Railroad, on the east by the Red Fork Association, and on the west by the Providence of God." The mission field extended far into New Mexico.

The charter members of this church were Messrs. and Mesdames R. B. C. Howell, F. M. Parks, Tom Leverett, T. L. Pearson and Seat Turner, and Mr. Thomas E. Smith.

The first church building was erected in 1892. This small wooden building was enlarged several times, and in 1926 it was torn down and a new brick building was erected on the corner of Eighth and Austin Streets.

The following ministers have served as pastor: Dr. I. B. Kimbrough, T. A. Moore, Henry E. Summers, T. P. Speakman, L. T. Mayes, R. E. Gillon, I. E. Gates, Millard P.

RELIGIOUS HISTORY 133

Jenkins, Harlan J. Matthews, H. L. Street, O. L. Hailey and Pat Horton.

The Calvary Baptist Church was organized at Plainview Dec. 16, 1910, by Rev. Charles R. Lee, of Hale Center, and S. W. Smith of Plainview. Its charter membership consisted of seventy-seven Baptists who withdrew from the First Baptist Church. A church was built at the corner of Eighth and Columbia streets. Two years later, a union of the two churches was perfected and the membership reunited with the First Baptist Church.

The Hale Center Missionary Baptist Church (now called First Baptist Church of Hale Center), was organized in 1901 by Dr. I. B. Kimbrough in the Epworth School House. Dr. Kimbrough served the congregation as pastor, preaching once a month. The Baptists shared the Methodist church building from 1902 until 1907, when the Baptist church was built. In 1935 this building was replaced by a new church which was dedicated January 1, 1936. Among the charter members were Messrs. and Mesdames J. H. Calvert, Jack Hamilton, A. D. Wallen, F. M. Lester and J. T. Weaver.

The following ministers have served as pastor: Dr. I. B. Kimbrough, J. W. Winn, D. N. Poole, Chas. R. Lee, T. P. Speakman, Quimby Brown, Richberg, J. J. Lively, Turnage, W. R. Triplett, T. J. Fouts, I. E. Gates, J. H. Lougan, G. B. Airhart, Waldrup, C. E. Painter, J. H. Vinson, W. R. Underwood, C. A. Joiner, Joe Wilson, M. E. Fairchild and W. R. Burnett.

Primitive Baptist Church of Plainview was organized Nov. 11, 1933, by the following Presbyters: Elders H. G. Richards, of Anton, Texas, J. H. Alldredge, of Lubbock, C. J. L. Bolinger, of Ralls, and S. J. Ellis, Silverton, and Deacons J. B. Jackson, of Anton and J. W. Huey, of Floydada. The charter members were: Mesdames Lena Phillips, Mary Gipson, and Cora Rickley, Mr. and Mrs. G. C. Miller and Miss Lora May Miller.

Pastors of this church were Elders H. G. Richard, G. C. Miller and S. J. Ellis.

Other Baptist Churches in Hale County are Plainview College Heights Baptist Church, Calvary Baptist Church of

Cotton Center, and Baptist churches at Seth Ward, Happy Union, Lakeview, Halfway, Valleyview, Runningwater, Cousins, Liberty, Prairieview, Abernathy and Petersburg.

The Menonite Church at Snyder was organized in May, 1908, by Bishop David Garber, of La Junta, Colorado. The Snyder School House had been established in 1907 and named in honor of Rev. P. B. Snyder, who became pastor of the church. A Menonite settlement was established in the Snyder community, which for many years was known as the Menonite colony, the colonists coming together from points in Minnesota, Ohio, Kansas, Pennsylvania, Virginia, Illinois and Colorado. Menonite teachers were employed in the school, and the school house was used for a place of worship.

Charter members of the Menonite Church were as follows: Messrs. & Mesdames P. B. Snyder, John Snyder, Andrew Brenneman, John Hartzler, H. Near, Joseph K. Hartzler, Benjamin Martin, Jonas Kreider, Ferd Rastetter, Joel Gimrich, Perry Smith and Aaron Good; Mr. John Snyder, Susie Snyder, Orville Snyder, Mr. H. E. Landis, Rebecca, Martha and Lucy Near, David Hartzler, Ellen Hartzler, Bertha and Ida Kreider.

P. B. Snyder was pastor of the church for many years and was a trustee of the Snyder school. In 1922 the Menonites began to move away and in 1925 the church was disbanded.

The Pentecostal Mission was organized in 1908 by Ferd Faulkner. Its charter members were Messrs. and Mesdames Ferd Faulkner, Ben Sebastian, Taylor, Joe Scott, B. B. Burroughs, Will Fairris, T. Coppage and Dr. and Mrs. J. D. Hagood, Mrs. A. J. Chambers and Homer Faulkner.

A small building was erected on the present site of the Fort Worth and Denver Depot, where many series of revival meetings were held in the early days of its organization.

The Church of the Nazarene was organized in 1909 with the following charter members: Messrs. and Mesdames Riley Brannon, J. B. Posey, Wm. Sewell, Charlie Johnson, Joe Waggoner, Coke Fullingim, O. C. Fluke, W. L. Hogue and George Nicholson, and Messrs. Edmondson, A. J. Chambers and George Russell.

A small wooden building was erected for a church which was used until 1928, when, during the pastorate of Rev. R. M.

Hocker, when prosperity was at its height and the building boom was at its peak and large loans could easily be secured, the congregation erected a beautiful brick church on the corner of Seventh and Fresno Streets. The church thrived until the financial crash of 1930, when many of the people were thrown out of employment and the heavy church debt became too heavy a burden for the members to carry. The church building was sold, and the congregation procured other place for worship. Plans are under way for the erection of a smaller church building.

The following ministers have served as pastor: Geo. W. H. Russell, George Nicholson, Eason, W. H. Phillips, Riley Brannon, Miss Nora Gehris, J. P. Ingle, S. L. Wood, R. M. Hocker, Youngman, W. D. McGraw and T. C. Ingram and D. W. Simpson.

The Pilgrim Holiness Church was organized in 1935 by T. C. Ingram, and meets at 215 East Seventh Street, with T. C. Ingram as pastor.

The Catholic Church—St. Alice Mission—was organized in 1909, by Father Dunn, of Amarillo, who organized the parish at Amarillo. Services were held first in the home of Mr. and Mrs. J. G. Seipp, later in the I.O.O.F. Hall in the Wayland Building. The first church building was erected in 1912, dedicated July 10, 1912, by Rev. Bishop J. P. Lynch of Dallas. A new brick church was built in 1928 under the supervision of Father Krarkut. This Mission was allotted to the Sacred Heart Parish of Amarillo. Later it became a parish.

Members of the first congregation included the following: Joe Keliehor, Mr. and Mrs. Charlie Jueske, Mr. and Mrs. J. G. Seipp, Miss Geneva Seipp, Mrs. C. C. Gidney and Mrs. D. M. Neal.

The following persons have served as pastor: Rev. Krarkut, Francis M. Kaminsky, W. E. Robinson, and W. F. Bosen.

The Protestant Episcopal Church—St. Mark's Mission —was organized in Plainview by Rev. Edwin Weary, of Amarillo, Archdeacon and General Missionary, working under Bishop Alex C. Garrett, of Dallas. The charter members were: Thos. Abraham, (Warden); J. A. Graham (Secretary) Dr. and Mrs. J. C. Anderson, Mrs. Atterwood, Mr. and Mrs.

Robert W. Brahan, Mrs. J. J. Bromley, Mrs. Wm. Catto, Miss Lucile Flint, Mr. and Mrs. E. H. Humphrey, Mrs. P. D. Hunsaker, Miss Edna Mayhugh, F. C. Vickery, R. C. Ware and Mrs. P. J. Wooldridge.

After worshipping first in the Methodist Church, then in the Christian and Presbyterian Churches and occasionally in homes, a Church building was procured and moved to the corner of Seventh and Columbia Streets. A rectory was built in 1925. From its inception, the Episcopal Church's program in Plainview and throughout the District of North Texas has been made possible by appropriations from the Domestic and Foreign Missionary Society of the Protestant Episcopal Church in the United States of America, supplementing the contributions of the membership.

Ministers who have served the Plainview mission are as follows: Edwin Weary, Jesse S. Wicks, William Garner, E. H. J. Andrews, Frank B. Eteson, Charles Harris, Jr., E. E. Madeira, Warwick Aiken, and Donald Ellis.

The Assembly of God Church of Plainview was organized in August, 1928, by Rev. Ralph Foster. The first members were Mr. and Mrs. Dan Seals, Minnie, and Betty Mangus, Mr. and Mrs. Starks, Mr. Bonds, Mable, Ward, and Ethel Starks. Pastors of this church have been Revs. Hennegar, Ford, Thorn, Oscar Jones, Scott Mitchell, Mont M. Walker and H. M. Reeves.

St. Paul's Evangelical Lutheran Church in Plainview was organized on May 25, 1930, by Rev. Wm. H. Emmert under the direction of the Mission Board of the Texas District of the Evangelical Lutheran Synod of Missouri, Ohio, and other States. The church building was completed in December, 1930, at the corner of Ninth and Oakland Streets. The charter members were: Albert Bertelson, G. J. Dieter, Edwin Kokel, Arnold Kokel, E. B. Kunkel, H. Kunkel, Adolph Obenhaus, Walter Obenhaus and Ernest Rohne.

Wm. H. Remmert and C. A. Gaertner have served this church as pastor.

The Seventh Day Advent Church of Plainview was organized on May 25, 1935, by Elder R. L. Benten, President of the Union Conference. The charter members were: Messrs. and Mesdames. C. A. Walgren, E. B. Kitching,

Harold Colburn, H. A. Bledsoe, E. N. Muse, and J. E. Woodward; Mesdames: Louise Cole, J. E. Schneider, M. L. James, T. M. Elder, Ora Fletcher, Cale Farris, Alton Stroman, and F. H. Selden; Misses Jessie Landrum, V. O. Brooks, Cecil James, Dorothy Farris, Ione Kitching and Mildred Farris.

The services are held at the church on the corner of Galveston and Thirteenth Streets each Saturday. C. A. Walgren is pastor and H. D. Colburn Assistant.

The Foursquare Gospel Church holds services in the Old Post Office building. Miss Daisy Beard is pastor.

The Salvation Army was officially opened in Plainview on February 16, 1929. The first officers were Adjutant and Mrs. Charles Brennan and Captain Verna Davis. On August 28, 1932, the resident officers were moved and the work was supervised from Lubbock until December 12, 1935, when Captain Guy Hepler was appointed as Commander of the Post. The Post was declared officially open at a mass meeting held Dec. 14, 1936, when Captain Hepler received the post color from Major William G. Gilks, Dallas Salvation Army divisional commander.

The Pastors Association was organized in Plainview on Feb. 24, 1911. The following pastors were charter members: Jewell Howard, C. N. N. Ferguson, H. H. Street, C. E. Hastings, W. A. Posey and Chas. R. Lee. Rev. Jewell Howard was elected President and Rev. C. N. N. Ferguson Vice Pres. and Chas. R. Lee Secretary-Treasurer. The purpose of the organization was that the ministers of the various denominations might work more effectively in the interest of Local Option in Hale County, and the first work was the outlining of a campaign for prohibition. The Association was reorganized in January, 1936, after having been inactive for some time, and Rev. Fred S. Rogers was elected President.

CHAPTER XII

Lodges and Fraternal Organizations

For many years the Lodge was a vital factor in the lives of the people of Hale County. It afforded a medium by which the people came together, the spiritual teachings enriched the lives of the members and the joy of the contact with friends kept the interest high. Lack of a quorum was unheard of, and often members traveled many miles, consuming several days in going and coming in order to be present in the early years.

The Ancient Free and Accepted Masons, Plainview Lodge No. 709, was the first Lodge organized in the county. On September 9, 1890, the Grand Master of the Grand Lodge, A. S. Richardson, granted a dispensation for this Lodge to function until the convening of the Grand Lodge of Texas. The story of the organization was given by Sterling P. Strong, as follows:

"The Dispensation was granted upon the application of J. W. Smylie, Sterling P. Strong, Z. T. Maxwell, W. L. Smith, R. A. Ford, R. C. Ware, A. J. Welter, R. W. Martine, L. G. Wilson, J. H. Bryan, and W. H. Portwood. The above named organized the Masonic Lodge at Plainview with A. J. Welter Worshipful Master, Sterling P. Strong SeniorWarden, R. A. Ford Junior Warden, and the Lodge functioned until the Grand Lodge of Texas met in Houston in December, 1890, when Sterling P. Strong went as representative of Plainview Lodge and secured a Charter from the Grand Lodge, which was dated December 12, 1890.

"The Grand Master, of Texas, appointed Wm. C. Turner, who then resided at Amarillo, Texas, District Deputy Grand Master to set Plainview Lodge to work under the charter. This was done on January 1, 1891. The first annual report to the Grand Lodge by Plainview Lodge showed the following officers and members: Sterling P. Strong W.M., J. C. Pipkin S.W., L. S. Kinder J.W., R. W. Martine Treas., R. M. Morris

FRATERNAL ORGANIZATIONS 139

Secretary, R. A. Ford Senior Deacon, P. F. Bryan Junior Deacon, J. N. Donohoo Senior Steward, C. W. Marsalis Junior Steward, A. Jones, Tiler, C. R. Bailey, J. H. Bryan, J. T. Chapman, W. G. Conner, F. Faulkner, W. P. Herbert, Z. T. Maxwell, J. Phillips, W. H. Portwood, W. L. Smith, J. W. Smylie, W. C. Turner, R. C. Ware, L. G. Wilson and A. J. Welter.

"Early in 1890, plans were perfected to build a frame school building, and the Masons of Plainview and surrounding country joined in this, building an upper story to the school building, and using same for the meeting place of the Masonic Lodge. The lumber and material for this building was hauled from Amarillo by freight wagons.

"Under Masonic Law, the three principal officers of a newly constituted Lodge must go to the nearest Lodge for examination. It was decided by the Masons interested at Plainview that the Masonic Lodge at Vernon was the nearest Lodge to Plainview, so A. J. Welter, R. A. Ford and myself went to Amarillo by horse-drawn wagon, took the train to Vernon, and was examined as the law provided by Vernon Lodge. Our examinations were satisfactory to Vernon Lodge, but when same reached the Grand Master, we were notified that there was a Masonic Lodge nearer to Plainview, which was located at Margaret, in Hardeman County. We prepared a chuck wagon and camping outfit and drove through the country to the town of Margaret, consuming fully a week to make the trip, but our examination was accepted, and the Dispensation which I have already mentioned was granted.

"Plainview Lodge No. 709 was the first Masonic Lodge organized on the Plains of Texas. After the organization of Plainview Lodge, myself and others of same were appointed by the Grand Master to set other Lodges to work, those being at Della Plain, Tulia, Canyon and Amarillo."

"For information concerning the organization or early history of the Masonic Lodge at Plainview, will say I wrote the Grand Secretary of the Grand Lodge, Ancient Free and Accepted Masons, of Texas, and he gave me records which have refreshed my memory concerning the early history of Plainview Lodge."

(July 3, 1935)   (Signed) Sterling P. Strong.

Pastmasters of Plainview Lodge No. 709 are as follows: A. J. Welter, Sterling P. Strong, J. C. Pipkin, R. W. Lemond, Harry Brown, R. Holland, Wm. Bain, S. W. Meharg, Jas. R. Delay, W. A. Todd, C. E. McClelland, H. A. Wofford, W. C. Longmire, J. C. Goodwin, H. C. Von Struve, Claud Daniel, W. E. Settoon, W. O. Anderson, P. L. Kemble, W. B. Martine, R. P. Smyth, C. S. Williams, S. W. Waddill, R. J. Frye, C. F. Vincent, J. C. King, E. Graham, E. A. Gilbert, V. V. Beck, J. A. Peret, R. W. McDaniel, O. B. Short, D. P. Everett, A. H. Schrock, R. H. Leatherwood and Clem Ross, W. M.

Plainview Chapter No. 228 of Royal Arch Masons was chartered Dec. 4, 1901, with the following officers: R. Wm. Lemond, High Priest, R. Holland, King, and J. H. Wayland Scribe.

The following were charter members: N. M. Akeson, H. Brower, Harry Brown, R. S. Crawford, L. L. Dye, S. N. Hix, R. Holland, S. L. Hunter, L. A. Knight, W. C. Kenyon, R. Wm. Lemond, R. West Lemond, W. P. Lash, C. E. McClelland, Chas. McCormack, W. B. Martine, W. C. Silvey, J. A. Stegald, R. C. Ware, J. R. Wright, J. H. Wayland, L. C. Wayland.

Plainview Chapter No. 164 Royal Select Masters was chartered Dec. 3, 1907, with the following officers: C. E. McClelland Thrice Illustrious Master, L. S. Kinder Right Illustrious Dep. Master and Chas. McCormick Illustrious Principal Conductor of the Work.

Plainview Commandery No. 53, Knights Templar, was chartered April 22, 1909.

The charter members were as follows: R. C. Andrews, V. Andrews, T. M. Bartley, J. B. Bartley, R. C. Childers, J. F. Cline, B. Crump, J. C. Cantrell, Jas. R. DeLay, W. A. Donaldson, H. V. Edsell, W. W. English, J. N. Farris, W. H. Flamm, J. A. Glenn, E. Graham, G. S. Hardy, D. C. Hoover, E. B. Hughes, R. Holland, L. S. Kinder, Jno. C. La Prade, W. P. Lash, J. M. Lemond, R. W. Lemond, G. A. London, J. P. Neason, D. F. Morgan, T. Montgomery, W. T. Montgomery, C. E. McClelland, D. B. McCleskey, Chas. McCormick, J. R. McGhee, J. E. McCune, W. W. Nelson, E. F. Ousley, M. C. Overton, A. A. Peoples, N. R. Porter, K. A.

Pederson, W. Peterson, J. F. Robinson, W. E. Schott, Lee Shropshire, J. H. Slaton, R. B. Smith, W. R. Spencer, J. D. Starks, T. P. Steen, R. L. Stringer, H. C. Von Struve, C. Surginer, W. A. Todd, T. M. Tomlinson, J. L. Vaughn, C. F. Vincent, R. C. Ware, T. D. Webb, J. W. Willis, S. C. Wilson.

Petersburg Lodge No. 1126, Ancient Free and Accepted Masons, was organized on December 4, 1918, by R. W. Lemond. The first officers and charter members were as follows:

J. C. Boyd Worshipful Master, A. L. Bailey Senior Warden, W. M. Featherston Junior Warden, M. J. Gregory Treas., W. R. Buchanan Secretary, A. V. McCarty, R. C. Hannah, R. B. Hannah, J. W. Montgomery, W. A. Stoddard, Wm. Britt, J. R. Davis, H. H. Roberson, W. R. Buchanan, James A. Thompson, R. L. McDaniel, Ernest Shelley, J. H. Howell, C. E. Buchanan, D. M. Pipkin and A. M. Becton.

Past Worshipful Masters are J. C. Boyd, H. A. Hegi, R. L. McDaniel, W. M. Featherston, Clarence Thorpe and J. V. Newton.

Lemond Lodge No. 832, A. F. & A. M., Hale Center, was set to work under Dispensation by Right Worshipful R. C. Andrews, District Deputy Grand Master on Oct. 13, 1899, and charter was granted Dec. 7, 1899, with the following principal officers and charter members: J. W. Smylie Worshipful Master, W. N. Claxton Senior Warden, R. A. McWhorter Junior Warden, F. M. Lester, W. E. Porterfield, B. O. McWhorter, J. A. Syfrett, W. M. Glover, L. J. Harral, J. S. Highsmith, E. P. Earhart and W. D. Crump.

Past Masters are: J. W. Smylie, R. W. Lemond, N. M. Akeson, R. West Lemond, F. Bridges, A. T. Howell Jr., W. W. Laney, L. T. Dent, W. N. Claxton, W. T. Lemond, B. F. Oatis, G. L. Akeson, W. R. Ferguson, Will H. Casey, D. C. Shepard, G. H. Bryant, W. L. Townsen, Jas. T. Smithee, W. H. Lemond, Silas Maggard, J. L. Monroe, Carroll Bird, J. Frank Triplett, J. M. Mills, W. C. Wilhite, J. P. Loving, J. E. Miller, Walt W. Larson and D. H. Jerrell.

Hale Center Council of Royal and Select Masters No. 261, was chartered Dec. 5, 1910, and set to work May 24, 1911. The first principal officers were R. W. Lemond T.I.M., N. M. Akeson R.I.D.M., and R. West Lemond I.P.C.W. Those who have served as Thrice Illustrious Masters are R. W. Lemond, N. M. Akeson, G. L. Akeson, W. L. Townsen and Howard Lemond.

Hale Center Royal Arch Chapter No. 325 was chartered Dec. 5, 1910, with R. W. Lemond High Priest, N. M. Akeson King and R. West Lemond Scribe. The Chapter was put to work Feb. 22, 1911, by Companion R. Holland, of Plainview, acting as Deputy Grand High Priest. Those who have served as High Priest are: R. W. Lemond, N. M. Akeson, W. T. Lemond, R. J. Woofter, R. West Lemond, W. B. Price, W. H. Lemond, G. L. Akeson, J. T. Smithee, Nils H. Akeson, Carroll Bird, W. C. Wilhite, J. P. Loving and C. C. Scrogging.

Plainview Chapter No. 37 of the Order of Eastern Star was organized on Aug. 16, 1896, in the Masonic Hall in Plainview, by R. W. Lemond, of Hale Center. The Chapter worked under Dispensation until a charter was granted on Nov. 10, 1897. The first officers and charter members were as follows: Mrs. Mary V. Dye Worthy Matron, R. W. Lemond Worthy Patron, Mesdames: Bettie Knight Associate Matron, Mittie Workman Treasurer, Lena Ware Secretary, R. M. Morris Warden, R. W. Lemond Conductress, R. E. Burch Associate Conductress, Lou Lester—Ada, Miss Ione Burch—Ruth, Mesdames Florence Harrington—Esther, Ella McWhorter—Electra, Frances Wilson, Mary Kinder, Lizzie Burch, Lou Donohoo, Mary Martine, Kate McWhorter, Lena Lemond, and Isabella Howell, and Messrs. R. W. Lemond, L. T. Lester, B. O. McWhorter, W. B. Martine, L. A. Knight and L. Lee Dye.

Past Worthy Matrons are as follows: Mary V. Dye, Bettie Knight, Lizzie Burch, Mary Martine, Margaret Todd, Lena Ware, Mary R. Kinder, Emma Nelson, Ella McWhorter, Margaret Coleman, Eva Penry, Carrie L. Pipkin, Josephine Keck, Etta Brahan, Zetta Lash, Julia Collins, Helen Vincent, Effie Peret, Adella S. Drew, Mattie Thompson, Mary E. Anderson, Ann Kelly, Louise Andrews, Minnie Woodall, Alice Abbott, Nora Rice, June Terry, Annie Standifer, Hannah Reinken, Fay C. Smith, Nadine Story, Lettie Rogers and Henrietta Wall. Worthy Patrons were: R. W. Lemond, W. E. Porterfield, W. B. Martine, L. A. Knight, Chas. McClelland, James R. DeLay, C. F. Vincent, R. P. Smyth, D. F. Morgan, Claude Daniels, C. C. Stubbs, H. G. Vaughn,

R. E. Rampy, Paul Summers, Arch Keys and Charles Reinken.

Lemond Chapter No. 38, Order of the Eastern Star, Hale Center, was granted a charter Oct. 7, 1900. The Chapter was organized and set to work by R. W. (Uncle Bob) Lemond. The first officers and charter members were as follows: Mrs. Mattie Smylie Worthy Matron, Robert West Lemond Worthy Patron, Mrs. Flora Harrington Assistant Matron, Mesdames: Nena Claxton, Lena Lemond, Leonora Ferguson, Ella McWhorter, Margery Highsmith, Annie Lemond, M. A. McWhorter, Kate McWhorter, Mary A. M. Syfrett, Rena Akeson, Messrs. Nils Akeson, W. N. Claxton, J. L. Ferguson, W. L. Harrington, R. W. Lemond Jr., J. S. Highsmith, B. O. McWhorter, J. W. Smylie, J. A. Syfrett and R. W. Lemond.

Past Worthy Matrons of the Chapter are as follows: Mattie Smylie, Florence Harrington, Ella McWhorter, Hattie Alley, Lena Lemond, Annie Lemond, Kate H. McWhorter, Nena Claxton, Alice Bull, Tilla Akeson, Artie M. Shepard, Gertrude Hunt, Anna Akeson, Carrie Wall, Rena Akeson, Hattie Quisenberry, Bessie Sanders, Sallie Lemond, Luella Porter, Sue Mag Maggard, Harriet H. Triplett, May Smithee, Rena Belle Akeson, Rosa Underwood, Lula Gage, Grace Louthan, Kate Payne, Mrs. J. Bailey Pinson, Aubrey Ivey and Lourane Jerrell. Worthy Patrons have been R. West Lemond, B. D. Woodlee, R. W. Lemond, N. M. Akeson, A. T. Howell Jr., J. M. Bull, A. L. Anderson, G. H. Bryant, G. L. Akeson, Howard Lemond, C. A. Joiner, Silas Maggard, J. T. Smithee and Nils Akeson.

Abernathy Chapter of Eastern Star was organized Oct. 19, 1921, by Miss Willie I. Pearson, Deputy Grand Matron. The following were charter members and officers: Mrs. Grace Gage Pinson Worthy Matron, Joe M. Ramsey Worthy Patron, Mesdames: Irma Jones Assistant Matron, Ulrika Schroeter Secretary, N. C. Hix Treasurer, Jewel Richter Conductress, Frankie Fitzgerald Assistant Conductor, Lillie Bledsoe Chaplin, and Fannie Arnold—Marshal, Miss Pearl Roberson organist, Mesdames Sallie Crow—Adah, Minnie Stambaugh—Ruth, Pearl Bledsoe—Esther, Nannie Smith—Martha, Frankie Snider—Electra, Vallie Ramsey Warden and Mr. L. R. Pinson Sentinel. This Chapter was afterward dismissed.

Plainview Lodge No. 12, I. O. O. F., was organized in Plainview on January 24, 1902, by E. S. Prentiss, of Amarillo, with the following officers and charter members: W. M. Shelly Noble Grand, George Fair Vice Grand, J. M. Carter Secretary, H. J. Sewell Treasurer and Q. D. Hoyle.

Past Noble Grands are as follows: W. M. Shelly, E. M. Carter, George F. Fair, R. H. Williamson, J. B. Maxey, Roy J. Frye, A. A. Hatchell, A. B. Rosser, J. O. Burch, A. H. Estes, G. C. Keck, O. W. Bryant, A. J. Chambers, E. R. Anderson, E. C. Baker, H. C. Randolph, C. S. Hefner, H. D. Hyde, A. E. Allen, W. J. Mitchell, I. W. Elliott, F. B. Gouldy, H. O. Conner, Geo. J. Martin, R. F. Hubbard, L. D. Griffin, J. J. Guyer, Geo. Ward, H. H. Rogers, J. C. King, R. F. Free, J. A. Peret, B. G. Morton, Geo. L. Kelly, E. I. Asher, C. H. Perkins, J. E. Dye, E. S. Aylesworth, L. H. Jones, M. S. Keller, J. F. Rice, S. H. Schaal, Belton Dodd, J. G. Terry, K. M. Bates, A. B. Cherry, R. O. Mayo, O. L. Harrington, H. O. Cordell, A. L. Stark, G. R. Stovall, J. C. Stovall, T. C. Hunt, J. M. Bell, Roy G. Wood, Solon James and Oscar Hill.

Plainview Encampment No. 58, I. O. O. F. was organized by C. C. Pangle, D.D.G.P., of Amarillo, on August 22, 1909, and the charter was delivered October 15th of that year.

The first officers and members were: G. F. Stephens, Chief Patriarch, Rev. G. F. Fair, High Priest, W. W. Jones, Senior Warden, A. A. Hatchell, Junior Warden, G. C. Keck, Scribe, J. N. Jordan, Treasurer; F. B. Gouldy, J. O. Burch, George R. Cox, A. B. Rosser, Lee Massingale, Elmer R. Anderson, A. H. Estes, E. Harlan, Henry DeJarnatt, C. S. Williams, Dr. J. H. Wayland, E. D. Hayes, A. B. Barkis and J. W. Vines.

A. A. Hatchell and Elmer R. Anderson received the decoration of Chivalry in 1915 and 1925 respectively. Elmer R. Anderson served as Grand Patriarch of the State in 1932-1933.

Plainview Rebekah Lodge No. 309 was organized Dec. 4, 1907, by Mrs. W. A. Bennett, President of Rebekah Assembly, with the following officers and charter members: Mrs. Connie Wayland Noble Grand, Helen Keith Vice Grand, Mamie Johnston Secretary, Beulah Winn Treasurer, Mesdames: L. W. Dalton, G. F. Fair, B. H. Towery, W. W. Jones, G. C. Keck, D. D. Shipley, May Vines, Ella Shelton,

FRATERNAL ORGANIZATIONS 145

Addie Brown, Berdie Brown, and Hoyle, Misses Margaret Boone and Celia Johnson, Messrs. J. M. Carter, L. W. Dalton, G. F. Fair, W. W. Jones, A. A. Hatchell, Jno. G. Hamilton, J. N. Donohoo and H. C. Randolph.

Past Noble Grands are as follows: Connie Wayland, Helen Keith, Ella Waldrop, Emma Keck, Etta Fitzgerald, May Vines, Melissa Nash, Gena Estes, Mary R. Anderson, Alice Rogers, Maud Jackson, Maggie Elliott, Mary L. Cox, Sarah Kerr, Lettie Rodgers, Ella Hunter, Eva Wilson, Annie Allen, Eva Hyde, Jessie King, Alice Abbott, Edith Johnson, Golda Anderson, Lucy Griffin, Adella S. Drew, Mona Green, Dollie Miller, Effie Peret, Mary Miller, Ella Munger, Victoria Asher, Nancy Stradler, Minnie Richardson, Annie Miller, Oma Laird, Eula Jeter, Minnie Woodall, Eula Mae Terry, Bessie Cole, Essie Mae Stovall, Winnie Reed, Dorothy Peret, Vesta Bates, Dena Madge Casey.

Lodge No. 1175 B. P. O. Elks, Plainview, was instituted Nov. 27, 1909, and charter was granted July 13, 1910. This was the fourth Elk Lodge organized on the plains. The following is a list of charter members and officers: J. W. Grant Exalted Ruler, Earl C. Keck Secretary, J. H. Slaton Treasurer, Levi Schick, E. Dowden and T. B. Carter Trustees; J. L. Vaughn, J. N. Donohoo, R. E. Burch, Charles McCormack, George W. Carter, J. H. Wayland, Reuben M. Ellerd, John J. Ellerd, Thomas B. Irwin, J. Walter Day, L. S. Kinder, E. H. Perry, E. B. Hughes, E. M. Carter, James R. DeLay, L. A. Knight, J. W. Pipkin, W. P. Dowden, Frank F. Hardin and L. C. Wayland.

The following have served as Exalted Ruler: Dr. J. W. Grant, James R. DeLay, E. H. Perry, Frank Hardin, J. W. Pipkin, W. J. Klinger, T. E. Shepard, E. B. Miller, E. H. Bawden, H. S. Hilburn, Casey Hughes, Ben Smith, J. J. Bromley, W. E. Settoon, Bain McCarroll, H. V. Tull Jr., R. E. Hooper, C. R. Ivey, J. P. Woodward, C. A. Butcher, W. R. Taegel, H. M. LaFont and Arthur Reinken.

1050 persons have been members of the Elks Lodge in Plainview since organization. The Elks Home was built in 1911-12.

The Woodmen of the World, Camp No. 877, Plainview, was organized Dec. 20, 1900. The first officers were J. Winford Hunt, Consul Commander, and Leslie Maupin, Clerk. Among other charter members were S. S. Sloneker, D. L. Hammer, Jeff Pipkin and J. D. Hagood. The following persons have served as Consul Commander: J. Winford Hunt, S. S. Sloneker, Jeff Pipkin, J. L. Dorsett, I. W. Elliott, Chas. Clements, D. L. Hammer, Joseph Martin, B. F. Moore, J. H. Johnson, F. E. Teague, L. D. Griffin, C. H. Mangum, Manley Bell and C. W. English.

The Woodman Circle was organized in Plainview June 6, 1908, by Henrietta Thomas, of Fort Worth, State Manager of Texas, with the following officers and charter members: Melissa Nash Guardian, May Sloneker Advisor, Minnie Grant Secretary, Margaret Coleman Banker, Louise Lindsay Attendant, Alice Johnson Chaplain, Katie Dyer Inner Sentinel, James Lash, Outer Sentinel, L. C. Wayland Physician, Harvey Wofford and Effie Johnson. The following persons have served as guardians: Melissa Nash, Margaret Coleman, Susan Leslie, Allie Bull, Alma Jones, Kate Dorsett, Lalla Meador, Alice Johnson, Maggie Adams, Fannie Pearson, Lassie Flack and Lucy Griffin.

Camp No. 12416, Modern Woodmen of America, was organized in Plainview Feb. 4, 1908, by H. Ragsdale and C. B. McConnell, Organizing Deputies. The charter members and first officers were as follows: J. D. Hanby Consul, J. J. Roberts Secretary, T. E. Jarman, G. T. Puler, August M. Hamilton, W. E. Ragland, J. F. Watson, W. S. Maggard, Tom Shafer, W. L. Welch, H. Broom, C. L. Gilbert, C. T. Pendley, Earl C. Keck, A. L. Hamilton, John Cowart, R. P. Mayhugh, P. D. Windsor, L. A. Kerr, and J. C. Morgan (Beneficiary Members) and L. C. Wayland (Social Member).

The following members have served as Consul: Jos. D. Hanby, Cecil Whipp, A. J. Chambers, H. J. Dillingham, Geo. A. Runyon, J. J. Guyer, Geo. J. Martin, J. C. Abrams, W. W. Thompson, W. Oliver Anderson, Fred L. Brown, Wm. G. Formby, Claude A. Martin, Royce Giles, Lewis B. Wimberly, Elmer R. Anderson and R. M. Franklin.

Camp No. 5217, Royal Neighbors of America, was organized at Plainview Feb. 20, 1908, by District Deputy Emma Hoagland. The following were the first officers and charter members: Etta Fitzgerald Oracle, Addie Broom Recorder,

Etta Pipkin Receiver, Vice Oracle Melissa Nash, Anne Graham Chancellor, J. H. Wayland Physician, Mamie Meador, Jewell Meador, Ida Jones, Unah Webster, Ada Webster, Lettie North, Bertie Hatcher, Mary Butts, Minnie Hester, Ethel Hammer, James Wayland, C. Johnson, Eva Hanby, Ida Timm, Mollie Rook, Connie Wayland, Mabel Barnes, Sallie Wayland, Katie Dyer, William Dyer, Berta Richardson, Ruby Chambers, Lula Butts, Lallah Meador, Ola Smith, Lettie Rodgers, Abby White, Mrs. J. O. Oswald, Tom Shafer, Henry Barnes, Louis W. Smith, Margaret Vebech, Helen Keith, Effie Waddill, John Roberts, Flake Garner, Fannie Stout and Honie Broom.

Plainview Lodge No. 321, Knights of Pythias, was organized on Apr. 20, 1903, by S. B. Tadlock. Charter was granted on March 14, 1904, on application signed by H. C. Randolph Chancellor Commander and J. W. Ware K.R.S. The first officers and charter members were as follows: W. N. Wardlaw Chancellor Commander, J. W. Campbell V. C., J. G. Wayland Prelate, Wm. Bain Master of Work, J. W. Ware Keeper of Records and Seals, H. E. Skaggs, Master of Finance, J. R. DeLay Master of Exchequer, T. A. Kinder Master at Arms, T. B. Carter Inner Guard, Lee Shropshire Outer Guard, S. J. Murray, W. W. Toney, Jno. B. Shannon, L. S. Kinder, L. W. Dalton, S. W. Meharg, Chas. McCormack, C. F. Vincent, A. M. Lycan, J. D. Hagood, C. E. McClelland, R. B. Tudor, J. H. Wayland, J. A. Stone, W. B. Martine, H. C. Randolph, L. Lee Dye, Geo. L. Mayfield and B. H. Towery.

This lodge was active for more than twenty-five years. The charter was surrendered on Apr. 24, 1928, however it was reorganized Nov. 29, 1929, and was suspended in 1934. Chancellor Commanders since reorganization in 1929 were as follows: C. H. Parsley, Dr. W. N. Lemmon, P. A. Wampler, B. L. Lawrence, Earl Lockhart and J. F. Wilmeth.

The Praetorian Lodge was organized in Plainview in May 26, 1908, by D. W. McGlasson with seventy-eight applicants for membership. The Lodge was an active social organization for a number of years and was finally disbanded.

Local Union No. 1081, Carpenters and Joiners of America, was organized in Plainview Oct. 23, 1917, with the following charter members: H. L. Byers, W. O. Wellborn,

Glenn A. Keen, George E. Palmer, Bain McCarroll, Ed Hays, Rupert Andrews, G. E. Duckworth, John Duncan, J. J. Guyer, William Bohannon, W. T. Burk, Henry DeJarnatt, T. C. Adams, Roy Maxey, John Jones, F. M. McCarroll, Emmett Dement, Sam Waddill, R. L. Hankal, W. T. Wilmeth and J. S. Hayes.

The following persons have served as President: H. L. Byers, J. J. Guyer, Bain McCarroll, Rupert Andrews, G. E. Duckworth, E. M. Hatton, A. L. Mitchell, F. B. Hoefer, R. A. Eslinger, H. P. Brooks and A. T. Thompson. The organization was discontinued in 1932.

The Journeyman Barbers International Union of America No. 818, was organized Apr. 2, 1923. Charter members were: B. G. Martin, J. E. Dye, O. P. Crow, George Sides, O. E. Galbroth, R. H. Green, W. B. Luna, C. M. Stapp, Charlie Davis, J. L. Estes, J. L. Galloway, T. W. Hendrix and R. F. Free. Those who served as president are: J. L. Galloway, T. W. Hendrix, R. F. Free and R. E. Hooper.

CHAPTER XIII

CIVIC ORGANIZATIONS

The Chamber of Commerce and Agriculture, first called Commercial Club, later Chamber of Commerce, was first organized in Plainview in 1907, with J. E. Lancaster President and James R. DeLay Secretary. The organization was later discontinued. In 1910 it was again organized, with J. O. Wyckoff President, O. M. Unger Secretary and W. A. Parker Treasurer. The outstanding achievement of Mr. Wyckoff's administration was the discovery and development of irrigation. O. M. Unger succeeded Mr. Wyckoff as President and served in that capacity until October, 1913, when E. Dowden became President and Mr. Unger Secretary. During his term of office, Mr. Unger it is said "literally worked night and day," used his own car and gave his own time, and brought to pass many things for the development of Plainview and Hale County. A few years later the organization became inactive. Several years later The Chamber of Commerce consolidated with the Young Men's Business League and employed as the first paid Secretary of the Chamber of Commerce a Mr. Long, who was then employed as Secretary of the Young Men's Business League, which then was discontinued.

The following persons have served as President of the Chamber of Commerce: J. E. Lancaster, J. O. Wyckoff, O. M. Unger, E. Dowden, E. H. Perry, R. A. Underwood, R. P. Smyth, A. E. Boyd, C. S. Williams, E. O. Nichols, J. B. Cardwell, A. G. Hinn, R. Q. Silverthorne, Glenn A. Smith, O. J. Sexton, Louis Jacobs, Sherman Umphress, Walter Thatcher, Marion Peters and B. C. Camp.

The following persons have served as Secretary: James R. DeLay, O. M. Unger, Z. E. Black, E. H. Perry, H. M. Mason, Mr. Long, John Boswell, Maury Hopkins, Grady Ship, Ed Bishop and Pete Smith.

The Plainview Fire Department was organized in March, 1909, under the authority of the City Council of Plainview.

During the first two years after the City of Plainview was incorporated, there was no organized fire department. When a fire was discovered, the alarm used to herald the news was a gun fired in rapid succession of shots. The people rushed to the fire and did what they could or thought about, with no one to direct their efforts. Many times people became excited and little was accomplished. When the Jordan Gin burned, during the early part of 1909, a group of young men, all eager to render assistance, saw the disadvantage of having no one to direct or take charge in case of fire. They talked the matter over and decided to go before the City Council and ask for authority to organize. On March 1, 1909, Richard Herbst and W. J. Klinger appeared before the City Council and received permission to organize a Volunteer Fire Department in Plainview. The following became members of the original Fire Department: Richard Herbst, Chief; J. A. Hamilton, Assistant Chief; W. J. Klinger, H. F. Klinger, J. R. DeLay, Clete Connell, Henry Halsey, J. A. Peret, J. W. Pipkin, and A. H. Estes. The first equipment was a two-wheel hose cart which was fastened to the back of any passing motor car or hand-drawn by the firemen, if need be. On April 5, 1909, the first apparatus, ordered from American La France Company was a combination horse-drawn, hook, ladder, hose and chemical. It was delivered August 18, 1909, at a cost of $1,900. The first team of horses was bought in the spring of 1910. These horses were the pride of the Fire Department and were trained and driven by D. T. Bolinger. This was the forerunner of the modern equipment of the present time.

The Young Men's Business League was organized July 18, 1913, at the County Court House, for the purpose of studying trade problems and to further the interests of the business men. W. J. Klinger was elected President, B. O. Brown Secretary and J. W. Willis Treasurer. The following business firms were represented at the organization: Richards Bros. & Collier, Duncan Pharmacy, Plainview Hardware Co., R. A. Long Drug Co., G. W. Graves Saddlery, The City Bakery, Rucker Produce Co., S. L. Seay Grocery Co., Watson's Second Hand Store, New Necessity Store, Warren & Scudder Grocery, Blassingame & Klinger Confectioners, J. W. Willis Drug Co. and the Hale County Herald.

The Board of City Development of Plainview was estab-

CIVIC ORGANIZATIONS 151

lished by the City Council of Plainview on April 6, 1920. It had been made possible by a provision in the Constitution of the City of Plainview for the establishment of a Board of City Development, according to the City Charter granted March 29, 1917. The following persons were appointed first members of the Board: Dr. J. C. Anderson, A. G. Hinn, R. S. Beard, W. A. Donaldson, G. V. Smith, W. Holbrook, W. E. Risser and R. P. Smyth.

The following persons have served as President of the Board: Dr. J. C. Anderson, L. S. Kinder, W. E. Risser, Frank Butler, C. A. Pierce, Charles Reinken, W. Holbrook, W. J. B. Gouldy and R. Q. Silverthorne.

The Kiwanis Club of Plainview was organized May 15, 1920, with the following officers and charter members: H. S. Hilburn President, P. B. Randolph Vice Pres., R. A. Underwood 2nd V. P., W. J. Klinger Secretary, C. E. Carter Treasurer, Directors: L. Lee Dye, John Lucas, A. G. Hinn, R. M. Crabb, T. Stockton and J. A. Testman; R. C. Ayers, R. S. Beard, L. P. Barker, A. E. Boyd, J. J. Bromley, H. C. Barrow, J. E. Burkett, W. H. Berryman, H. E. Bullock, T. O. Collier, M. A. Cram, Riley P. Duff, J. F. Duncan, Dr. J. A. Ferguson, M. P. Garner, H. L. Grammer, Dr. J. L. Guest, A. C. Hatchell, Willard K. Harp, J. G. Haltom, E. H. Humphries, T. O. Halley, C. L. Largent, Dr. W. J. Lloyd, Homer Looper, M. C. McGlasson, W. C. Mathis, S. P. Miller, R. H. Knoohuizen, E. B. Miller, D. D. Neal, Dr. E. O. Nichols, C. A. Pierce, C. E. Richards, W. E. Risser, Chas. Reinken, E. E. Robinson, T. C. Shepard, C. C. Stubbs, E. F. Sansom, Will Stockton, T. J. Van Arsdale, C. F. Vincent, C. S. Williams, J. E. Watson, S. R. Ware, P. J. Wooldridge, J. M. Waller and J. B. Maxey.

The following members have served as president: H. S. Hilburn, R. A. Underwood, C. A. Pierce, A. E. Boyd, W. Holbrook, L. P. Barker, R. H. Knoohuizen, E. B. Miller, W. J. Klinger, T. C. Shepard, R. Q. Silverthorne, T. O. Collier, O. J. Sexton, R. E. Boen, S. B. Kelley, Olin Brashear and E. H. Ezell.

The Plainview Rotary Club was organized February 23, 1921, by H. C. Pipkin, of Amarillo, Representative appointed by Governor H. J. Lutcher Stark, of Orange, Texas, with J. C. Anderson, of Plainview, organization chairman. The first meeting was held in April, 1921, and the Charter was received May 17, 1921. The first officers and charter members were: J. C. Anderson President, C. D. Wofford V.P., Guy Gibbs Secretary, A. B. DeLoach Treas., E. Dowden Jr., Sergeant at Arms, Directors: J. C. Anderson, C. D. Wofford, Guy Gibbs, A. B. DeLoach, L. S. Kinder, D. Hefflefinger and F. J. Hurlbut; R. E. Horn, M. Howard, Dr. D. P. Jones, A. M. McMillan, L. C. Pace, A. L. Putnam, R. S. Ziegler and Col. R. P. Smyth.

Those who have served as president are: J. C. Anderson, C. D. Wofford, Frank Butler, Meade F. Griffin, R. B. Sparks, L. S. Kinder, D. D. Bowman, C. B. Harder, J. L. Nisbet, Maury Hopkins, W. F. Lowe, Elmer E. Winn, Frank Day, Walter Thatcher, L. W. Kiker, Pat Horton and Frank Caves.

The Lions Club of Plainview was organized in October, 1929, by District Governor H. Halcomb, of Dalhart. The first officers and charter members were: Edwin McMath President, Dyer Slaton Secretary-Treasurer, C. M. Anderson, A. N. Bratton, Olin L. Byers, P. Flaxman, J. M. Forbes, H. M. Fields, Claude Furr, Bob Harder, Abie Jacobs, Warren Jeffus, Royce Oxford, Roy Phillips, Lon Robinson, John Roundtree, T. J. Settle, J. W. Stewart, C. B. Thomas, Lewis F. Thompson, J. Frank Triplett, B. S. Winkels, Joe H. Webb, H. Vandenberg, Bill Taegel, Jess Lockhart, David Bates, Frank Clarke and Dr. Gaffney. The following have served as president: Edwin McMath, Earnest Fletcher, J. P. Weyman, Sherman Umphress, W. W. Evans, S. J. Burrows, Dave McCurdy, and A. R. Nisbet, Jr.

The Panhandle Plains Dairy Show was organized on November 19, 1927, at which time thirty-five breeders, County Agricultural Agents and Chamber of Commerce Secretaries met at Tulia for the purpose of effecting such organization. W. L. Stangel, Superintendent of Animal Husbandry at Texas Technological College at Lubbock, called a meeting for Dec. 8, 1927, at Lubbock, at which time details for the organization and plans for the first dairy show were made. At a meeting held at Tulia Dec. 16, 1927, the following officers were elected: D. F. Eaton, Lubbock, President; Bob Anglin, Secretary. The first dairy show was held at Plainview during the first week in April, 1928. It was decided to make Plainview the permanent location for the dairy show and a building was erected at

Plainview for the permanent housing of the Dairy Show. The following persons have served as president of the organization: D. F. Eaton, Lubbock; O. L. Stansell, Floydada; S. J. Payne, Tulia; P. C. Bennett, Amarillo; W. L. Stangel, Lubbock; Geo. P. Grout, Panhandle; Joe Vaughn, Tulia; H. B. Hales, Amarillo, and J. W. Heavin, Plainview.

The American Red Cross, Hale County Chapter, with headquarters at Plainview, was authorized August, 1917, and the following officers were elected: Mesdames: Tom Carter, Chairman, J. W. Pipkin, Vice Chairman, R. A. Underwood, Treasurer, H. C. Randolph, Secretary. Branches of the chapter were organized at Abernathy, Hale Center, Littlefield and Olton. A number of auxiliaries were also formed to assist with the production of hospital garments, surgical dressings and knitted articles needed during the World War, of which the chapter produced the following: Knitted articles 4223; surgical dressings 94953; hospital garments 5887; refugee garments 5995.

Since the War the chapter has carried to the community the services of the National Organization in its peace-time program. Outstanding in these services were the Chapter's participation in drouth relief in 1930 and 1931, and the distribution of government wheat and cotton in 1932 and 1933. In the distribution of government wheat and cotton turned over to the American National Red Cross, the Hale County Chapter assisted approximately 900 families with 1170 barrels of flour, and approximately 2000 families with the following materials made available from the government cotton: 12,100 yards of cloth, 136 yards of sheeting, 240 blankets and comforters, 603 dozen garments and 72 dozen sweaters, the yardage being made into garments and supplies by women paid from relief funds.

The following persons have served as chapter chairmen: Mrs. Tom Carter (1917-1920), Mrs. J. A. Ferguson (1921); Mr. A. B. Martin (1922-1923), Mrs. Carl Brown (1924-1925), Mrs. Frank Jarvis (1926-1932) and Mr. John Lucas (1933 until the present time).

The Hi-Y was organized at the Plainview High School in October, 1928, by Grover C. Good, of Dallas, State Secretary, assisted by T. J. Hawkins of Plainview, Sponsor, and J. T. Fielder. The following persons have served as President:

Raymond Seal, Glenn Flake, James Hatch, Jim Boswell, Jack Madison, James Wallace Davenport, Louis Simpson, Jo Billy Dillon.

The Junior Hi-Y was organized at the Junior High School of Plainview by Grover C. Good, State Secretary, in 1930, assisted by C. D. Wofford Jr. and E. M. Ballengee. This organization was without a sponsor for two years and then Ernest Ratliff became sponsor. Charlton Stovall and Richard Shirley have served as president.

The Boy Scouts organization was perfected at Plainview April 23, 1912, at the City Hall, through the influence of the members of the Civic League. The first patrol was organized at that date with James R. DeLay, Mayor of Plainview, as Scoutmaster. Ten boys were present, and the following officers were selected: Grady Vaughn Patrol Leader, Gratz Hunter Assistant Patrol Leader, Harold Knupp Secretary and Walter Thatcher Sergeant at Arms. E. B. Miller became Scoutmaster and served from 1913 to 1919. The Boy Scouts were active in the sale of Liberty Bonds and Thrift Stamps during the World War. W. J. Klinger became Scoutmaster in 1919. O. J. Offlighter served in that capacity from 1920 to 1922, after which the organization was inactive for several years. Lloyd Roberts, District Scout Executive with headquarters in Plainview, served as Scoutmaster from 1928 to 1930. J. T. Hatch served as Scoutmaster for several years. The Boy Scouts Council for the Staked Plains was organized in 1928, with Judge L. S. Kinder as its first president. W. J. Klinger succeeded Judge Kinder in this office.

The South Plains Council, Boy Scouts of America, was organized in 1937, with Earl M. McCure Scout Executive, with headquarters at Lubbock. Alex R. Nisbet is District Chairman. Committees from the Lions, Rotary and Kiwanis Clubs of Plainview and the American Legion are active in promotion of the Boy Scout movement under the new set-up. A training camp and cabins have been set up at Lubbock and Boy Scouts of the South Plains have access to them. A trained Scoutmaster visits each organization, and schools for training local Scoutmasters are held from time to time.

The Boy Scouts organization in **Hale Center** was perfected in January, 1937, with G. C. Tiner Scoutmaster and D. L. French Assistant.

CHAPTER XIV

Women's Clubs

The dawn of the Twentieth Century was also the dawn of a new social order. The score of years that followed witnessed rapid changes. Plainview had shaken off the dust of a frontier cowtown and was assuming metropolitan proportions. Men were busily engaged in building railroads, laying off new townsites, building homes and developing new industries. The old order was passing and there was much need for spiritual and cultural advancement as well as material development. The women did their part by organizing clubs to broaden their views and to co-ordinate their efforts.

The Pioneer Club of Plainview was organized by Mrs. W. E. Armstrong, on Nov. 12, 1905, at the home of Mrs. A. E. Harp. It was first called the Mystic Club, however, the members never studied the occult as indicated by the word "Mystic," and the name was later changed to Pioneer Club, which was peculiarly fitting inasmuch as it was the first Woman's Club organized in Hale County and is also said to be the second study club organized in the Texas Panhandle. It federated in 1906.

The house in which this club was organized was of pioneer setting, having been built for a ranch home by George Slaughter, a wealthy stock man of an early day. While it stood on the Slaughter Ranch twenty miles west of Plainview, it was often the scene of gracious and generous hospitality. The house was afterwards moved to Plainview and at the time of the organization of the Pioneer Club, it stood on the block where the Texas Theatre now stands.

The following ladies were present at the first meeting and became the first officers and members: Mrs. S. W. Meharg President, Miss Lula Pitts V. P., Miss Beulah Speakman Recording Secretary, Mrs. W. E. Armstrong Corresponding Secretary, Mesdames A. E. Harp and T. J. Jordan and Misses Myrtle Haynes, Clevie Dupuy and Bessie Parr.

The membership was limited to twenty and included most of the leading women of the town. The club soon became exclusive and to belong to it gave prestige to the members. For many years its courses of study were selected with a view of broadening the lives of its members and giving them an insight into the writing and lives of authors both past and present.

The following members have served as president: Mesdames: S. W. Meharg, W. E. Armstrong, E. Graham, R. W. Brahan, T. P. Whitis, C. W. Tandy, H. W. Harrell, L. A. Knight, L. Lee Dye, Marshall Phelps, D. F. Sansom, J. O. Rountree, L. S. Kinder, R. E. Meyers, Hal Wofford, A. L. Putnam, Chas. Malone, L. B. Platt, G. W. McWhirter, W. B. Martine, and A. B. Cox.

The Junior Pioneer Club of Plainview was organized in 1927 by Mrs. D. C. Laird, Club Mother, who selected the personnel of the club. Mrs. E. Graham assisted with the organization. The following were the first officers and charter members: Mesdames: **J. L. Hunter**, President, **Buddy Webb** Secretary, **H. C. Galloway, Hubert Scott, Lon Robinson, F. D. Blocksom, J. L. Matlock, Walker Brickey, Arthur Reinken, Dyer Slaton** and **Roy Elliott.**

The following members have served as president: Mesdames: J. L. Hunter, H. C. Galloway, Hubert Scott, Lon Robinson, F. D. Blocksom, Burns Noble, J. L. Matlock and Jack Bristol.

Junior Pioneer Club No. 2, Plainview, was organized April 15, 1933, at the home of Mrs. E. Graham, by the Senior Pioneer Club, with daughters and adopted daughters of members of the senior club. Mesdames E. Graham, L. D. Harrison and E. E. Weise were sponsors. Charter members were: Mrs. Harroll Laird President, Misses Ella Mae Giddons and Evelyn Weise and Mesdames Jim Bryan, Kelly Harrison and Bush Stone. Others who have served as president are Mrs. Hazel Davis and Miss Mae Boswell. The club federated with the County Federation of Women's Clubs in 1933.

The Civic League of Plainview was organized in 1906, with Mrs. Mary V. Dye as president. The principal projects of the League were Health Promotion and City Beautification. Clean-up campaigns were waged year after year personally supervised by the members. In a state health campaign, the president of the Civic League was appointed pure food inspector for Plainview and sanitary measures and improvements were put into effect. Funds were raised by the women by various projects besides solicitation of moneys for city beautification. Trees were purchased and planted on the school grounds and along the streets. Homes were visited and home-owners pledged to cooperate by planting trees. As a result of the labors of the Civic League, many thousands of trees were planted in Plainview over a period of years which tower above the once barren prairie a memorial to these pioneer women. The League ceased to function when the Board of City Development was organized which took over the work they were doing.

The Cemetery Association of Plainview was organized in connection with the Civic League on October 7, 1909. The following officers were elected: Mrs. J. N. Donohoo President, Mrs. W. E. Armstrong Secretary, Directors: Mrs. Will Knight 1st Ward, Mrs. L. Lee Dye 2nd Ward, Mrs. W. A. Todd 3rd Ward, Mrs. E. B. Hughes 4th Ward and Mrs. J. F. Garrison 5th Ward. Improvement and beautification of the Plainview cemetery was the objective of the organization. The work of the Association also included the raising of funds to finance the improvement and up-keep of the Plainview Cemetery. Mrs. Mary V. Dye is the President of the Association at this time.

The As You Like It Club was organized as a study club in the fall of 1911 by Mrs. H. C. McIntyre at her apartment in the Ware Hotel at Plainview. The following were charter members: Mesdames J. F. Garrison, W. L. Harrington, H. C. McIntyre, C. W. Tandy, S. S, Stevens, Tom Whitis, J. J. Bromley and H. C. Randolph.

The following members have served as president: Mesdames: H. C. McIntyre, E. F. McClendon, L. C. Wayland, Joe Fowler, Hal Wofford, J. B. Scott, Farris Frye, George Saigling, E. H. Perry, T. B. Carter, Arilla Peterson, J. D. Steakley, G. W. McDonald, J. W. Walker, Frank Daugherty, O. B. Jackson, J. Harvey Hansen, F. B. Cave, Marsh Watson, A. B. DeLoach.

The Browning Club of Plainview was organized Nov. 18, 1911, at the home of Mrs. J. C. Anderson, for the purpose of studying the poems of Robert Browning. For more than ten years the club continued to meet at the home of Mrs. Anderson. The first officers and charter members were as follows: Lena Williams President, Rebecca Longmire Vice President, Burr Goode Secretary, Allene Smith Treasurer, Mabel Wayland Critic, Bertha Hinn, Pattie Estes, Alma Cobb, Docia Cowan, Mamie Outz and Mrs. J. C. Anderson Matron.

The Junior Browning Club was organized in Plainview by the Senior Browning Club in 1934, with Mrs. C. E. Carter, sponsor, assisted by Mrs. D. H. Collier. Officers and charter members were as follows: Annette Collier President, Katherine Aiken Secretary, Allene Thompson, Margaret Crews, Mary Earle Sansom, Claire Jeanne Branham, Jane Powell, Latrell Richardson, Jean Gouldy and Margaret Alexander. Katherine Aiken later served as President.

The Parent Teachers Association in Plainview was first organized in October, 1911, at the Central School, by the teachers of the public schools and mothers. Miss Ellen Robinson, Superintendent of City Schools, was in charge of the organization. 75 names were enrolled as charter members. The following officers were elected: Mrs. Alex Anderson President, Mrs. A. W. McKee Vice Pres. and Mrs. J. F. Owens Secretary.

The Lamar P. T. A. was organized in Plainview in October, 1913, at the Lamar School House, with A. G. Harrison, Principal of the School, in charge of the organization. The following officers were elected: Mrs. Chas. Flack President, Mrs. F. W. Vanderpoel Vice Pres., Miss Maud Brandon Secretary and Mrs. W. B. Martine Treasurer.

The Runningwater P. T. A. was organized March 3, 1925, by Miss Augustine B. Stoll, Red Cross Public Health Nurse for Hale County, and Miss Kennedy, Red Cross Supervisor for the District. Mrs. L. T. Mayhugh was elected President.

The Travel Study Club was organized in Plainview October 8, 1912, at the home of Miss Edna Mayhugh, with the following officers and charter members: Mrs. L. T. Mayhugh President, Rosa Fowle Secretary, Mesdames: Thomas Abraham, W. B. Joiner, J. W. Longstreth, J. W. Pipkin and J. W. Ryan, and Misses Edna Mayhugh, Amy Glenn, Ella Mallow, Byrd Roebuck and Lena Williams. The first year's study was Oriental Countries, text book Stoddard's lectures. Travel studies have included a vast scope of educational features.

The following members have served as President: Mesdames L. T. Mayhugh, L. Lee Dye, R. S. Charles, J. W. Pipkin, E. F. Sansom, O. B. Jackson, Chas. A. Malone, J. Murray Malone, B. H. Towery, E. C. Hunter, Nine McComas, L. P. Davis, Jo Wayland, B. M. Sims, W. J. Klinger, Guy Bounds, H. W. Visor, J. L. Dorsett, W. E. Thatcher, J. M. Malone, and M. E. Dement.

The Junior Travel Study Club No. 1 was organized through the Senior Club in 1932 by Mrs. Guy Bounds. Frances Mayhugh was the first President. The club is federated with the State and National.

The Junior Travel Study Club No. 2 was organized in 1936 by Mrs. L. T. Mayhugh, sponsor. Mary Sam Lock was elected President. This club is federated with State and National.

The City Federation of Women's Clubs of Plainview was organized in 1912, with Miss Rosa Fowle President. Mrs. T. P. Whitis succeeded Miss Fowle in 1913. The object of the organization was the unification of the Women's Clubs of Plainview for the promotion of social, intellectual, artistic, civic and philanthropic work. The federation included the Civic League, Pioneer, Browning, Travel Study and As You Like It Clubs. The starting of the public library was the main objective.

The City Federation was reorganized in the fall of 1920 after having been inactive for some time. Officers then elected were as follows: Mesdames Tom Carter President, R. A. Underwood 1st V.P., C. A. Malone 2nd V.P., George Saigling Recording Secretary, A. L. Putnam Corresponding Secretary, S. W. Meharg Treasurer, Hal Wofford Parliamentarian, Meade F. Griffin Press Reporter and C. E. Hunter Auditor. The organization federated with the County and State Federations in 1921. Besides the sponsoring of the Public Library, other civic work has been done, among which was the inauguration of the Annual Flower Show in September, 1921, which was taken over by the County Federation in 1925, Home Beautiful Contests and tree planting programs and participation in the City Park Movement. The City Federation organized the Women's Auxiliary to the Chamber of Commerce in 1927.

The following persons have served as President since reorganization: Mesdames: Tom Carter, Nine McComas, A. L. Putnam, R. A. Underwood, Carl Goodman, Hal Hamilton, Jr., Louis Frogge, C. S. Williams, Bob Meyer, Wallace Davenport and Marsh Watson.

Hale County Federation of Women's Clubs was organized at Hale Center Nov. 21, 1914, by Mrs. E. Graham, of Plainview, District Chairman for the Seventh District. Mrs. Graham had been appointed by the late Mrs. Phoebe K. Warner, of Claude, Texas, then State Chairman of Rural Extension Work, and who later became National Chairman.

The State of Texas was divided into seven Districts and Mrs. Graham was given the Seventh District, then composed of some eighty counties, and assigned the duty of organizing County Federations in each. In the pioneering of this work, Mrs. Graham encountered varied and ofttimes amusing experiences in organizing the county groups. Four or more letters were written to persons in each of the eighty counties in the interest of the work. As two of the counties were not organized at that time, Mrs. Graham wrote to the Postmasters of each and requested the names of some woman who would make a suitable County Chairman for the work. The responses to two of these letters depict the skepticism on the part of the men toward the Women's Club movement. One reply was as follows: "We don't want no sich foolishness as this in our Co." signed "Postmaster." The other read, "We don't want our wimmin folks to learn how to cut any new didoes." signed "Postmaster." Needless to say, in less than twenty-five years, the work begun by "The Little Brown Wren of Texas" (beloved Phoebe K. Warner) has spread to all counties of the state and regardless of early masculine prejudices, the eighty counties have fallen into line.

The Clubs which constituted the organization were as follows: Travel Study Club, As You Like It Club, Mystic Club, Lamar P.T.A., Central P.T.A. of Plainview, Civic League, Browning Club, Hale Center Needlework Club, Mothers Club of Hale Center and the Priscilla Club of Woodrow. The purpose of the organization is to advance and encourage Hale County Women in culture and to encourage fraternal intercourse among Women's Clubs. The first officers were: Mrs.

J. W. Longstreth, Plainview, President, Mrs. B. M. Johnson, Hale Center, V. P., and Miss Rebecca Longmire, Plainview, Secretary-Treasurer.

The following persons have served as President of the organization: Mesdames: J. W. Longstreth, B. M. Johnson, Nine McComas, Carl Goodman, O. B. Jackson, W. B. Price, Silas Maggard, Paul Johnson, K. C. Sterrett, L. T. Mayhugh, J. W. Walker and Mrs. W. L. Porter.

The Junior Council of Federated Clubs was organized in Plainview by Mrs. L. T. Mayhugh on April 1, 1937, with Mrs. Douglas Earthman President. It was organized for a service club and consists of two delegates from each Federated Club who constitute the working body. This organization has the distinction of being the first Council for Junior Federated Clubs in the state.

The Cotton Center Club was organized in the spring of 1914 by Mrs. W. O. Ball, at the Norfleet School House. It was first called Friendship Club and was organized solely as a social center for the community. The name was changed to Anchor Needle Club and later to Cotton Center Club. The work of the club was made to cover every phase of community need. During the World War, the club took up Red Cross Work, and in recent years has been very active in Home Demonstration work.

The following persons have served as president: Mesdames: W. O. Ball, Floyd Ruddick, J. C. Sturdivant, Earlton Harp, Jno. Payne, J. C. White, Forrest Sageser and E. E. Matthews.

The Home Economics Club of Plainview was organized in the fall of 1915 at the home of Mrs. G. Graham, with Mrs. E. Graham as organizer. The following were charter members: Mesdames: G. Graham, Jimmie Duncan, A. M. McMillan, Ben Sanford, George Saigling and W. J. Patten. Among its past presidents have been: Mesdames George Saigling, J. D. Steakley, Claude Powers, Meade F. Griffin, R. H. Knoohuizen, D. P. Jones, Carl Goodman, J. B. Wallace and E. F. Sansom.

The Plainview Delphian Club, later changed to Delphin Club, was organized in August, 1917, in the home of Mrs. W. C. Mathes by Miss Stella Huntington, of Fort Worth, who was Field Secretary. The charter members and first officers were: Mrs. E. F. McClendon, President, Mrs. T. Stockton,

Vice Pres., Miss Clara Hooper Secretary, Mesdames R. A. Underwood, Farris Frye and Dickenson Advisory Board. J. B. Scott, Mary Effie Murphy, J. B. Maxey, E. J. Morehead, A. B. Martin, O. B. Jackson, and E. M. Carter and Misses Josephine Rosson and Alma Armstrong.

The following persons have served as President: Mesdames: E. F. McClendon, J. B. Scott, R. A. Underwood, A. E. Boyd, E. M. Carter, A. B. Martin, G. W. McDonald, O. B. Jackson, C. S. Williams, L. M. Frogge, R. R. English, S. W. Reynolds, W. B. Davenport, and L. R. Bain.

The Beta Delphin Club of Plainview, first called Junior Delphin, was organized in October, 1925, at the home of Mrs. R. A. Underwood, by the Senior Delphin Club, under the direction of Mesdames A. B. Martin, O. B. Jackson, R. A. Underwood and G. W. McDonald. The membership was composed of daughters and adopted daughters of the Senior Delphin Club. The charter members and first officers were: Josephine Wayland President, Ruth Hooper V. P., Elizabeth Williams Secretary-Treasurer, Louise Warren, Pauline Mitchell, Helen Jackson and Beulah Boney. Those who have served as president are as follows: Josephine Wayland, Helen Jackson, Ruth Hooper, Mesdames Clint Herring, E. J. Turner, Sam Curry, W. K. Gamble, R. S. Miller and Rayford Daniel, Miss Virginia Keys, Mrs. Elmer Turner and Mrs. Roy Davis.

The Gamma Delphin Club was organized in Plainview through the Beta Delphin Club by their chairman, Mrs. L. T. Mayhugh, on April 1, 1937, with Janet Green President.

The Hale Center Delphian Club was organized on September 14, 1917, at the home of Mrs. Nick Alley, with the following charter members and first officers: Mesdames R. W. Sanders President, Wm. Price Secretary, W. L. Porter, R. F. Alley, Nick Alley, R. A. Miller, Shepard, O. C. Sanders and R. W. Ferguson, Erie Wall, Sallie Kerr and Allie Ralls.

The N. O. N. Club of Plainview was organized in 1921 by Miss Lula Blair Neal, then a member of the As You Like It Club. The club was named by Miss Neal, who chose the three letters that are the first letters of three Latin words that, translated, indicate progress and service. Originally the study course was Dramatic Art and Citizenship, but later was changed to a miscellaneous study program.

The Business and Professional Women's Club of Plain-

view was organized in the spring of 1927. It grew out of an organization known as the Daughters of Ruth Guild, which was organized on Oct. 13, 1925, by Mrs. John W. White, at the Presbyterian Manse, with Mrs. Vivian Graham as the first President. Mrs. P. Flaxman became the second president in October 1926. During Mrs. Flaxman's administration, in May, 1927, the club was reorganized and the name changed to Business and Professional Women's Club. The club federated with the State and National organizations of B. & P. W. clubs in the fall, with the following charter members and officers: Mesdames: P. Flaxman, President, Adella S. Drew, Secretary, J. F. Metcalf V. P., Vivian Graham, Katherine Snell, W. E. Thatcher, and Ivy Hart, and Misses Opal L. Wood, Nell Ayres, Jewell Eiland, Edith Smith, Josephine Wayland, Maxine McCallon, Joyce Carl, Eula and Inez Roper, Vivian Favor, Juana Jane Reeves, Carrie Bier, and Mary and Dorothy Cox (former members of the Daughters of Ruth) and Lena T. Glenn, Mrs. C. A. Lyle, Mrs. A. C. Bledsoe, and Ouida Youngblood.

This club is classed as a Women's Service Club. One objective of this club has been the sponsoring of the Annual Pioneer Round Up of Hale County, instituted in 1929. The Centennial Celebration in 1936 with Governor James V. Allred as speaker was an outstanding celebration. The Round Up in 1937 was the occasion of the unveiling and dedication of the Mackenzie Trail Monument.

The following persons have served as President of this Club: Mesdames P. Flaxman, Adella S. Drew, Julia E. Kelly and E. M. Ballengee and Misses Jewell Eiland, Vaneta Cross, Lucile Marr, Mable Vore, Lena T. Glenn, and Mrs. E. F. Miles.

The Music Study Club of Plainview was organized Feb. 17, 1927, by Mrs. Arilla Peterson, its object being the study of music as a means of intellectual culture and to encourage the highest musical standard for the community. The charter members and first officers were: Mesdames: Arilla Peterson, President, Guy Gibbs 1st V. P., C. C. McGlasson 2nd V. P., Carl Goodman Secretary, Clinton Walter Treasurer, R. B. Davidson critic, Guy Jacob, Horace Belew, R. H. Knoohuizen, J. D. Steakley, Robert Meyers, R. W. O'Keefe, Peyton Randolph, Tom Carter, A. G. Hinn, B. F. Wolff, and Misses Carrie Bier and Jane Stinson.

The following persons have served as President. Mesdames

Arilla Peterson, Carl Goodman, Horace Belew, Myrtle Smith, R. H. Knoohuizen, A. H. Mabry, and C. R. Hooton.

The Schubert Music Club of Plainview was organized January 31, 1929, with the following officers elected and charter members: Miss Carrie Bier, President, Mrs. Jack Birdsong 1st V. P., Miss Vada Bussell 2nd V. P., Mrs. J. V. Buchanan Secretary, Miss Juanita Largent Treasurer, Mrs. John Shinn Parliamentarian, Miss Josephine Stocking, Agnes and Frances Bier, Mesdames R. P. Holmlund, J. T. Koon, T. C. Meinecke, Elmer Turner, and Bruce Hardeman, and Misses Mary Angeline Russell and Louise Warren. On May 10, 1930, the club became a member of the Texas Federation of Music Clubs. Its study course is outlined by the National Federation of Music Clubs.

The Women's Auxiliary to the Plainview Chamber of Commerce was organized by the City Federation of Women's Clubs at the Public Library on Feb. 25, 1927. The purpose of the organization was to assist the Chamber of Commerce and the Board of City Development in Civic projects. The first officers were as follows: Mrs. W. J. Klinger President, Mrs. J. D. Steakley Vice Pres., Mrs. Earnest Fletcher Secretary, Mrs. E. E. Coleman Treasurer. All members of federated clubs in the City Federation and all P.T.A.'s were members of the Auxiliary. The executive board was composed of one representative from each of the various clubs. The first work of the Auxiliary was to have the names of the streets painted on the curbstones at street crossings. Other civic projects included tree-planting programs and city park beautification, the main objective being the building of the House of Friendship in the Park, this being formally opened on May 1, 1931.

The following persons have served as president: Mesdames: W. J. Klinger, Alex Nisbet, Nine McComas, P. Flaxman, E. H. Perry, L. J. Halbert, Lewis Kiker, R. B. Underwood and G. R. Mabry.

The Plainview Garden Club was organized on March 8, 1930, by Mrs. R. S. Ziegler, at the home of Mrs. L. J. Halbert. Its purpose was to stimulate greater interest in home gardening and to foster civic beautification. The first officers and charter members were as follows: Mesdames: R. S. Ziegler President, Tom Carter V.P., L. J. Halbert Secretary, E. B. Thomas Cor.

Secretary, J. L. Nisbet, Meade F. Griffin, L. B. Platt, E. Harlan, Wilbur Roberts, J. C. Owens, Oscar Collier and J. F. Duncan. The following have served as president: Mesdames: R. S. Ziegler, Tom Carter, L. A. Knight, J. F. Duncan, Jo W. Wayland, E. E. Weiss, R. S. Stewart and Carl Donohoo.

The Llano Estacado Chapter, Order of the United Daughters of the Confederacy, was organized in Plainview October 29, 1930, by Miss Johnnie Colbert. The charter members and first officers were as follows: Mesdames Sarah Elizabeth Lester Knight—President; Mary Alice Vincent Dye —Vice President; Ada Browning Cantrell, Treasurer; Nancy Hines Milsap Slaton, Mary Belle Tudor and Harriet Frances Duckett Wayland, and Miss Johnnie Colbert. This Chapter cooperates with the American Legion in the Memorial Day services each year and assists in the preparation and placing of floral decorations on the graves of both Union and Confederate veterans of the Civil War, the Mexican, Spanish American and World Wars.

The Civic Culture Club of Petersburg was organized in January, 1932, by Mrs. Jack D. Wester. The charter members were: Mesdames L. S. Claitor, Victor Blassingame, Sam Mason, Jack D. Wester, John Gregory, O. H. Heard, R. A. Jefferies, M. K. Simpson, W. M. Vernon, Clyde Martin, Ted Schuler and E. R. Gibson, with Mrs. L. C. Claitor Club Mother. The following members have served as president: Mesdames: Jack D. Wester, L. S. Claitor, Clyde Martin and Sam Mason.

The 1935 Study Club of Abernathy was organized in July, 1935, by the President and Official Board of the Hale County Federation of Women's Clubs. The first officers and charter members were as follows: Mesdames: Ray Pinson President, L. A. Harral Vice President, R. A. McAlister Secretary, C. E. Givens Treasurer, Frank Andrews Reporter, Jim Bledsoe, O. D. Crow, Ed Hardesty, J. W. Harris, Chas. Johnson, Vic Lamb, G. W. Ragland, A. B. Reid, W. A. Richter and L. Wright. Mrs. L. A. Harral succeeded Mrs. Pinson as President and Mrs. R. R. Struve is President elect.

The Camp Fire Girls—Prairie Fire Group—was organized in Plainview Feb. 21, 1916, under the Guardianship of Miss Elizabeth Briggs, with 10 girls in the group. This group was active until Aug. 31, 1917. Miss Carrie Bier organized the second group,—Wetomachick,—with 6 girls, on July 17, 1925, which was active until Nov. 30, 1926. In 1931 and 1932, the following groups were organized by the following Guardians: Tingtinatata, Golda Anderson, (10 girls); Tejas, Mrs. Cecil Bell (17); Cheskchamay, Carrie Bier (6); Apalechi, Dorothy Black (12); Nowetompatimmin, Julia Bralley; (15); Tejas, Elisabeth Cox (7); Wetomachick, Marjorie Flaxman (14); Lahoma, Eleanor Griffin (4); Nnilawisti, Blanche Joyner (11); Navosoyo, Elsa Kirchoff (18); Abohahanta, Betsy Largent (8); Thunderbird, Juanita Long (13) and Otyokwa, Bernice Thompson (6 girls). All of these groups ceased to be active by fall of 1933. No new groups were organized. One of the members of the first group to be organized in the county was Miss Ruby B. Lattimore, who now holds the position of Associate Field Secretary, Camp Fire Girls Incorporated, with office in New York City, she having joined the National Field Department of Camp Fire Girls in 1926. Much of her time is spent in training adult volunteer leaders for leadership of Camp Fire groups. The work of the Camp Fire Girls ceased in Hale County only for lack of leaders.

The Girl Scouts was organized in Plainview on January 23, 1936, by Mrs. Winfield Holbrook. Fifty girls were enrolled in two troops, Mrs. Irene Ayers being Scout Leader of Troop 1 and Mrs. E. M. Anderson Scout Leader of Troop 2. Much interest is taken by the girls, progress in the work being retarded only by lack of leaders.

CHAPTER XV

Military History

Co. L, 4th Inf. T. N. G.

Company L, a unit of the 4th Infantry, Texas National Guard, was organized in Plainview on Dec. 2, 1913, by Capt. Ben Golding with three officers and 53 enlisted men. This unit was in the service continuously from organization up to and including the World War.

The Texas National Guard was ordered to mobilize on the Mexican Border on May 10, 1916, pursuant to the call of the President of the United States and the regiment was mustered into Federal service May 17, 1916. Company L, 4th Texas Infantry, was mobilized at Company rendezvous at Plainview. The 4th Texas Infantry was scattered to stations in the Big Bend on May 28, 1916, the regiment being distributed over many hundreds of miles of territory, from Sanderson to Sierra Blanca and territory south to the Rio Grande. Company L was located at Sanderson and Marathon, Texas, from May until November, at which time it was moved to Harlingen, where it served until February 11, 1917. The regiment was mustered out of service on March 25, 1917, by order of the President.

On March 31, 1917, six days after being mustered out, the 4th Regiment, T.N.G. was called back into Federal service under call of the President. On May 23, 1917, Co. L, 4th Texas Infantry, was sent to station in the Brownsville District of Texas, with regimental headquarters located at San Benito, and on August 5, 1917, was drafted into service for the World War. The regiment was relieved from duty in the Brownsville District at the end of September, 1917, and was moved to Camp Bowie for a period of training preceding its movement overseas.

The status of this unit can be followed from its organization up to and including the re-organization and designation of its members as troops of the 144th Infantry, which was formed at Camp Bowie in September, 1917, from the 4th Texas Infantry (less Machine Gun Company) and the 6th Texas Infantry. Company L, 4th Texas Infantry, was combined with Company E, 6th Texas Infantry, to make Company H, 144th Infantry. Capt. Lee Otus Shropshire was transferred to the Cavalry as the result of this consolidation. The first Infantry Brigade of the 36th Division consisted of the 2nd, 3rd, and 4th Regiments Texas Infantry, of which Company L was a component, was commanded by Brigadier-General Henry Hutchings. The second Brigade, which consisted of the 1st, 5th and 6th Regiments, was commanded by Brigadier-General John A. Hulen.

The Regiment, as a part of the 36th Division, arrived in France July 30, 1918, and with the exception of the artillery was sent with other units of the 36th Division to the 13th Training Area in the vicinity of Bar-sur-aube. It remained in that area until Sept. 26, 1918, when it moved by rail to the Area between Epernay and Chalons, Division Headquarters being established at Pocancy, Department of the Marne. There it remained for ten days with other units as a reserve of the French group of Armies of the Center, being attached to the 5th French Army for supply purposes. The 36th Division was transferred to the 4th French Army on Oct. 3, 1918, and the regiment participated with other units in the Meuse-Argonne Offensive (Champagne) October 7, 1918, to Oct. 26, 1918. The regiment as a part of the 36th Division entered the lines on the night of October 9th, relieving the 6th Regiment of Marines, 2nd Division, on Blanc Mont, just north of Somme Py. In conjunction with other troops of the Division, the Regiment attacked North on October 10th, advancing some 21 kilometers in the next three days, generally through the St. Ettiene-et-Arnes, Machault, Vaux Champagne, to the south bank of the Aisne River, suffering its heaviest casualties on October 13th between Givry and Attigny. During the combat period, Company H, 144th Infantry, was actually commanded by then Captain Ira F. Sproule. The relief of the 36th Division was completed October 28, 1918.

After assembling in the Suippes-Somme-Suippes Area, the Division moved to the Triacourt Area, establishing Headquarters at Conde'-en-Barrios. Here with other units of the 36th Division the 144th Infantry remained as a unit of the First American Army until the signing of the Armistice. The Division was visited on April 9, 1919, and inspected by General John J. Pershing, Commander-in-Chief, A.E.F. During the ceremonies, General Petain, Commander of French Armies of the East, conferred the French Croix de Guerre on two members of old Company L, 4th Texas Infantry, ie. 1st Lieut. Carl C. Brown and 1st Lieut. Nelson Perdue.

Shortly after the conclusion of hostilities, the Regiment with other units of the 36th Division moved to the 16th Training Area around Tonnere. Hope of an early return to the United States was shattered by a semi-official announcement that the 36th Division would remain overseas indefinitely as a part of the Army of Occupation, but on April 10, 1919, orders suddenly came directing the Division to prepare to return home. Troop ships bearing the entire Division with the exception of the artillery, embarked from Brest. A stormy voyage harassed the troop ships on the return home. A severe storm was encountered, the wind reaching the velocity of ninety-six miles an hour, and two men were swept overboard and drowned when big waves completely swept the decks of the liner Pueblo. The Division landed at Hoboken on June 4th to 6th, 1919. After a short stay in rest camps near the ports, the various organizations entrained for Camp Bowie, where the Regiment was demobilized, on June 21, 1919.

The officers and personnel of the original unit, Co. L, 4th Infantry, T.N.G., at organization on Dec. 2, 1913, was as follows:

Captain Ben Golding, 1st Lieut. Lee Otis Shropshire, 2nd Lieut. Charles D. Powell, Elmer R. Anderson, Ralph C. Arnold, Charles W. Barnes, William S. Barnes, Edward P. Blair, Thomas C. Blakemore, Tom E. Brooks, Carl C. Brown, Nolan Brown, James W. Broom, Lee R. Bryan, Ernest B. Burchett, Russell J. Clark, Conrad Cornell, Carl L. Curtis, Clarence Dishon, Mason Dillingham, Liston H. Dunaway, Harold R. Fluke, Earnest A. M. Fowler, Caswell Franklin, Alsey N. Gardner, Raymond D. Gibbs, Charles F. Gilley, Malcolm L. Graves, Clarence C. Green, Jesse Hamilton, William A. Heard, Melvin G. Hilton, Alva H. Hooper, James

K. Hooper, Thomas F. Kincannon, Walter J. Klinger, Robert H. Knight, Ralph L. Maggard, Arthur L. Mitchell, Fred Mitchell, William J. Mitchell Jr., Lewis M. Mise, Bain McCarroll, Morey C. McGlasson, John E. McVicker, Jerome K. Nash, Samuel O. Nations, Erle G. Owens, William E. Palmer, Floyd S. Pearson, Lee Roy Pearson, Nelson Perdue, William J. Smith, Elliott E. Terry, John B. Wade, James B. Williams.

MILITARY HONORS CONFERRED UPON HALE COUNTY
VETERANS DURING THE WORLD WAR

Hilburn, Herbert S. Captain, 359th Infantry, 90th Division,

Distinguished Service Cross, Legion of Honor, Croix de Guerre with Palm, Australian Star.

Near Villers-devant-Dun, France, Nov. 2, 1918, G.O. No. 46, W. D. 1919.

"Under heavy machine-gun fire, he repeatedly went to the rear of his company to rally and reorganize it, and then rushed forward to lead his men on. Having taken the town of Villers-devant-Dun and the crest beyond, he held it with only 16 men until the next morning against a superior number of the enemy."

"Created Chevalier May 9th in Consideration of services rendered in France during the War. Has also D.S.C. and Croix de Guerre."

Brown, Carl C, first lieutenant, 144th Infantry, 36th Division.

French Croix de Guerre with silver star, under Order No. 15,252 "D", dated April 1, 1919, General Headquarters, French Armies of the East with the following citation:

"He displayed extraordinary heroism in the combats near St. Etienne from October 8-10, 1918. A skillful leader of men, he was able, thanks to his qualities, to assure the success of the operations."

Residence at appointment: Plainview, Texas.

Perdue, Nelson, first lieutenant, 144th Infantry, 36th Division.

French Croix de Guerre with silver star, under Order No. 15,252 "D" dated April 1, 1919, General Headquarters, French Armies of the East, with the following citation:

"He displayed extraordinary heroism in the combats near St. Etienne from October 8-10-1918. A skillful leader of men, he was able, thanks to his qualities, to assure the success of the operations."

Residence at appointment: Plainview, Texas.

Fletcher, Robert S., second lieutenant, 142nd Infantry, 36th Division.

French Croix de Guerre with gilt star, under Order No. 15,340 "D", dated April 3, 1919, General Headquarters, French Armies of the East, with the following citation:

"An officer of great bravery. He led his men on during a long advance, encouraging them by his boldness and intrepidity. He reached all the objectives that had been assigned to him.

Residence at appointment: Plainview, Texas.

MILITARY HISTORY

Stoney, Tom Joseph (deceased), 1498260, private Company "H", 23rd Infantry, 2nd Division.

French Croix de Guerre with gilt star, under Order No. 12,742 "D", dated January 5, 1919, General Headquarters, French Armies of the East, with the following citation:

"From October 3-9, 1918, near St. Etienne-a-Arnes, as a liaison agent under a violent bombardment, he displayed coolness and courage. Was killed during the action." (Next of kin: Mrs. Joseph Stoney, mother, 285 Myrtle Avenue, Brooklyn, N. Y.)

World War Dead

The following is a list of Hale County veterans who lost their lives in the services of the United States during the World War, as furnished by the Adjutant General of the State of Texas.

Name		*Residence*	*Organization*	*Date of Death*	
Abrams, Clarence,		Plainview,			
Anderson, Wm. Jennings,	2 Lt.	Plainview,	20 FA	Apr.	13, 1918
Barton, Joseph J.	Pvt Lcl	Bartonsite,	Co. D 360 Inf.	Nov.	4, 1918
Blakemore, Ray,	Pvt.	Plainview,	Co. A 305 Inf.	Nov.	1, 1918
Brahan, Robert W. Jr.	2 Lt.	Plainview,	372 Inf.	Sept.	29, 1918
Cooper, James A. Awarded DSC	2 Lt.	Hale Center,	2 Brig. Mg Bn	July	19, 1918
Cunningham, James A.	Pvt.	Plainview,	MTC Repair Unit 312	Oct.	18, 1918
Dice, Garrison B.	Rct	Plainview,	As Sig. C Unassgd. Fort Sam Houston	Jan.	14, 1918
Fitzgerald, George,	Cpl	Plainview,	Co D 7th Inf.	Aug.	1, 1918
Iverson, Elmer H.	Pvt.	Abernathy,	1 Co. 1 Bn 161 Dep. Brigade	Oct.	10, 1918
Kuykendall, Samuel A.	Pvt.	Plainview,	Co. A 356 Inf.	Oct.	28, 1918
Miers, Dan,	Pvt.	Ft. Griffin,	Co. F 359 Inf.	Sept.	26, 1918
McDaniel, John F.	Sgt.	Plainview,	36th Div.	Oct.	8, 1918
Stoddard, Chester V.	—	Plainview,	Co. U Recruit Dept.	Nov.	4, 1918
Stoney, Tom Joseph	Pvt.	Brooklyn, N. Y.	Co. H 23 Inf.	Oct.	1918
Turner, Thomas J.	Pvt. LCL	Abernathy,	Co. E, 34 Inf.	Dec.	31, 1918
Webb, William E.	Pvt.	Plainview,	Co. C 4 Engrs.	Sept.	29, 1918
West, William L.	Pvt.	Petersburg,	Amb. Co. 10 FT Bliss, Texas,	Feb.	27, 1919

Battery A, 131st F.A., T.N.G.

Battery A, 131st Field Artillery, Texas National Guard, was organized in Plainview and Federally recognized April 7, 1922. The regiment was designated "131st FA" to perpetuate the history of the 131st FA, 36th Div. A E F. Battery A, at Plainview was the first unit organized in the reorganization. No units of the old 131st FA were located at Plainview. Officers assigned to the unit at Plainview were Captain Thomas A. Bay, 1st Lieut. Ethelbert Dowden, 1st Lieut. Chas. W.

Scruggs and 2nd Lieut. William P. Dowden. Battery A is still located at Plainview.

American Legion

Ray Blakemore Post No. 260, American Legion, at Plainview, was named in honor of Ray Blakemore, a Hale County Veteran who was killed in action on Nov. 1, 1918. The charter was granted Oct. 29, 1920. The following were charter members: D. W. Covington, Clyde L. Cox, Thos. M. Fletcher, F. A. Greene, Meade F. Griffin, E. F. Hood, J. K. Hooper, R. E. Horne, Norman Mosely, W. H. Munn, A. W. Otto, C. M. Reynolds, Homer Rook, G. W. Rosser and Roy A. Upton. The Legion Home was erected in 1929.

Commanders of the Legion have been: Meade F. Griffin (1920), H. S. Hilburn (1921), Carl C. Brown (1922), E. O. Nichols (1923) E. W. Thomas (1924), J. E. McVicker (1925), Guy Gibbs (1926-27) A. R. Nisbet (1928), Pat Connelly (1929-1930), E. C. Kuykendall (1931), Jim Jordan, (1932), John Dubose (1933), John Burt (1934) John Scott (1935), and A. B. Cherry (1936-1937) Elmer R. Anderson (1937-).

Adjutants have been: Guy Gibbs, F. A. Greene, Earl F. Miles, J. K. Hooper, W. Oliver Anderson, Hugh L. Murphy, Roy G. Pearce, F. J. Hurlbut, Roy Lippert, Roy Wood, A.B. Cherry and Ervin Grisham.

American Legion Auxiliary

The American Legion Auxiliary, Ray Blakemore Unit No. 260, was organized March 16, 1921, with the following charter members: Mesdames: W. P. Dowden, R. A. Felfenstine, R. W. Otto, P. T. West, T. Hammond, J. C. Hooper, Elmer R. Anderson, Meade F. Griffin, E. T. Willard, A. H. McGavock, L. L. Russell, F. A. Greene and A. A. Beery.

The following persons have served as President: Mesdames: W. P. Dowden, Eva B. Dowden, T. Hammond, W. Oliver Anderson, Lloyd Carlton, Elliott E. Terry, E. R. Anderson, C. D. Hardesty, Roscoe Snyder, Mrs. Jenna Mae Hart.

World War Veterans

The following is a list of Hale County men who were inducted into service of the United States Army and Navy through the Local Draft Board and through Company L,

MILITARY HISTORY 173

Fourth Infantry, T.N.G. during the World War, and a partial roll of enlisted men, a complete list being unavailable.

Clarence Abrams, John Q. Adams, Charles W. Akers, Claude E. Akers, H. M. Akers, Earnest Allen, James W. Allen, Jesse Allen, Lonnie H. Allen, Robert E. Allen, Willie Allen, Tilmon C. Alexander, Elmer R. Anderson, William Jennings Anderson, Oliver Anderson, William H. Anderson, Edwin B. Andrews, R. G. Andrews, Rupert W. Andrews, Geo. D. Applewhite, Lawrence K. Armstrong, Ural S. Armstrong, Stanford W. Arnett, H. G. Atwood, Thomas Aguirre,

Walter T. Babb, J. J. Bachhofer, Guy Hearne Bailey, J. L. Bailey, Odelia M. Baker, William Leon Baker, Harold H. Bain, Robert E. Bain, Mikie Barbin, Hubert F. Barham, Decker Lee Barnes, Will E. Barnes, Joseph J. Barton, Joe C. Baty, Frank R. Baxell, William F. Beard, Fred G. Beckman, Carlos Belcher, James C. Bell, John H. Bell Jr., Grover C. Bent, Burgin Bird, Ed P. Blair, Wm. H. Blakemore, Ray Blakemore, Leo Boedeker, William Bohanon, Frank Bolin, Juan Edward Bolton, J. Lee Boswell, Robert E. Boyd, Lonie Bracken, Robert W. Brahan Jr., Olin E. Brashears, Claude H. Bray, William Britt, W. F. Brooks, Mack Brookshire, Carl C. Brown, Charles C. Brown, Elbert Benton Brown, Grover C. Brown, Nolan Brown, P. B. Brown, Wingo Brown, William E. Bryan, William Jennings Bryan, Otis Buchanan, Compton Bull, John C. Burke, Thomas A. Bunch, W. E. Burgess, Fred W. Burke, Robert D. Burroughs, George K. Burt, Herbert Burt, John H. Burt, Charlie W. Byers,

James M. Carpenter, W. H. Casey, P. G. Chauncey, Ray P. Cecil, Henry E. Child, Lilburn S. Claitor, Robert L. Claxton, Carl S. Clark, Wm. W. Collings, Patrick Connelly, Edwin M. Cook, Abner C. Cooper, Claude W. Cooper, Henry G. Cooper, Jas. A. Cooper, Leon L. Cooper, T. E. Cooper, Wm. H. Cornett, David Covington, Homer A. Covington, Judson A. Covington, Alban Robert Cox, Clyde L. Cox, Fred E. Cox, Kenneth L. Cox, Littleton H. Crawford, B. S. Culpepper, James A. Cunningham,

Sam P. Dalmont, Allie E. Davis, Virgil Daughetee, John E. Dement, George M. Denham, Garrison B. Dice, Algie E. Dick, Roy E. Dick, Wylie Dickerson, D. T. Dillingham, Clarence Disheon, Taras E. Doak, Frank H. Dodson, George W. Dodson, Archie Duckwall, A. W. Duckwall, Dave Duncan, Thomas J. Duncan, Liston H. Dunnaway, Jas. O. Durham, Gus B. Dye.

E. C. Ebeling, Leo R. Ebeling, Wm. C. Edmondson, Arthur D. Ellerd, John J. Ellerd, Oscar D. Ellerd, John H. Empie, Barber Eubanks, Walter Evans,

O. W. Felty, Joseph E. Fields, George W. Fitzgerald, Mitchell Flake, Paul E. Flake, Robert S. Fletcher, Thomas M. Fletcher, Robert F. Formway, James W. Fort, Lawrence Fort, R. H. Fort, Oscar C. Foss, George A. Foster, Paul Foster, Uld Fox, George C. Franklin, I. N. Freeman, Earnest Fowler, Wm. C. Ferguson,

O. B. Garner, Johnie B. Garrett, David R. Garrison, Henry G. Gentry, Guy A. Gibbs, Warren E. Gibbs, J. B. Gibson, James R. Gilbert, Lester Gill, George Gillespie, Arthur Gilliland, Craig Gilliland, Fred Gilley, Jasper L. Gipson, Henry Glisson, Reuben J. Goode, Paul Golla, Ford Gough, James V. Graham, William Z. Graham, Homer L. Grammar, Malcolm L. Graves, Lawrence R. Gray, Richard L. Griffith, D. H. Guinn,

Dewitt T. Hale, George C. Hammack, David E. Hankins, Earl Harmon, Gordon W. Hanson, A. N. Hardesty, E. C. Hardesty, Joseph W. Hardman, Edgar G. Harp, Robert F. Harp, C. E. Harrison, John B. Harrison, Jno. T. Hartwell, Ray I. Hartzler, E. E. Hatchett, Hardie Hay, Roger Q. Hay, Marion D. Haynie, H. D. Heath Jr., Luther C. Heath, John J. Hegi, Frank Henderson, Jas. E. Henderson, Floyd C. Heneks, James W. Herrell, H. S. Hilburn, Jas. R. Hill, Robert G. Hill, Willie D. Hinds, George Hoenig, Forest C. Hoffman, James B. Holland, John T. Holland, Jason C. Homan, Alva H. Hooper, Chester W. Hooper, James Kelly Hooper, James L. Howard, Frank Dyer Howell, J. Bennett Howell, B. B. Huckabee, A. A. Hudgins, George Casey Hughes, Harold C. Hughes, Harry C. Huguley, David R. Humbler, W. O. Hunt, Carrol D. Hunter, D. G. Hunter, H. L. Hyman,

Amos C. Ivey, Sylvan R. Jackson, George L. Jay, Fred C. Janzen, Franklin S. Johns, Alma C. Johnson, Johnnie C. Johnson, M. C. Johnson, Wm. F. Johnston, Hartwell H. Jones, Ray B. Jones, Sam Jones, Stephen P. Jones, Virgil Jones, Joe M. Jutson, Grover C. Jordan, James E. Jordan,

Glenn A. Keen, D. E. Kelly, Homer Kelsoe, James A. Kelsoe, E. G. Kerr, Lewis Roy Kier, Howard M. King, Walter L. Knight, Price Kirkland, Samuel Kuykendall,

Elbert D. Lamb, August Laney, Carl Laney, Fred Lanford, Hugh A. Lattimore, Karl C. Lea, Grover C. Leary, James A. Leckliter, Thell C. Lee, Wm. E. Lewis, C. E. Ligon, Roy M. Lipscomb, Jack Little, Frank M. Locke, Jesse D. Lockhart, Willie R. Logan, Walter C. Longmire, C. F. Longstreet, G. W. Louthan, Wm. M. Loveless, Wm. V. Lundy, C. W. Luellen, Travis E. Lutrick.

Newton B. Magill, Lester F. Magness, Leroy Mahagan, Robert B. Maroney, Jay B. Marshall, Clyde E. Martin, Richard C. Martin, Sam C. Mason, John T. Mathes, W. C. Mathes Jr., Frank Maulding, Virgil Merrell, Leslie Eugene Mickey, Dan Miers, James E. Miller, John W. Miller, Sidney P. Miller, Quince C. Millsep, A. M. Milstead, Arthur L. Mitchell, Earnest Mitchell, Jesse R. Mitchell, Wm. H. Mitchell, C. W. Moon, Furd M. Moore, Wm. M. Moore, Roy L. Morton, Leslie L. Morrison, Barney E. Moseley, Leland T. Mounts, George B. Murphy, S. F. Murphy, Lloyd Wm. McBride, Bain McCarroll, John R. McCavey, Geo. J. McCeig, M. B. McClain, Edgar F. McClendon, Alva C. McDaniel, Charley C. McDaniel, J. F. McDaniel, James R. McDaniel, Roy Lee McDaniel, Morey C. Mc-

MILITARY HISTORY

Glasson, Harvey B. McGuire, John J. McGough, Robert L. McGough, Lee McGown, Wm. J. McHan, John G. McKallip, Daniel N. McLaughlin, James K. McVey, John E. McVicker,

Sam O. Nations, David W. Neal, J. B. Nelson, A. H. Newman, Andrew J. Newman, Samuel Newman, Hugh W. Nicholl, Wm. F. Nix, Robert H. Noles, John E. Norman, Frank E. Norfleet, Harry B. Nottingham,

Albert W. Oberste, DeWitt T. Oliver, Ira W. Ott, A. W. Otto, Erle Gray Owens, Jamie C. Owens, John M. Overall,

Frank J. Pachta, Homer B. Pack, Joseph O. Patterson, Hum Patrick, David N. Pearce, J. C. Pearce, Lee Roy Pearson, George T. Perdue, George W. Perdue, Nelson Perdue, Julius E. Peterson, Wendell D. Phillips, James W. Pierce, James R. Pierson, Paul V. Pierson, John W. Pinkeard, Robert Lee Pinckard, W. B. Pettus, Charles D. Powell, E. E. Powell, Eugene Thomas Powell, Jack J. Pritchett, Thomas F. Preston, James V. Proctor.

George R. Quesenberry,

George W. Ragland, James C. Rallings, Tommie L. Rape, Robert Ray, Archie F. Real, Clyde Reid, Cecil J. Rhodes, Jeff A. Richardson, Wilhelm A. Richter, Buren Rightmire, Harl Rightmire, Nathan Riddle, John G. Robinson, M. F. Rodgers, Homer A. Rook, Guy Rosser, Lucius Stokes Rosser, Joe G. Rosson, S. E. E. Rosson, Shawver Rowe, James M. Rowls, H. D. Rushing, O. T. Rushing, Charles E. Russell, Lewis Russell,

Forest S. Sageser, Wilhelm Sammann, Jesse E. Sanderson, Earnest E. Sanford, Geo. H. Sargent, Lark T. Sargent, Charley E. Saunders, T. B. Saxon, George M. Schick Jr., Jesse T. Scott, Oliver O. Scott, I. M. Seaman, Wm. F. Seaman, John W. Sears, Elmer E. Sellers, Robert Sharp, Carter Shaw, Ray E. Sheffy, S. E. Sheffy, Oliver Shelton, C. B. Sheppard, Arthur W. Sherley, C. A. Shook, Leo Shore, Lee Otus Shropshire, Charles Simpson, Nelson H. Smelzer, Edward Smith, James W. Smith, Joseph W. Smith, Roy Joseph Smith, Wm. G. Smith, Wm. Gladstone Smith, Homer C. Smithee, T. C. Smithee, Joe R. Snyder, Mark G. Snyder, J. A. B. Soffle, Everett Spann, Walter A. Spence, George S. Stanford, H. E. Stalcup, Troy D. Stambaugh, Thomas G. Stansell, Sidney B. Steen, Fred L. Stevenson, Baxter H. Stewart, Chester V. Stoddard, Wm. E. Stoddard, Tom Joseph Stoney, Robert E. Story, Frank Stultz,

Jesse Lee Taylor, Walter Taylor, B. B. Tedford, Herman A. Tedford, Henry L. Terrell, Marvin Terry, Alvin Thomas, Arthur L. Thomas, E. B. Thomas, Everett C. Thomas, Samuel H. Thomas, Norris T. Thompson, Wm. R. Thompson, Cecil Tidwell, O. A. Toaker, Edward J. Torres, H. V. Tull Jr., H. A. Turner, Henry A. Turner, Thomas J. Turner,

Roy Upton, Truman Van Fleet, George James Vance, Bert M. Vaughn, Grady M. Vaughn, Wm. W. Vencil, Thomas F. Vines, Floyd Visor.

D. D. Wallen, Roy E. Wardlow, Cecil C. Warren, Talmage Watkins, John Henry Wayland, Charles D. Webb, Eugene Thomas Webb, Samuel J. Webb, George Weemes, Carlton H. Wells, Wm. L. West, Geo. C. Westcoat, E. M. Weller, Henry J. Wheeler, Newton A. Wheeler, C. E. Whitacre, John G. Whitacre, Fred White, Henry White, Jim C. Whiteley, Charles C. Williams, Clay G. Williams, Earnest Williams, E. R. Williams, Milton L. Williams, Thomas B. Williams, Charles S. Wilson, Halard Wilson, Lewis C. Wilson, Lloyd R. Wilson, Virgil R. Winn, Wilbur C. Winn, J. E. Woolverton, W. E. Woolverton, Charles O. Woodson, George W. Wyckoff, Byron Yancy, Moses Yowell, Matt F. Zollicoffer.

Memorial

The following is a list of veterans of all wars buried in the Plainview Cemetery whose graves are decorated each Memorial Day by the American Legion.

Mexican War: Stephen R. Heard and Jesse L. Sanders.

Civil War: B. T. Ansley, R. A. Barrow, J. L. Boswell, J. O. Brown, J. H. Bryan, J. C. Burch, J. H. Calvert, V. C. Cannon, W. C. Clements, H. S. Cox, J. L. Craig, Edwin W. Dyer, Jas. R. Goodwin, A. J. Harp, H. W. Harrell, Jno. E. Hardin, Jas. A. Hooper, A. T. Howell, W. P. Long, R. W. Martine, John T. Mayhugh, Hugh McClelland, John L. Morlton, A. F. Nash, H. S. Pearson, John Pendley, James T. Phelps, John N. Phenis, Adam B. Powell, Franklin A. Pickford, W. M. P. Rippey, A. B. Roberts, J. L. Robinson, C. Sewell, W. B. Sheffy, I. B. Shelton, J. M. Shropshire, J. L. Smith, John W. Stewart, C. W. Tandy, J. P. Toney, J. L. Vaughn, S. D. Waddell, W. S. Waddell, W. S. Wasson, Joseph H. Wayland, F. M. Wells and J. W. Winn.

Spanish American War: J. M. Braselton, F. M. Joyner, John Meisterhons, and Dr. E. F. McClendon.

World War: Clarence J. Abrams, Jim Corbett Aldridge, John A. Anderson, William Jennings Anderson, Roger Mills Ayers, Leon Baker, Joseph J. Barton, Tannehill E. Beek, W. H. Collins, Pat Connelly, Clell C. Cotchell, A. E. Cousineau, Wm. Henry Craig, Park N. Dalton, Sidney R. Davis, Algot W. Engdohl, Claude Denzell Goen, Malcolm Graves, Alvah Hooper, Robert H. Knight, Jno. Elmo Leatherwood, Randall R. Moreland, Cecil Munger, Samuel D. Naylor, Edgar Smith, George A. Smith, William H. Snell, John R. Snyder, Chester V. Stoddard, Joseph Otho Walker, George Wyckoff, and Foy Yancey.

Siberian Expedition, William D. Dodson.

Aviation Corp, Heber G. Vaughan, Arthur Bert Rigler.

STREET SCENES IN PLAINVIEW
(Upper) 1897, (Lower) 1937

CHAPTER XVI

TALES THE OLD TIMERS TOLD
THE PLAINS BUFFALO
By L. S. Kinder

There are very few among us today who have any personal knowledge of the history of the country prior to the year 1876. Up to about 1873 or 1874, the Indians were still a serious menace to the few people who were then in the country, and the buffalo hunters were about the only white people in North West Texas until about 1876. The Indians fought the encroachment of the settler and hunter into the country mainly for the reason that they feared that they would be deprived of their food supply, which was the buffalo, that furnished them meat and raiment. From time immemorial they had derived an inexhaustible supply of food from the countless numbers of these animals that grazed this part of Texas. This part of the North-American continent had been for ages the grazing ground of the buffalo. Today we cannot comprehend the extent of the great herd of these animals that ranged throughout this part of Texas.

Mr. Goodnight, who knew as much about this animal and its habits as any other man, said that there were two great herds: the Northern and Southern. He says there were marked differences in those of the two herds. Those of the Northern herd he called the Northern Bison, and the other herd he designated as the Southern Buffalo. It seems that these herds never inter-mixed, nor encroached on each other's range. The Northern herd never ranged South of the Arkansas river, and the Wichita Mountains; and the Southern herd stopped in their migrations northward, where the other herd turned back. Mr. Goodnight wrote an interesting article, "What I know about Buffalo," and the writer is fortunate in having a copy. He states that almost every year in the sixties, he passed through the Southern herd. When he had traveled about fifty miles Northwest of Ft. Belknap in Young County, he would generally strike the herd on the waters of the Brazos river. Their range covered the entire country between the Cross Timbers and the Staked Plains.

According to his estimate the herd extended about 125 miles North and South and about 25 miles wide and were as close together as they could graze and when they passed on not a particle of vegetation was left. Well informed buffalo hunters were of the opinion that there were eight or ten million of these animals in the Southern herd. A well known army officer, in writing about the buffalo, said that he and some hunters in the sixties were traveling over the Santa Fe trail and they took a position on the Pawnee Rock, at that time a well known land mark in Kansas, and at a single view they believed that they saw as many as a half million of these animals. It is beyond comprehension that this enormous number of animals could have been so quickly exterminated. There were very few left in the eighties; mankind however can be destructive to a very marked degree when his mind is turned in that direction.

The Comanche Indian claimed as his hunting ground all that country extending from the Canadian river on the North, to the Rio Grande on the South, and for years bitterly contested the settlement of that territory by the white man. This tribe was one of the most numerous and warlike of all American Indians, and gave the pioneer more trouble than all others of the Southwest. No wonder they contested any movement upon the part of the whites that might deprive them of the fruits of this wonderful hunting ground.

BUFFALO HUNTING IN THE SEVENTIES
By Levi Schick

A young man came to me in 1872 wanting a job. I was engaged at that time in furnishing beef for the Government at Dodge City. At that time there was very little buffalo hunting, for it hadn't commenced then. There were soon, however, a good many in the field who came in the fall about the time the railroad reached Dodge City. I made arrangements with my partner to look after the beef contracting business and I went buffalo hunting with Wright Moar, for that was this young man's name. We were out about three weeks, I guess, on that first trip, where we hunted buffalo on Mulberry Creek of the Arkansas River. I did the killing and he did the skinning and we got quite a few hides, about $1100 worth. Then we went Northwest from Dodge City, and down the country which had just been burned off. Of course there were very few buffalo, and they were traveling at that time. So we went back to Dodge City where we found his brother, John Moar, waiting for him. I went back to my Government job and Wright and John Moar went off together hunting buffalo. Wright Moar got to be a famous buffalo hunter. I think he told me that at one time he had sixty men working for him. In eighteen months he killed about 6500 head. The way they hunted was interesting. They would locate a bunch and get as close to them as they could. There was always a leader in a big herd. If they could pick out the leader and kill it, the others would stand around and they could kill quite a few before they scattered. Sometimes they would knock the buffalo down thinking they had killed him when they had only creased him. Then it was dangerous for the buffalo was always ready to fight when he got up. There was no buffalo hunting worth mentioning after 1878, though there were quite a few small bunches of from fifty to two hundred scattered around for several years after that. Colonel Goodnight finally gathered a few when they were just about gone and perpetuated the species when they were about to become extinct, by starting the famous Goodnight Buffalo Herd.

BUFFALO DAYS
By J. W. Smylie

In 1877 four friends and I rigged up an outfit and went to Fort Worth, where we bought supplies and started out to hunt buffalo. We came through Weatherford, Graham, Fort Griffin, Old Phantom Hill and on west through Stonewall County to the Double Mountains. Here we spent the winter of 1877-1878 killing buffalo. On Christmas Eve, 1877, between twenty and thirty buffalo hunters got together and decided to come up on the Plains. We followed the divide between Salt Fork and Double Mountain Fork of the Brazos and camped just beneath the caprock expecting to come up on the Plains the next day. That night there came a snow storm which covered the whole country with seven inches of snow. At that time we all thought the Plains was but a great sand desert and on seeing the snow we were afraid to venture forth. I know now that we were in the eastern part of Crosby County. That winter was about the windup of the slaughter of the buffaloes. Hides were very cheap, bringing from $1.50 to $3.00 and a few robe hides bringing as high as $5.00. The hides of the buffalo were gathered at Fort Griffin and freighted from there to Fort Worth by team. Near the northwest corner of Jones County was a trading post called Remel City. Conrad and Rath had a supply house and bought the hides. There was a restaurant, two or three saloons and a large dance hall made of sod walls and covered with buffalo hides, with a plank floor. Buffalo hides were the currency for there was no money. In 1880 I spent several months on the waters of the Colorado River. While the engineers were staking the road bed to Big Springs, there was a man camped at Big Springs piling up buffalo bones. At the time I saw him he told me he had collected eighty tons. I later heard that when the railroad reached Big Springs that he sold his buffalo bones for four thousand dollars. Hale County was still strewn with buffalo bones when I moved here in 1887.

PIONEER DAYS AS A TEXAS RANGER
By W. F. Meador

It was in February, 1882, that I came up from Jacksboro to Blanco Canyon and enlisted in a Ranger company. This gave me a chance to scout all over these Plains. There were no Indians here to amount to anything then, though once in a while a bunch would pass through going across from Mexico to the Oklahoma Reservations. We went on a little scout very often. Once the report came to the camp that there were Indians at Four Lakes. That was in New Mexico a little bit southwest from here. Old Captain Arrington was with us, and there were twelve of us went across. It was sixty or seventy miles southwest of the Yellowhouse, not far over the Mexico line. We rode in there one night and camped. In the morning there were no Indians there though we saw signs of them. They had not been gone long. They had left the night before and gone across by way of Tulia, where they killed a Mexican. Then they went on across to Oklahoma. The last bunch I knew anything about came through close to the old Ranger Camp. They never did any devilment. They knew the way to go through, and knew the watering places. They were mighty shy, just passing through, and didn't give any trouble. It wasn't long before the ranches were opened up, and I started to work on the Plains as a cowboy.

CHIEF LONE WOLF VISITS THE MORRISON RANCH
By J. N. Morrison

It was in the summer of 1881 that Lone Wolf, the famous Kiowa Chief, came to the Morrison Ranch in Hale County. Guests were very few in those days and frontier hospitality was extended to the Chief and his party. In the group were several Indians, one of whom was their old Medicine Man, two or three Indian Squaws, and two white men who were acting as guides to keep the white people from killing them. Only seven years before this, General Mackenzie had defeated Lone Wolf and his bands in the Battle of Palo Duro Canyon and sent them to the reservations. In 1881 the Indians were as much afraid of the white people as the white people were of the Indians, and naturally both the Indian and the white man made it a point to shoot first. It seemed the Indians in the Reservations were preparing for some sort of religious ceremony in which they needed a buffalo hide, so they had come in search of a buffalo, as there were still a few roaming on the Staked Plains. They finally located the buffalo. Since it was the duty of the Medicine Man to do the killing, the aged Indian mounted a fast horse in regular Indian fashion, bareback and without bridle or halter, and guiding the horse with his knees he pursued and killed the buffalo with his bow and arrow. Immediately after the buffalo had fallen, the squaws rushed forward and skinned it. It was always the squaw's duty to skin the buffalo and Lone Wolf had brought them along for that purpose. They had brought their own tepees with them and it was a fascinating experience to me to watch the squaws putting up the poles and stretching the covering over them. They stopped at the ranch house to eat while they were on this hunt. The squaws always waited until Lone Wolf had helped himself before they took any food. They watched him closely while he ate and imitated his actions throughout the meal. When the buffalo hide had been secured, Lone Wolf quietly went his way, leading his party back to the Reservations. My mother, who was the first white woman to come to Hale County, gravely watched her guests depart, sincerely hoping they would not return.

MOVING THE SLAUGHTER CATTLE
By George D. May

I came to Hale County in the spring of 1883 and went to work on the Circle Ranch when the Morrisons and Slaughter formed a partnership. Morrisons put up the land and Slaughter put in 10,000 head of cows and calves and R. W. O'Keefe was the first foreman. I helped O'Keefe trail these cattle from the Slaughter Ranch at Big Springs. We made three herds of it, with 3,000 in each of the first two trips and 4,000 in the last trip. It was a 200 mile drive from Big Springs to the Circle Ranch and we could only travel six or eight miles a day, or possibly ten at the most.

When we were coming up here with a herd—I think it was the second trip—we did not find any water for the cattle until we reached the Lubbock Yellow House. The cattle were very thirsty for we had made a dry drive as the water had dried up in the lakes on the route O'Keefe had planned. The night before we reached the Yellow House, every man in the outfit stayed up all night trying to hold the cattle. If they were lying down and a puff of wind came up, they would jump up and smell. It would take hard riding for a while to quiet them. Then they would be all right until another puff of wind came. On that dry drive we made, we didn't have any water to drink ourselves, and we would ride up to the chuck wagon and eat some canned fruit or tomatoes to quench our thirst. The cook carried a keg of water on each side of the wagon to cook with, but he wouldn't let us have it to drink.

Usually when we watered a big herd, we would cut them up into groups of two or three hundred so that in case they broke loose and ran to water we could handle them better. If we didn't they would run into the water and jump on top of one another, packing them down and drowning a lot of them.

Before we reached the Yellow House, a little breeze came up and wafted across the prairie the odor of water. When they got their first whiff of it they started to run. They were so excited that the man in front of them couldn't stop them. On they went and all we could do was to follow. They kept running until they reached the lake and went right into the water. That time they sure every one of them got in. Rufe O'Keefe and I stayed with them until we pulled them all out of the bog that night and we broke up all our rope pulling them out. The other boys all went to sleep but we worked on, and we had the cattle all out by two o'clock in the morning and didn't lose a one.

Lots of the country was not usable those days on account of lack of water. I could have bought land at 50¢ an acre but we didn't think there was any water anywhere. We didn't know you could drill anywhere you wanted to put down a well and get water. It was funny about finding all this water and having windmills all over the country when we didn't think there was any water to be had on the plains. All the water we knew about then was in the Runningwater Draw. It runs from the head of it in New Mexico down to within four or five miles of Plainview, and I have heard it said that the water went under the ground then and came out at Blanco Canyon. A few would drill a four inch well and get water along the Draw, but we had no idea there was any water on the Plains away from the Draw.

The freighters on the ranch worked oxen, linked one wagon behind another, and went to Colorado City after groceries. Sometimes they would be gone two or three weeks after supplies. The Plains were strewn with buffalo bones and the freighters would gather up the bones and take them down to Colorado City and sell them and bring back a load of supplies on their return. The boys used to take the heads of the buffalo and scallop the wagon, putting buffalo heads all around the top of the wagon and filling in the wagon box with bones. It looked pretty to see the wagon scalloped that way. They carried worlds of bones to Colorado City and sold them to be ground up and shipped east for fertilizer. The prairies once were white with buffalo bones but they are all gone now.

But the most amazing thing when I think of it is the

bounteous water supply underlying these fertile Plains that we once thought a desert.

HORATIO GRAVES—FIRST SETTLER
By Amy Graves

It was in 1877 that my father, Horatio Graves, made his first trip to Hale County. At that time we were living in Ausable Forks, New York, where my father was pastor of a Methodist Church. The lure of cheap land and a desire to establish his wife in a home where the winters were more mild than in New York State were his reasons for coming. He had read in the New York Christian Advocate about the cheap land for sale which had been allotted to the railroad companies for the building of railroads in Texas, and about the fine climate in Texas. He left New York in the fall of 1877 and arrived at Eastland where he made arrangements with Connellee and Ammerman to make a trip to the Staked Plains with a surveying party. On this trip they located the Bottle Corner, which was for years the controlling corner in Hale County. They first went to Lubbock County, as father wanted to look at some land there. As they were surveying to locate this tract of land their field glasses revealed in the distance a band of Commanche Indians. The redskins got off their horses and so deployed themselves in the rise that to the unaided eye they looked like a great company. The sight of those Indians caused father to decide to take the Hale County land. The tract of land they located in Hale County, as I remember, was about twenty five sections, obtained by locating "railroad scrip." Father kept for himself about sixteen sections. Father came again in 1878 to locate a big tract of land in Texas for speculators in the east. After he had got his start by locating lands for speculators, he felt that he was safe in bringing his family to the frontier.

MEMORY PICTURES
By Lottie Graves Layer

It was in March, 1883, that our family moved to our new home in Hale County. A year had passed since we left our home in New York. The first part of our journey was by train to Eastland, where we lived until July, 1882. In two covered wagons, with two cows tied to the rear wagon, we started for the Staked Plains. Heavy rains impeded our journey and we were a month enroute. We were compelled to ford several swollen streams before we reached our journey's end. We spent the fall and winter at Estacado while father was preparing our home, and attended the first school on the Staked Plains, which was taught by Ruth Emma Hunt in the fall of 1882. When we moved to our new home in 1883, the grass was just turning green. There was water in the lakes for it had been wet all winter. There were wild horses in great numbers and many buffalo trails led down to the lakes. The vastness of the prairie, the blue vault of the sky meeting the earth in the wide circle of an unbroken horizon was impressive, as was the sunrise and sunset and the deep blue heavens shining with brilliant stars at night. There were unusually brilliant sunsets in the summer of 1884. I think this was a world-wide phenomenon. Mother read that they were attributed to violent eruptions of Mt. Vesuvius. Soon after we arrived at our new home, one Sunday morning my sisters and I walked to the west hill which overlooked a deep basin, where a large herd of antelope were grazing. Some of them noticed our approach and came toward us. We stood still, expecting them to run away, but their curiosity led them to move cautiously toward us. A buck came to within a dozen feet of us. Then we could no longer restrain the dog that accompanied us and at sight of him the entire band scampered away out of sight. One Sunday evening father shot a buffalo from the kitchen door. All day they had been feeding in the north and south basins, but father would not go out because it was Sunday. But when they came so near the garden he felt he must frighten them away.

In the late spring Mr. Alpheus Dyer came out from Troy, New York to live in the second house which father had built not far to the west of ours. Being a dentist he brought his dental chair and tools and a very good microscope. It was a great treat to look at his large collection of slides. After two years he moved to Estacado and Mr. A. E. Adams and his family lived in this house until they could build their sod house.

These are just a few memory pictures which I recall of our coming and settling in Hale County.

FRONTIER HARDSHIPS
By D. N. Shepley

My father, D. L. Shepley moved his family from Snyder, Texas, arriving in the old Epworth community in Hale County in March, 1886. Father drove out on a section of land, dug a hole, put up cedar posts around it, stretched a tent over them and declared it his home. We didn't have room in our one wagon to bring many groceries when we came with our household goods, so father had to go immediately to Colorado City for supplies. He gathered buffalo bones enroute and sold them there for $21.00 per ton to get money to buy groceries as that was about the only way we had of making a living at that time. While he was gone there came a terrible rain and the hole in our tent was filled up level with water. The whole face of the earth seemed to be under water. There we were, alone in the worst mess you ever saw. The bed was under water and we children stood up on the bed and cried, while mother waded about waist deep in the water, putting everything up as high as she could to keep it dry. We felt so helpless and forlorn out there on the prairie, but mother did the best she could. When father returned he got cedar trees from the breaks and built us a dugout. He placed a big ridge pole across the dugout and rested split poles on it. Then he put all the dirt he had dug out of the ground on top for a roof. There was nothing to be seen but a pile of dirt, but a cyclone could not tear it up. We had no windows, but left the door open for light. Later we built a sod house which was a great improvement, but we were the happiest family that ever lived in this world the first day we got into the dugout. We got our water from A. E. Adams's well a mile and a half distant. Father hauled the water in a barrel when he was at home, but we children had to get it while he was away. So he put a bolt in each end of the barrel, tied a rope to them and we pulled that barrel across the prairie to the well, where Mr. Adams helped us fill it, for we were too little to do that. Then we would roll it a little way and sit down to rest, as it was all we could do to pull it. It took us half a day to get a barrel of water. Father started to dig a well soon after we came, digging on it whenever he had time. Mother and we children would dig while he was away and it was about a year before we got it finished. I shall never forget the day he struck water. He was down about fifty feet and was digging away when the water began to trickle in. He called up, "O Emma! Come here! I've struck water!" She was so excited she had to see for herself, so we children let her down into the well with a rope. Then we happened to think—we had mother and father down in the bottom of the well and they couldn't get out unless we pulled them out, so we made them promise all kinds of things before we would pull them up. That was a great day of rejoicing and that well of water was the best anybody ever drank.

Once while father was away we ran out of anything to eat. His wagon broke down and he was delayed. Mother ground corn in the coffee mill to make bread with, and we cooked some corn and tried to make hominy, but it was a very poor way of existing. One of my most vivid recollections of those pioneer days is of my mother, standing on top of the old dugout in the evening, watching for father. Maybe he would come that day, and maybe not for several more. The first year we were on the Plains, father made seven trips to Colorado City for groceries and thirteen trips to Quitaque, fifty miles away, for wood, before mother finally learned to burn cow chips.

Z. T. MAXWELL
By William E. Maxwell

Z. T. Maxwell left Montague, Texas, in April, 1885, with a small bunch of cattle and arrived in Blanco Canyon in May of that year. He sold his holdings in the spring of 1886 and traded his cattle to Anson Cox of Estacado for 2000 sheep. Then he made a prospecting trip westward into Hale County in search of a location. Finding the two hackberry groves, he proceeded to dig a well in the draw between the two groves and built a sod corral for the sheep which we moved up in the first part of September. Father returned to the canyon to move the family up, leaving Perry Balch and me to care for the sheep. I shall never forget that first night. We penned the sheep, ate our supper and made our bed on the bank of the draw. While we were getting ready for bed, Perry brought a leg of mutton and placed it under his pillow. I asked him why he did it and he said he was trying to keep the wolves from getting it, though they might, anyway. He placed a loaded Winchester by his side and we went to sleep. Some time during the night I was awakened by the explosion of that gun. When I asked what was wrong, Perry replied, "Well, they got the meat, but I don't know whether I got the wolves or not." Just then we heard a tremendous fight among the wolves some distance away.

Our family moved up and we built a half dugout, half sod house in the bank of the draw between the two hackberry groves. My sister Edna was born there December 28, 1887. In the spring of 1887 the lakes were full of water, the grass was green and Hale County was the most beautiful country I ever saw. It was this fact, together with the splendid shallow water and healthful climate that caused the early and rather rapid settlement of this particular section. There were a few families in the country when we moved there. I remember a Mr. Graves who lived about twelve miles south and a Mr. Gray several miles up the draw. At the time we moved, my grandmother, Mrs. Elizabeth Duncan, my two uncles, W. V. and W. E. Duncan, and my aunt, Mrs. Edith Clark, moved four miles south of us. Bill Marsalis was two miles south. In the spring of 1887 Mr. McClelland came with his family and camped near us in a tent for a time. He had a store in Plainview in the early days. Among the early comers were E. L. Lowe, Horace Griffin, J. C. Burch, J. H. Bryan and Uncle John Pendley. I am not sure when Mr. Lowe came, but he must have come after my father did or he would have taken the land with the trees on it, for so far as I know, these were the only trees in the country. Maxwell and Lowe started the town of Plainview and helped to organize the County. It was in September, 1892, that my father moved to the Indian Territory.

E. L. LOWE
By Virginia Lowe Quillen

My father, Edwin Lowden Lowe, was born in Lowden County, Tennessee. After my grandparents died he went to live with an older brother in Hamburg, Ashley County, Arkansas. There he practiced law and soon became a member of the State Legislature. There he met and married my mother, Virginia Archer, the daughter of a wealthy plantation owner of Louisiana.

Due to ill health my father was seeking a higher and dryer climate, so some time in the eighties, we set out for the Plains of Texas. Our family consisted of my father and mother, a sister five years older than I, and myself. We made the trip in covered wagons. I do not remember any of the journey to the Plains, but we must have stopped for several months at Buffalo Gap, where my mother died. I am told that her death was caused by lack of proper medical attention. She was buried there and we continued on our journey, with my faithful old Auntie who made a home for us and our heart-broken father. Upon reaching the spot which is now Plainview, my father felt that he had found what he was seeking—a healthful climate and pure water.

We lived in tents before we built our dugout home. The wolves came at night and gnawed the harness of our horses, and did whatever damage they could. One night when my father had gone to meet some men on business, Auntie, upon hearing the cry of a panther, let down the tent flap, which served as a door. Then she took a seat just inside to await the coming of the panther. All the while my sister and I slept. She later explained to us that she thought if the panther came first, perhaps by the time she was eaten my father might come in time to save us. It was courage in those days, but in thinking of it now, it seems pathetically humorous. Our dugout home was comfortable. It consisted of three rooms —one room was used for kitchen and dining room, and the other two for bed rooms. We had not lived in the dugout very long until we built a frame house. I believe it was the first one built in Plainview. This home consisted of four rooms downstairs and one large room upstairs and a cellar.

Until there were stores where food and clothing might be bought, our supplies came from Colorado City. As it was months between times, when some one could make the trip, materials were bought by the bolt, apples and flour by the barrel, and other necessities in proportion. I remember when the wagons were due how eagerly I watched from an upstairs window. How many times a tiny speck in the distance proved to be just an animal of some kind! On the day, however, when the object grew larger and larger until the wagons and teams could be outlined, my joy knew no bounds.

My father died soon after our frame house was built. I remember one day Auntie and I had been visiting my Aunt Jule Griffin (the Horace Griffin family). They lived a mile or more away. As we were returning home a storm came up. The wind blew with such force that we had difficulty in standing up, having to hold to each other in order to do so. As we neared our home we could see father coming from town in the opposite direction. He would walk a while, then stoop down and rest. We reached him as quickly as possible and helped him home and put him to bed. I do not remember that he ever walked again. Crowds of people came to our home to have church during his illness before his death. Father was much loved by every one that knew him. He was a Mason and was given a Masonic burial. I remember the crude procession as it wended its way to the graveyard. I sat on the front seat of a rickety wagon of some kind, which was drawn by one horse. It was lonely without my father, and that night the schoolhouse bell tolled for him.

Auntie continued on after father died, sent us to school and had us taught music, paying for our lessons with town lots when money was scarce. We went religiously to church and Sunday School. The most that I can remember of church was sleeping through the sermon and being awakened at the close by my beloved Aunt's shouting. She was certainly a shouting Methodist.

The work of building up the town was continued after my father died. An uncle, Charles Henry Gilbert, was administrator of our estate and Auntie Lowe was appointed our guardian. Together they worked for the good of the town, giving away many more lots. I really feel that a large part of Plainview was built upon the love I had for this dear old couple, for years later I quit-claimed it seems to me hundreds of lots to clear titles to that land.

After several years—the managing grew to be a burden to Auntie, and so our Fort Worth relatives sent for us—I went to make my home with my mother's only sister, Mrs. R. H.

Tucker, who had wanted me since my mother's death. My sister went to make her home with a more distant relative, and dear old Auntie went back to Arkansas.

THORNTON JONES' GROCERY STORE
By Thornton Jones

I was in the mercantile business with Stringfellow and Hume at Estacado in 1886 and 1887. In the spring of 1887 Maxwell and Lowe decided to start a town on their claims and they offered me a number of lots if I would put in a grocery store in Plainview on or before the first day of June, 1887. In order to comply with this, I started my store in a tent 18 x 24 feet and left my brother Will in charge until I could arrange my business to take charge of it myself. In September of that year I was appointed Postmaster of Plainview. Antelope were plentiful in those days. On the 14th day of January, 1888, during a snow storm, a large bunch of antelope drifted in from the north. Standing in the doorway of my store, I shot one about where the Court House now stands, and I killed three before they got out of my reach. I freighted lumber from Colorado City and erected a store building 20 x 40 feet, which was located on the southeast corner of the present Court House Square. A number of settlers came into the country in the summer and fall of 1887 and soon we had quite a little settlement at Plainview.

FIRST VISIT TO PLAINVIEW
By W. L. Harrington

In July, 1887, I stopped at the Rock House in Blanco Canyon on my way to New Mexico with a bunch of cattle. We had difficulty in getting through the large ranches with our cattle, so I told Hank Smith I wished he would give me a way-bill so I could find some water in crossing the Plains, so I could get into New Mexico with my bunch of cattle. Uncle Hank said to me, "You go right up this Runningwater Draw to a little place they call Plainview." He told me how far it was and I followed the Draw, driving as close along the banks of it as I could, and the first thing I knew, I was right on top of a dugout. A woman came running out all excited to see what had happened. I said, "I beg your pardon. I am looking for a place they call Plainview." "Well," she said, "Mister, you are right on top of half of it right now!" That was Mrs. Maxwell. I asked her to direct me to the Circle Ranch, which she did, and I went on.

THOSE EARLY DAYS
By Mrs. J. W. Smylie

Mr. Smylie and J. M. Carter came west prospecting in July, 1887. We had gone through a three years drouth in Runnels County and they were so impressed with the possibilities of the unsettled country in Hale County that each one filed on homestead land. Mr. Carter's land was where the depot now stands and Mr. Smylie's across the draw south of town. I have often said that I helped to lay out Broadway in Plainview, for Mrs. Carter and I were such close friends that we wore a path between her home and mine. There were several dugouts and sod houses in Plainview. Mr. Rawlings had moved a one-room house from somewhere and started a store. The first of February, Mr. Smylie built us a shack to live in. The sides were of boxing planks. The ends were of sod and it was covered with wagon sheets. We built a fireplace in one end and surely did enjoy it, for that first winter was very severe. The dirt floor was covered with rugs made of gunny sacks. It was here that our oldest daughter was born. Mr. Smylie had gone back to Runnels County for some cattle and our household goods and I think that loneliness and anxiety caused her premature birth. We had no doctor at Plainview, and in fact there was none in the County. This was two years before the first physician came. On March 22, 1888, I stood in our doorway and saw the first grave dug in the Plainview cemetery. It was for the infant sons of the Portwoods. Later on there were two other little graves made—one for the Moore's baby and the other for the Bradford's little son—and then E. L. Lowe, our County Clerk, was buried.

Fuel was a great problem when we first came to this country, and surface coal, or cow chips, was our standby. None of us thought it condescending on our part to help bring in the fuel or to use it. The long distance to the railroad for coal and the high price of it and shortage of money, made the use of it necessary.

In the early days the mirages were "questionable" and unusual in appearance. Large lakes of water were a common sight to see in the distance on cold mornings. Early one morning I came to Plainview, and when within a few miles of town I looked, and behold! Plainview was a city built upon a hill. The old Baptist church standing in the southern part of town looked like a castle, and every window had the appearance of something extraordinary. The draw or creek that curves around the west and south of Plainview was a broad river and the houses in town were reflected in the river. The view was magnificent, but faded away as we drew nearer. Several years after seeing this mirage, I was in my yard one cold morning and I saw a train going from Hereford to Canyon. The track seemed to be elevated and the train was very distinct as it glided along. The distance from the railroad to my home was about seventy miles, but the train was distinctly reflected. We saw many beautiful mirages. If anyone doubts my veracity, I refer them to our old pioneers.

I wish to speak of our well remembered friend, Mr. R. C. Ware. He was indeed a friend to the needy and practiced the Bible quotation, "He that asketh of thee, turn not away." I have never heard of anyone in need going to him for help and being refused while he was in the mercantile business. Many of my old friends have fallen by the wayside. I wish I could tell you of their nobility and endurance of character. Among those I want to mention are Mrs. Thornton Jones, Mrs. Sheffy and my beloved friend, Mrs. J. M. Carter. "None knew her but to love her; none named her but to praise."

EARLY BUSINESS FIRMS IN PLAINVIEW
By W. B. Martine

The first business houses in Plainview were built of lumber freighted by wagon from Colorado City or Amarillo. Thornton Jones operated the first store in a tent on the lot cornering the Court House square on the southeast but it was not long until he built a wooden building. When I came to Plainview in the early nineties, A. Vince had the Post Office in his store on the lot cornering the square on the southwest. A. J. Welter had a shoe shop in the same building. The Hesperian Hotel stood on the corner of the block south of Vince's store and was first run by Pearson & Hughes and afterwards by R. W. Martine. On the west side of the square and across the street north of Vince's, R. C. Ware had a general store. Mrs. Fowle put in a millinery store north of Ware, and next to that was the Wayland Drug Store, then Williams Bros. store operated by J. F. and Quincy Williams, Dye's Drug Store (Dye had bought the Atkins Drug Store) Ben Sebastian's Barber Shop and J. D. Dobbin's Tin Shop. J. N. Donohoo bought an interest in R. C. Ware's store and the Donohoo-Ware store moved farther north in the block. Hugh McClelland then moved his store from the southeast corner of the square, Thornton Jones' old stand, to the building vacated by R. C. Ware. Uncle John Pendley had a blacksmith shop on the "First National Bank corner," cornering the square on the northwest. On the north side W. B. Knight had a livery stable and wagon yard which covered the west three lots. Jumbo Canterberry afterwards operated this. Next on the east was the Herald Office. Harry Brown had a restaurant toward the middle of the block and Pipkin & Donaldson's store was east of it. On the east side of the square M. V. Rallings had a store toward the south end of the block. Col. R. P. Smyth built his office just north of Rallings. Z. T. Maxwell had a livery stable south of the lot cornering the square on the southeast and he had a hotel across the street west. This was the first hotel in Plainview. W. Z. Hamilton's blacksmith shop was south of Maxwell's livery stable. On the south side of the square, Nathan Lapowski, of Colorado City, built a long building on the west lot later on, into which A. Vince moved and went into partnership with C. O. Leach. At that time A. J. Welter moved his shoe shop to the Rallings building. Kinder and Wilson had a law office about the middle of the block. All those wooden buildings on the west side were eventually destroyed by fire and the rest of the buildings through the years were either torn down or burned, and fire proof buildings now surround the Court House. The Herald is still operating but under a different management. Hamilton's Blacksmith Shop is the only one of these pioneer firms still doing business in Plainview.

"UNCLE JOHN" PENDLEY, BLACKSMITH
By Stella Pendley Garner

"Uncle John" Pendley is the name by which my father was known to the early settlers. He came to Plainview in September, 1887, bringing his family, which consisted of my mother, brother and myself. Coming from Anson, in Jones County, by wagon, we followed the Mackenzie Trail to Plainview. Thornton Jones had a tent near the present site of the Court House Square in which he had a store and kept a few groceries. We drove up to the tent but found no one there. We got what groceries we wanted and put the money for them in a cigar box. It seemed a lonesome, desolate place. Mother began to cry and said, "Let's go back." Father said "No, I came to stay and am not going back." We camped that night on what is now the First National Bank corner. The next day we drove out three miles east of town where father found some land that suited him. We lived in our wagon until he could dig a dugout. Soon afterward he provided another room for us by digging another dugout right beside the first, leaving a two-foot wall between with a connecting doorway. He afterwards built a three room plank house with lumber hauled from Colorado City. Father set out an orchard soon after we came and in a few years we had an abundance of fruit which we shared with others. There were lots of antelope then and brother often shot them from the dugout door as they ran past and this provided us with meat. We grew at home nearly everything we needed to eat except flour, sugar and coffee. We went shopping twice a year and freighted all our supplies from railroad points. Later father conducted a blacksmith shop on the corner where the Hale County State Bank stands. Brother and I did the farming. Brother walked and plowed the ground, planting with a wash pan tacked on a board fastened behind the plow with holes in the pan for the seed to drop through. I rode a horse dragging a rock to cover up the seed. We gathered the crop with a slide having a knife on each side to cut the feed, one of us catching the fodder while the other drove the horse. It was a primitive method but we had good crops. Father was one of the founders of the First Christian Church and was its first Sunday School Superintendent. He was also the first County Commissioner in Precinct No. 1 and was a member of the first school board. Every phase of community life and common interest had the support of "Uncle John" Pendley.

SURVEYING INCIDENTS
By Col. R. P. Smyth

It was in the fall of 1887 when I first visited the place where the town of Plainview is now located. I was on my way to the Circle Ranch and was following the dim road known as the Mackenzie Trail. I had reached a point about where is now the southeast corner of the public square in the town of Plainview when I observed a man about 300 yards to the right of the trail, who seemed to be walking around in a circle. From his actions I supposed he had got lost from some party of emigrants crossing the plains and had become crazed for the want of water. To drive on and leave him in the condition I supposed him to be in was not to be thought of, so I halted my team and awaited his approach. Walking up to the hack he introduced himself as Mr. Maxwell. Seeing in my hack the transit chain, ranging poles and other articles belonging to a surveyor, he remarked: "And I suppose this is Colonel Smyth." I asked him what he was doing out there so far from any settlements. He told me his family was camped in the draw below us and that he had been informed that there was a body of unsurveyed land in that section subject to pre-emption. If it did exist he intended to pre-empt 160 acres of it. I asked him what he was going to do with it when he got it. He said that it looked to him like a good place to build a town. Then I was sure that my first impression was correct.

A short time afterward, a deputy district surveyor, I surveyed a 160-acre pre-emption for Mr. Maxwell and along side of it another 160-acre pre-emption for E. L. Lowe. The survey of this land disclosed the fact that here was a body of unsurveyed land subject to location under the homestead laws of the State, giving each family 160 acres of land. All it cost them was the surveying fees, living on it for three years and paying $5.00 to the State for a patent. Such news travels fast and in less than a year all of it was occupied by settlers.

The day that J. M. Carter and J. W. Smylie came prospecting was one of our windy days. To get out of the wind so I could write their applications for them, it was necessary to place a box on the ground and lie flat on the ground with my head in the box to make out their applications. Judge Carter took the quarter north of the Lowe quarter and Mr. Smylie took the quarter south of the Maxwell quarter.

The first house in Plainview with a plank floor in it was the sod house owned by Horace Griffin. He hauled the lumber from Colorado City, and passing by where I was at work surveying, he told the boys working for me that if they would come over and help lay the floor we could have a dance on it. I put up my transit and told the boys to "nail her down." That night all the beauty and chivalry of Hale County was gathered at the sod house of Horace Griffin to have their first dance on a real plank floor. Back where I had come from, I had been for seven years president of the foremost dancing club in the city, so I thought I knew everything about dancing. The music started up—a fiddle short a few strings—but that was a little matter. We were there to dance on the plank floor and not on the fiddle. I led the belle of the ball out on the floor. I was a little mystified as to what the dance was to be. The noise from the fiddle did not sound like "The Blue Danube." A cowboy took his position near the fiddle as master of ceremonies and directed four couples how to take positions. It was the position for the dancing of an old dance long gone out of fashion, known as the waltz-quadrille. It was a quadrille without the waltz. The master of ceremonies called out "Salute your partners!" That was easy. Then came "All forward and back, first couple to the right, four hands round and round you go, ladies do si do and gents you know." Here was one gent who did not know, and the whole push had to be halted until it could be explained to this gent. Then on went the dance until early morn.

WHY WE ORGANIZED HALE COUNTY
By L. G. Wilson

I commenced the practice of law in Gainesville, Texas in the spring of 1887 in the office of Potter and Hughes. I came west in 1888 and my ticket gave out at Childress, where I first met Judge A. J. Fires. There I gave my last dollar to replenish the chuck box of a freighter with whom I crossed the range and arrived at Plainview May 1, 1888. The grass was green and covered with herds of antelope and wild horses, and I was convinced that it was the land Horace Greely referred to when he said, "Go west, young man, and grow up with the country." Plainview had been founded by Maxwell and Lowe and there were a few settlers who wanted me to locate. They said they had no money but would divide what they had—plenty to eat, cedar posts and work. I told them if they would give me an interest in the grub without the work and organize the county, I was located. We got to work and secured the signatures of all who passed to our petition for organization until we had 150 names and on July 3, 1888, I think it was, E. L. Lowe, Z. T. Maxwell, Henry Moore, J. M. Carter, Col. R. P. Smyth and I went to Estacado and secured an order for an election for countyseat and officers for Hale County. I was elected County Attorney when the County was organized. We hauled all the material from Amarillo at one trip to build our first court house, which consisted of a small one story building with a court room in front and a few small offices in the rear. That year our first mail line was started, a one-horse buckboard once a week from Amarillo. Those were frontier days, but we were healthy, happy and prosperous, with the latchstring on the outside of every door. Soon we had a daily mail each way with large hacks carrying not only mail but passengers and express and I have never seen a more enthusiastic crowd at any railway station to meet the train as gathered every evening to meet the incoming hack with mail, express and passengers.

CARRYING THE MAIL IN 1888
By W. L. Tharp

I carried the mail from Amarillo through Plainview to Estacado in July and August, 1888, and it took me six days to make the round trip. Bent Clisbee, who ran a livery stable in Amarillo, had secured the mail contract for two months and he hired me to carry the mail. The first trip I made was the first time I had been over the route, and it took me a day and a half to get to Plainview. There were no towns between Amarillo and Plainview then, though a Mr. Parrish had a post office which they called Tulie at his ranch about three miles up the draw from where Tulia is now located. There was a road from Amarillo to Plainview, then, a right smart of a trail, but the first morning out, I had to swim the Palo Duro Creek at the T Anchor Ranch.

I carried the mail for two months and when my contract was out, a man by the name of Bailey took the mail and delivered it to Plainview three times a week. When Bailey's time was out, I believe Clisbee got the mail again and put it into Plainview once a day, for a long time. Then Stant Rhea got the job from Clisbee and carried it himself for several years until they built the railroad into Canyon.

THE FIRST PUBLIC SCHOOL
By Alice Rosser Buntin

I arrived in Hale County in a covered wagon on May 15, 1889, with my brother and my aged mother from Gainesville, Texas. I can realize now how blue my mother was when she first got out of the wagon. She said there wasn't enough green grass for a goose to eat and that there was nothing here but coyotes, wild horses and antelopes. She wanted to take the back track, but we pitched our tent northeast of Plainview and each one of us took up a section of land.

The next day after our arrival, three of the neighbors came in, as they were interested in all newcomers. There were several large families of children in the community, and they were wanting a teacher. They found out I was a teacher, and before they left they had employed me to teach the Mapes School, which was later called Fairview and then Prairieview. This community was called the Missouri Settlement. The Public Schools had been established, so they employed me to teach a school in a brush arbor in the summer before the school house was built. The men of the community went in together and built a school house with lumber freighted from Amarillo. I taught in the new school house for ten months, and before school was out, there was an average attendance of sixty children.

I also taught at Epworth before Hale City and Epworth went together and became Hale Center. I brought my organ from Gainesville and kept it in the school house for the children to sing by. I also taught for a while in Plainview. I recall an incident while I was teaching at Plainview that is amusing when I think of it now. L. A. Knight had a colored woman working for his wife and Dr. J. H. Wayland had a colored man. Pretty soon these colored folk got married, and by and by along came a little black baby. It was a great curiosity for none of the children in Plainview had ever seen a colored baby, so the whole school was dismissed and we all went over to Knights to see the first colored baby that was born in Hale County.

FREIGHTING
By R. M. Irick

In the fall of 1875, I got stuck on an old man's daughter and got married. Her name was Mandy Caroline Meyers. The Indians raided the country in Jack and Wise County up until 1874, and by 1875 the white people moved farther west. We came to the Staked Plains, arriving on June 28, 1889, and settled down on the Draw twelve miles from Plainview, just in the edge of Floyd County, in what is known as the Irick Community. When my five girls got big enough to go to school, I moved my family to Plainview. I had ten yoke of oxen and a house-moving outfit, so I moved my house from Floyd County. E. W. Dyer and I went into the grocery business together. I hauled the goods from Amarillo and he sold them. I first used my ten yoke of oxen to freight with but it took me fourteen days to make the trip to Amarillo and back. Then I freighted with twelve mules for a good many years—until we sold out our grocery business. Once they had me summoned on petit jury at the opening of Court. Old Judge Cockrell was District Judge. They were questioning me as to any reason I might have for not serving on the jury. I told the Judge that I didn't know that I had any legal excuse, but that I was running a twelve-mule team hauling groceries for the people to eat, and if they kept me there a week the whole town of Plainview would be out of food. He said, "You get on the road as quick as you can." About that time we went to Amarillo, and a blizzard came while we were on the road. The snow got to be fourteen inches deep and we couldn't find the road. Ollie Davis was with me. That time we stayed eleven days, and when we left Amarillo we only brought half a load.

The people of Tulia were out of groceries and they stopped us and demanded that I let them have my supplies, as the whole town of Tulia was out. I told them, "You can't have this. I am taking it to Plainview for the folk there to eat." They said they would buy it if I would sell it, but if I didn't they would take it anyway. I said, "In that case I will divide with you," so they took half of it. When I reached Plainview every man in town was at the store waiting for me, for the whole town was out of groceries. As I unloaded the sacks of flour, I could see a man going in every direction with a sack of flour over his shoulder.

THE OLD CLISBEE STAGE LINE
By J. H. Lutrick

In 1888, or somewhere near that time, a resident of the great Panhandle of Texas known as Clisbee established a stage route from Amarillo to Plainview, both for mail and passenger service. From Plainview the route lay east to Della Plain. He had no set schedule, but the stage left Amarillo each morning and arrived sometime during the day at Plainview, according to the speed and ability of the mules and whether they had to race over mud or dry dirt on the way. Clisbee went to Old Mexico for his supply of mules, buying about 150 or 300 Spanish mules for this stage route. He needed a large number for the frequent change of teams at the different Post Offices that he visited between Amarillo and Plainview. Whenever changes of teams were made, Mr. Curry, the driver, and his sons, would tie them to a snubbing post until he got the collars, hames and tugs all on, and they were hitched to the coach. Just how many changes of the team were made on the route, I can't say, but stops were made at Canyon, Happy, Tulia and Plainview. Happy was usually the dinner stop. Tom Scott was on the route from Plainview to Hale City, Estacado and Old Emma in Crosby County. We who lived out here depended on this stage line for our mail each day and some of our supplies. The stage between Amarillo and Plainview ran each way each day. Fare on the stage was eight or ten cents per mile and the distance was about ninety miles from Amarillo to Plainview and about 160 from Amarillo to Old Emma. It was good traveling for those who could stand it, but the tenderfoot had to hold on for dear life, for every one of those mules was a full brother to the other and they were all rearing to go when they were hitched up. This stage route operated for nineteen years.

A CATTLEMAN LEARNED TO FARM
By J. W. "Blue" Stevens

All my life I've worked with cattle, off and on. Back in 1894 I quit my job on the XIT Ranch and rode horseback from Spring Lake to Boyd, Texas, to get married. It took me eleven days, stopping two Sundays, for the distance was some three hundred miles. After we married we stayed there for two years trying to farm, but I didn't know anything about farming. My wife had to teach me how. Why, she even had to show me how to set a plow. But I couldn't make a living there, so I traded fifty head of yearlings to Mac McClain for a section of land southeast of Hale Center without looking at it. We lived on it a year or so and then bought two sections where we live now so that we could get more grass for our cattle. Later we leased several sections and finally bought more, for to make money on cattle, you have to have grass for them. I used to lease up other land and graze my cattle on it during the summer and in the fall bring them back to graze on my own grass for the winter. But land was cheap in the early day and we didn't realize what a wonderful farming country we were in. It was not until a man from Kansas pointed out that we had an advantage over their land that we saw that we could make more money by growing feedstuff to fatten the cattle before shipping to market. So we began to break small acreages and plant row crops for winter forage for the cattle. Gradually people discovered that this soil and climate would grow anything and more and more farmers moved in. It grew harder year by year to find grass for the cattle, but we planted row crops and leased grass here and there for a long time. We were the last ones in this country to turn loose of range cattle, but in the early twenties we sold our cattle, plowed up all the land and I have learned to farm. My wife once said to me, "Why can't you plow up a hundred acres of land and rent it out to somebody? They would make us more on that than we can make grazing it with cattle." But I didn't want to work with tenants. I told her I had rather hear a cow bawl than a renter. The bawling of a cow doesn't keep a cow man awake. But the country's settled up now and we have learned to farm.

PIONEER DAYS AS A SHEEP MAN
By R. B. C. Howell

It was in October, 1889, that I came here from Breckenridge, Texas. The climate itself was what brought me here to settle —a climate where one could sleep in the summer time, cool at night, no matter how warm it got during the day. I realized there was plenty of water here, and rich soil to make the grass grow like it did, though none of us realized that we were in a farming country. The fact is, I came to get where I would never see a sack of cotton again while I lived. I didn't know I was getting to a better farming country than where I came from. I was in the sheep business and came here to find range and water. Immediately I built fences, and improved my place generally, putting up a shed for 6,500 sheep with lumber I had bought and hired hauled from Amarillo. Then I started up here with seven men in my outfit to bring the 6,500 head of sheep. When we got to Stink Creek, the sheep had been without water for three days and nights. It was in the hot summer time and they ran into that water—an alkali, gyp and salt stream—and 4,500 of them died from drinking it. So I reached the Plains with only 1,976 head of the herd I had started with—lean, sick sheep, badly damaged from drinking that alkali water. But these did all right, and I kept them until I paid out my land and got my family in easy circumstances. The struggle was not so hard because my sheep produced my living and I raised lambs regardless of the seasons and didn't depend on farming. The County had just been organized a few months before I moved here, and Mr. Groff told me that one of the voting places was through the window in the back of my dugout. Whenever the heel flies got after the sheep they would get up on top of the dugout and during lambing time, the lambs would fall down the chimney into the dugout faster than the children could carry them out.

THE MERCANTILE BUSINESS IN 1890
By J. N. Donohoo

It was in September of 1890 when I first came to the Panhandle of Texas, prospecting for a location for a mercantile business. I thought this was a lovely country and I couldn't understand why there were not more people living here. I was reminded that this was a new country and that that was the way the whole of West Texas was being built up. The few people that were living in the country mostly lived in dugouts, but I liked them. They were very hospitable and showed me around through the country. There were some few people who had raised a little truck in patches, but the great majority of them made their living by raising cattle. There were no fences and the stock was all branded and turned loose on the public domain to run together until the round up in the spring when they were gathered up and each man picked out his brand.

After I had stayed in Plainview for several days I felt so much better that I decided to bring my family from Tennessee and locate, for my family physician had told me that I was in the first stages of tuberculosis, and I had come west looking for a healthful climate where I might regain my health. I went to St. Louis and bought a little stock of such goods as I thought I could sell in Plainview. I knew a real dry goods store would not succeed because there were not enough people in the country —not enough women. A heap of the people were bachelors. R. C. Ware had a little grocery store then and I effected a partnership with him. We had a nice little trade for we carried a good stock. We sold a heap of goods on credit, and I have asked people their names so I would know who to charge things to. People came a long distance to trade with us—from Floyd, Lubbock and Swisher Counties, and from ranches still farther away. One day a fellow came in with an order from a ranch to buy some groceries and supplies for the camp. He gave me a list he had made of the things he wanted and I started to look over it to see how many of the articles I had. I hadn't looked far until I stopped. "You want five gallons of 'lick'. I don't sell whiskey here." He told me "lick" was the cowboy's name for molasses. I went on down the list. "Half a dozen sugans. What's a sugan?" He pointed to some bed-quilts,

"Them things hangin' up there." The cowboys had names of their own for a great many things. I can't remember all of their vocabulary, but they kept me puzzled a great deal of the time.

Amarillo was the nearest trading point and all of our goods that we sold were hauled in wagons ninety miles to Plainview. It is interesting to know how those wagons were loaded and freighted down here. A man would hitch half a dozen teams of horses or mules to a wagon and trail two to four wagons behind, all fastened to the wheel wagons and they hauled a tremendous load of stuff. All of our groceries, supplies and coal were hauled that way. If it rained and the roads were very muddy, they stopped and left the wagons standing in the road, sometimes for two or three weeks, waiting for the road to dry up. Nobody ever thought of stealing anything out of the wagons.

I have never regretted moving to Plainview, though a great many changes have taken place during the years since I came.

EARLY MEDICAL PRACTICE
By Dr. J. H. Wayland

During the thirty years of my general practice on the Plains, from 1891 to 1921, going almost day and night on this broad expanse of territory, many and varied were my experiences. For many years my practice extended south far beyond Lubbock, north to Amarillo and near Childress, as far southeast as Matador, west to the ranches in New Mexico and northwest to Hereford including the XIT Ranch,—a territory of two to three hundred miles across this vast Llano Estacado. Many times I have run over a fence, not knowing it was there until I struck it in the dark hours of the night, endangering my life no little. The first fence was sixteen miles west of Plainview and the next one west was thirty five miles farther, near the old Spring Lake Ranch Headquarters. O course we had no road to travel and I had to go to these various points by directions given me by the cowboys who came after me. Many a dark night I have been kept at my wit's end to keep the proper course and not get lost out in the wilderness. At such times if a star was in sight, I would watch it between my horses' heads. I soon discovered that I must find some way of making these long trips and not get lost in doing so. I sent to Montgomery Ward's for a pocket compass, which I carried in my pocket for twenty years as I would a watch, and I found it true and reliable in directing me. In those early days, large deceptive lakes, known as mirages, ever floated out before me. I have been fooled by them no end of times by seeing some object that looked close to me, but which was in reality many miles away. The cowboys and settlers were always very kind in piloting me across roadless sections to a trail or some place from which I could find my way home, but in such cases I never lost sight of the instinct of my horses, for when I headed homeward, regardless of road or section, they always knew how to go. Even the old schreeching windmills on the range were great mileposts for me and the cowtrails leading to them often told of my approach to a well where I might get a refreshing drink for myself and team. These old watering places were like a beautiful oasis of the desert. I always carried feed in the back of my buggy and fed my horses out of the old-fashioned morral—a feed bag tied to their heads. Occasionally at night I would lie down on the ground beside my buggy and take a few minutes rest. Oftentimes I have been aroused by wolves coming near and sniffing in my face hunting some morsel of food. Even a polecat bit my ear and awakened me one night.

I have often been called to see some sick member of a family in a tent, in a dugout or only a wagon body covered with a wagon sheet, as there were no houses on the Plains at that time. However, I made many pleasant discoveries. Highly educated people, with University degrees, with a great desire for getting a home for themselves and their families were very cheerful pioneers of this country and were charming hosts in their humble dugouts. Many of the good women would line their dugouts with tow sacks, whitewash the walls and do many things to make their homes attractive. There were no nurses in those days, and I was not only physician, but nurse, washwoman and cook for many of my lady patients and I always took pleasure in washing and togging up a new born babe with material furnished me. Many times no provision had been made and I would have to wrap the infant up in a sheet. But the Lord was always with us in the speedy recovery of the mother and growth of a fine baby. Of course we did not have the advantages of the present day, but with all respect to these latter day medical theorists, I challenge them to show better success than I had then.

FRONTIER DAYS AS A MISSIONARY
By Rev. J. W. Winn

I came west from Kentucky searching for a Missionary field and landed in Plainview in the first part of July, 1892. When the Baptist Association convened at the Irick School House in Floyd County, I met Dr. I. B. Kimbrough, who asked me to preach on Sunday, and when the Association Board met, they extended me a call as Missionary. I said to the moderator, "You had better give this work to one of these other preachers. I don't have my credentials with me, and you don't know whether I run off from Kentucky where I done some devilment I wanted to get away from, or whether I am here to locate". He laughed and said, "We're not interested in what you did before you came here—we are interested in what you do while you are here." I moved my family here that fall and located on the extreme south line of Hale County in the "Homestead Strip". I built a dugout three feet in the ground, thirteen feet wide and twenty-eight feet long with a partition in it, covered it with 1 x 12 boards and threw dirt on top of that for a roof —had two windows on each side and a door in each end. That first winter my married son, married daughter and six grand children stayed with us, and with myself and wife and eight unmarried children there were twenty of us wintered there in that little dugout. We had a garden, cows, and some pigs and we got through all right. While I was away in the mission work, my wife and children would gather up enough cow chips to use for fuel to run through the winter.

In the spring of the year I took up my mission work. I furnished my own conveyance and the State Board and Association each paid me $150 per year. My work was to look after the churches that did not have pastors and the first church I visited that did not have a pastor was the Baptist Church at Lubbock. They hadn't had any preaching there for more than a year when I came and the members had scattered. I held a series of meetings for them lasting a week or ten days and there were a few professions. At the close of the services we had a baptizing in Mr. George Bowles' tank east of Lubbock. A large per cent of the people who attended stated they had never seen a person immersed before. I went from there to Old Emma, the countyseat of Crosby County, and held a meeting there. I think there were about six or seven members there that went into the church as charter members. I preached as a Missionary there for five years before I found them a pastor. I preached the first sermon that was ever preached in Lamb County and organized a church after they built a school house. The next Sunday I preached in the northeast corner of Dickens County. It took me a week to go from one place to the other, visiting the homes as I went. When the wind blew severely in the winter time, I would go with the wind to my back. When I got up in the morning, whichever way the wind blew was the way I would travel. If it changed during the day, I would change my course accordingly. No one knows what I went through in those blizzards out on the open prairies and at times I almost perished, but I never got lost for my horses knew the way. When the Baptist Convention met at Dallas they launched a campaign to build the Baptist Sanitarium at that place. I was getting $300 a year, but I gave them $100 to start the Sanitarium. When I got home my wife met me with tears in her eyes, for she had read in the Dallas News what I had done. She said, "I believe you will give away everything you make." I tried to assure her that I would take care of her, but it was hard to convince her. A few weeks afterward, we received two Missionary boxes from Ladies Aid Societies —one from Virginia and another from North Carolina. They had made inquiries concerning my family and in each of these boxes were garments for each member of my family, including shoes, etc., and two heavy overcoats for myself. I told my wife to set a value on each piece and add them up. I had my $100 back and she priced them low enough, too. When I sold my homestead some years later, I built a ten room home in Plainview for my faithful wife and family and was finally able to give her the comforts she well deserved. There were hardships a-plenty in those early days and the wolves howled around my dugout door both literally and figuratively, but there were joys as well as hardships in the work of a frontier missionary.

PIONEERING THE "HERALD"
By J. M. Shafer

The first time I crossed these Plains was in 1878, while enroute from Denver, Colorado to Stephensville. There was not a living thing on the Staked Plains at that time except prairie dogs, rattlesnakes and jackrabbits between the Pecos River and where we struck the Concho. We drove for two days and nights without water. That was a desolate stretch of country we passed on that trip. In June 1890, I moved to this county from Stephensville. Plainview wasn't much of a town then. There was only one house in town that had a coat of paint. John G. Davidson had started a newspaper. He didn't run the paper but a short time until he sold to a Mr. Cates and I bought it from him. Cates starved out at it. Davidson did, too. I reckon I would have, if my wife hadn't kept boarders. I traded a pair of ponies and a wagon for the printing office and the lot and building. The office was fourteen feet square. It had a little old hand roller sausage grinder press, a small roller over a frame. I built it up with new type and press and new material. I had a boy old enough to look after the printing. I was kept pretty busy working to make both ends meet and had a pretty hard row to hoe for quite a while, but I got a nice advertising business out of Amarillo where I went once a month to collect on advertising and get new work. Later I lost my printing office by fire. The Plainview News allowed me to use their plant until a new one arrived. I hauled the brick from Amarillo to build the new Herald office. It was almost the first brick building in town.

When I first came here the wind used to howl across these open prairies and a tenderfoot, on losing his hat, would chase it for miles, while a cowboy would just sit down and wait for another one to come along. (That is what they used to tell, anyway.) Everybody, sooner or later, had a chase for his hat. It is strange, when a hat blows off it will stand right up on edge and roll like the wheel of a wheelbarrow. I was going home from the printing office one evening and there was a barrel traveling ahead of me, just rolling along. Finally it came to my fence and it jumped the fence. I was a-horse-back. I had to go through two gates to get to the pasture, and when I looked up, the barrel was nearly across the field. I started after it, but before I got anywhere near, it jumped over another fence and kept going. I couldn't get through the fence without riding a mile back so I gave it up. I don't know what became of that barrel. For all I know it may be going yet. The wind never came from the north long enough to bring it back.

THE GRASSHOPPER PLAGUE
By Anson Cox

Along about 1891 or 1892 there was noticed an unusual number of grasshoppers but no damage was done to the crops that year. The ground, however, was perforated with little holes, and the next spring as I was plowing, millions of little things about the size of fleas hopped up and down. Upon examination they proved to be grasshoppers. They soon became large enough to be noticed everywhere and began eating.

One of our farmers near Estacado had a beautiful field of wheat. The hoppers were more numerous in the grass, but soon left the grass as the wheat began to grow. Our farmer declared they should not eat his wheat. Having a large family of children and a load of brush on hand, he armed each child with a brush broom to kill the hoppers as they passed a furrow he had plowed around the field. Then he hitched his team to a large log and drove the horses at a trot along the furrow, crushing the hoppers as they gathered in the furrow. But all in vain. After an hour or two he gave up. The hoppers grew fast and ate every green thing in sight except Bull thistles and Yucca plants. They crawled right over sod houses or into them if the doors were opened. They seemed to go toward the east all the time. I thought I could save my garden. I had a large earth tank about two feet above the level of the land. I made a ditch around it and let the water in, but the hoppers marched in, filled the ditch with drowned hoppers, then others marched on over them and feasted on my garden.

There was desolation everywhere—everything green gone as bare as though there had never been any vegetation. Those who have never seen such a pest have no idea of the destruction they cause.

FIRST BUSINESS WOMAN
By Mrs. J. L. Vaughn

I came to Plainview in December, 1889, to visit my brother, Thornton Jones, coming from Lancaster, Kentucky by train to Amarillo. Mrs. Jones came with me and all the way she kept telling me about the dugouts. When we reached the place where Tulia is, they came to a little hole in the ground, stopped the team and got out. I thought they were playing a joke on me, but while they were trying to persuade me to get out, I saw a little woman come up out of that hole in the ground—the nicest, cleanest little woman coming up those steps. Well I got out and went into her dugout. She was Mrs. Truss Gray and she had the loveliest supper for us. I remember the nice juicy steak and delicious preserves she had with other things. She had little bedrooms curtained off and we stayed all night there. There was no house between Canyon and Mrs. Gray's, and only three buildings in Canyon. Plainview had just a few people and beyond Plainview was Estacado. I first moved to Dimmitt and remained until 1893, when I came to Plainview and opened a dry goods store, selling millinery, notions and ladies' furnishings. The women used to get together in my store in the afternoons and visit. At that time all the women wore bonnets and I sold some of them the first hats they ever owned. People used to buy a hat and make it last them several years and children's hats would be handed down from one child to another. There were no silk dresses in those days and women all wore calico or gingham. My store was on the west side of the square just north of where the Ware Hotel now stands. I ran my store here until 1898 and I never did lock it. In fact, I didn't have any lock. Anyone that wanted to could go in and get what they wanted, and leave the money. My brother, Thornton Jones, had a grocery store and he used to leave it with Brother Will when he had to go away. When Will didn't have much to do he would go over to Kiser's to visit with the girls and leave the store to run itself. One day a cowboy came by for some tobacco. It was the custom if there was no one at a store to go in, get what you wanted and leave the money or charge yourself up with it and go on. This cowboy was a mischievous fellow and he wrote a sign on the outside of the tent which housed the store, "If you want tobacco, go to Jones—if you want Jones, go to Kiser's."

TALMAGE'S SERMON
By J. Frank Norfleet

The first twelve months that I stayed on the Spade Ranch, I spent fifty five cents of my year's wages. I spent all that for stamps and stationery to write to my mother. Right there on that ranch I learned a great lesson. I didn't know I was learn-it then. I took a notion that I was not going to let the boys gamble in my camp, because I had seen serious difficulties arise over a game of cards, and to keep things from going that way, I refused to allow any gambling. The boys would come out there in bunches looking for work. They would leave home just before the spring term of court and most of them thought when they got away from home they had to "act like men." They wanted to be tough, and carry a six-shooter, and gamble, and they made themselves at home generally, so I had to take care of them and see that they didn't do things to get them into more trouble. I got hold of an old newspaper that had a sermon in it by Dr. DeWitt Talmage (I don't recall how I got it—perhaps my mother sent it to me) and while they were sitting around of a night I would get that out and read it to them. The text of it was "A Wayward Son is the Heaviness of His Mother." I want to tell you, I never finished reading that sermon to one single boy or bunch of them, but what just about the time I got through, someone would say, "Don't you reckon it's about time to turn the horses out?" and when they got outside the door I could see them get out their old big red bandana handkerchiefs and wipe their eyes. During the past few years I have met several of those boys that came to the old Spade Ranch in those early days and they said to me, "Norfleet, do you remember the first time I ever saw you? It was over at your camp on the Spade Ranch. Do you remember the night you read Talmages' Sermon to us?" Those boys never forgot that lesson, coming to them at such an unexpected time, and it has been a great lesson to me, for we never know what we are doing when we say the right things to a boy. "Mother" is a word that comes first with a boy, especially if he is away from home. To make him think of his mother at a time when he needs help most saves many a boy from ruin.

EARLY TRIAL BY JURY
By D. C. Lowe

When one of the large ranches was established, they found located in the finest of their holdings a man who had settled on a very desirable piece of property. They tried to buy him out, but he told them the property just suited him and that it was not for sale. He also told them that he would be glad to live with them in peace, but his friendly spirit did not appeal to the ranchmen. When they found they could not buy him out, they determined to run him out. In those days there were lots of Mavericks on the range—calves that had been weaned and had not been branded. The law was that a Maverick calf was the property of whoever first branded it. Well, the friction grew between the ranchers and the settler and finally they got some cases in court accusing him of putting his brand upon some thirteen of their calves. They thought they could get rid of him that way if by no other. All this country was attached to Hale County for Judicial purposes so of course they had to come to Plainview for trial. The lawyers representing both sides got together and agreed to try one case and let the decision of the thirteen cases rest on the decision of the one. When the jury was selected for the trial of the first case, Thornton Jones was selected as a juror. His sister, Mrs. Stringfellow, was visiting with Mrs. Jones while her husband attended the trial. The children were playing in the yard. They had a dug well near the house, about fifteen feet deep and it stood some four feet in water. While they were playing around it, one of the little ones fell in the well. Mrs. Jones jumped into the well to save the baby. She could stand up in the well and hold the baby out of the water, but she could not get out, and neither could Mrs. Stringfellow get her out. So one of the children ran to the Court House, right into the courtroom and straight up to the jury box where her father was sitting on the jury trying this case and shouted, "Papa! Mamma and the baby are in the well!" Jones did not wait to be excused or even to ask leave. He just ran out of there and made for home and the whole assembly—jury, judge and all —followed to a man to help get his wife and baby out of the well. When they came back and had assembled in the courtroom to proceed with the trial, the defense attorney arose with dignity and addressed the court: "Your Honor! Since my client has been on trial, the jury in this case has been permitted to leave the courtroom without proper guard and they have mixed and commingled with the world and are therefore no longer eligible as jurors in this case. I move the court that this case be declared a mistrial." The motion was granted by the court and the case was continued from time to time until it was finally thrown out of court. They had agreed that the decision of the remaining cases should hinge upon the decision of the first, so because the baby fell in the well, the whole thirteen cases were thrown out and the defendant went free.

THE JUMPING OFF PLACE
By Martha Glover

When we arrived in Amarillo on October 23, 1890, on our way to Hale County, we thought we were at the "'jumping off place." My invalid mother, my brother, Will Glover, and I had come with the Jim Harrel family. The rush of settlers started in June of that year and most of them lived in dugouts. But I told them we would be under ground long enough, so we built a box house. They said we would freeze in a house above ground, but we didn't. We had brought a month's supplies with us and my brother freighted and kept us in provisions for a year or so. In the next few years the drouth came, and the grasshoppers, and people were leaving. Some of our neighbors went to Plainview to get ready to leave and finally the time came when we planned to leave the next day. We had got all ready to go. Then Will met some boys from the XIT Ranch who told him they needed a man, so he went right out with them. He sent someone to tell us and asked that we send his clothes to him when the next freighter passed our way. For several years while my brother was working on the XIT Ranch, I worked and supported mother and myself so that we could put all the money

Will made into cattle. He would get off from his work long enough to put in our crop and then go back to the ranch. I would tend the crop and look after the cattle in his absence and in that way we got our start. We worked hard, but it takes hard work to accumulate anything, and we had lots of fun in those days along with our work.

The second morning after we came, there loomed one of those mirages. It was the sand hills, fifteen miles south of us, but they looked like they were right out in our field. I said, "Yonder it is, right over there!" For then I knew we had got to the jumping off place.

EARLY DAYS IN THE CATTLE INDUSTRY
By J. C. Hooper

When I came to Hale County from Gainesville in 1898, I located eight miles west of Plainview. I had sold my cattle before I came, and bought fifty head of whiteface cattle here to start my herd. I kept those and increased the herd from time to time until I had quite a few cattle. We had no fences for the cattle in the early days; the range was open and everyone ran the cattle together. Then at round up time we would gather them up and cut out each man's cattle according to his brand. I started to farm some in 1899 and raised some kafir corn and milo maize to feed to the stock during the winter. There was of course no market for farm products until after the coming of the railroad. Therefore, what little farming there was here prior to that was for the purpose of producing only what could be consumed on the farm or fed to stock. Cattle raising was for that reason the major industry from the time of the first settlement until the coming of the railroad in 1907 provided marketing facilities for the many other products which the Plains soil and water made profitable. There was not much fence building done until 1905. At that time I hauled my fence wire from Canyon and went to the breaks east of here and cut our cedar posts. In this way it cost us about $100 a mile to build fences at that time. Most fences in those days were just two wire fences, though around the fields we used three wires. The prairie fires were the terror of the early settlers, not only because they completely destroyed the supply of range grass for the cattle, but even in some cases burned the cattle themselves, as well as houses, windmills, etc. The first year I was here a prairie fire swept the country and burned all the way to the caprock before they could get it under control. The grass was high and burned faster than our horses could run. Everybody turned out to help fight it for though we couldn't stop the head fire, we could hold the sideline fire from spreading. Those who have never seen one cannot imagine the terror a prairie fire brought to the early settler.

CATTLE IN A STORM
By R. W. (Uncle Bob) Lemond

I have stood guard around cattle at night when the hail was as large as hen eggs, and one could see the lightning flash all over the herd. It would roll off their horns like balls of fire. The cattle would not run while it was raining or hailing, but would huddle up and wait until it was over. Then they would be sure to get scared at something and begin to run. I have actually rode around a herd and followed the cattle all night long. I would stop them for a while and they would run again; I would stop them again, and again they would run. But in this country when we had a stampede there was no possible danger except when your horse stepped in a prairie dog hole. There were no fences, ravines or gullies; still you couldn't help feeling a little uneasy when three or four thousand cattle were coming right behind you on a dark night. The cowboys, riding around the cattle, would sing to them to get them quiet. Two would ride at a time for two hours, then two more would go on for two hours, etc. These were called guards. The first and second guard were always considered the hardest because after that the cattle were usually bedded and quiet. The songs the boys sang most were "Bury me not on the lone prairie" and "Mable Clair." When a stampede came up in the night, the guard would call some of the boys out of their nice warm beds to go help with the cattle. Lots of times the boys would just get in their beds and be called right out and maybe when they came back the beds would all be wet; but that was a part of the cowboy's life, and he was always ready to help when needed.

MY "HOME ON THE RANGE"
By Mrs. J. E. Cox

We were married on December 28, 1898, and on the first of the year we moved to the little dugout home which Jim had prepared for his bride. Green Wilson and my husband had leased four leagues of school land together. Tom Wilson, Green's brother, moved out and was our only neighbor. The dugout was 16 x 18 feet, was four feet in the ground and built of plank a few feet above the ground to accommodate windows and was covered with a board roof. The furnishings consisted of a built-in bunk, built-in table made of plank, a little wood cookstove in which we burned cow chips and a little table behind the stove on which we always kept a jar of sour dough to keep it ready to make our sour dough biscuits. We lived in that dugout for four winters. There were weeks at a time that Jim and I wouldn't see a soul but each other. You can't imagine the quiet, serene happiness that we experienced those four years. There was a peace that is lacking in modern civilization.

I got much pleasure chasing the antelopes and killing them for meat. We would get them on the hard ground in the north end of the pasture away from the sand hills. I would ride ahead and turn them facing Jim, for they always ran in a circle. He would dismount and stand beside his horse, holding the bridle rein on his arm, while I would turn the circle of antelopes, each time getting them a little closer until they were in shooting distance. Jim had so keen an eye that he always let them circle several times, before he found one that he thought would be perfect meat. Often I thought they would get away from me before he would shoot.

The prairie fire was the dread of our lives, especially in the sand hills where the grass grew high. One night we were awakened by a big fire. We had a west window and the light from the fire illuminated the whole room. Jim's first thought was of his horse and saddle to go fight the fire. I was afraid to be left alone, but Jim hesitated to take me along for you never could tell how far away the fire might be. But he saddled Jim Lane with my sidesaddle, tied his slicker behind his saddle, and we met the head fire at Janes Brothers pasture twelve miles away. We rode the side of the line fire and Jim started fighting the fire, whipping out the flames with his slicker, while I held his horse. It was not long until more cowboys came, and at one time I was holding eight horses. A cowboy hung his bridle rein on the horn of Jim's saddle, and the next one who came hung his rein on the saddlehorn of the last horse, trailing a string of horses behind. Mack Huffman of the Spring Lake Ranch had some beeves killed and cut in quarters and the boys tied ropes to these and drug them one after the other on the flame to put out the side fire. The boys' faces were black from the burned grass and they were so fatigued they could hardly walk. I remember Sam Hooker, Ed Green, Mack Huffman and Jarret and John Janes went home with us for breakfast. I cooked for those boys and they drank coffee and ate sourdough biscuits faster than I could cook them.

THE METEOR
By R. A. McWhorter

One night in the fall of 1882, the Quakers going home from church were startled to see a meteor shoot across the sky, lighting the entire country. From the intensity of its light they concluded it had fallen to earth somewhere near Estacado, but they never found it. A year or so later a cowboy found it five miles north and a little east of the present town of Abernathy. It dug a hole in the ground where it fell, but it must have bounced out for it was lying on the ground a foot or more from the hole and was broken into two pieces. The large piece was wedge shaped and was about as high as a chair, and it weighed 650 pounds. The smaller piece weighed 300 pounds. After I moved out here in 1892, I carried it to my home in a wagon. It took several men to lift it. I brought it home with me and set it on the ground just outside my dugout and we used it for a washstand for a couple of years. I have had at least thirty people tell me they aimed to go get it and take it home, but they didn't do it, and it lay where it fell for ten years before I got it. I sent some little chips of it to the museum in Washington to see if they would pay me anything for it. They finally wrote me to wrap it up in tow sacks and label it "iron ore," and send a draft for

$500.00 with bill of lading, which I did. A few years ago Homer Minor said he was in the East and he saw it in the museum and it had my name on it. Of course we missed the washstand, as we had grown used to it standing there just outside the dugout, but that $500 came in pretty handy to help out with our living expenses.

THE INDIAN SCARE OF 1891
By Mrs. J. O. Oswald

The most startling thing that ever happened to Plainview was the Indian scare of 1891. After fifteen years of peace and quietness on the Plains, the terror of the savages had been forgotten. Suddenly out of a clear sky came the cry, "Indians are coming!" A messenger raced through the country heralding the news and notified the homesteaders and the people came from all over the prairie into Plainview for protection. The people rushed to the Court House and the men got all the lumber in town and built a barracks around the Court House. But there wasn't enough lumber in Plainview to build a barracks large enough to hold all the people, so a lot of them stayed in their homes and prepared to defend themselves with guns and clubs. A man went through the country with a wagon, picking up the women and children and bringing them to town for safety. He went past one place where an old woman lived all alone who was not afraid of the devil himself so he didn't stop to tell her. He knew she wouldn't pay any attention. At the next house he stopped and told the woman the Indians were in the breaks and were headed this way, that he was sorry but he couldn't bring her for his wagon wouldn't hold any more. She rushed over to that old woman's house and reported the news. The old lady said "Let 'em come! I'll protect you." And she barred the door and got her guns. They sat up all night with their guns pointed toward the door ready to shoot. I was spending the night with my cousin out in the country. My uncle came home all worked up for he firmly believed it, but they didn't go to town. Aunt wouldn't let us burn the light that night and we were afraid to go from room to room. I was worried for I knew my father had gone to the breaks to get a load of posts. After breakfast next morning I went home as quickly as I could. Mother said to us, "Well, children, the Indians are in the breaks and your pa is gone. I reckon we won't see him any more." We all broke down and cried. The people in Plainview stayed all night and the following day in the barracks waiting for the Indians to come. We never knew how the story started, but Indians never again molested the Plains.

WHY BOYS LEAVE HOME
By M. M. Day

When boys leave home, they generally have a reason for it. They don't just go. Something happened that they couldn't face. There's always a reason for it, and I'll tell you mine.

When I was a lad of fourteen a man lived near us whose horses had been getting into our corn all fall. Mother woke me and my brother about ten o'clock one night and told us to go out and get the horses out of our corn. We went down and got them out. About twelve o'clock mother heard the bell on the lead horse and called us again to get the horses out. About two o'clock she called us again. I was so sleepy and so tired of being awakened every two hours to drive the horses out that I had about enough. As we went out the gate, I picked up a piece of rawhide about four feet long, went out and caught this horse that had the bell on it, and tied a bundle of fodder to the horse's tail with the rawhide and set it afire. I thought it would scare her and she would soon kick it off and run away, and I went back to bed. But she couldn't kick it off for the rawhide drew up all the tighter when it got hot. She ran over the fence and all over the whole countryside and set the woods on fire for three or four miles around. Next morning I was awakened by my mother calling me. The old man who owned the horse was there and the whole country was burning. Mother asked me if I did it. I knew I had done wrong to do it, but there was no use to lie about it, so I told the truth. My Uncle Jack Broadfoot, who raised us boys, came up through the plum orchard just then. The old man and mother commenced to tell him. He said, "Marion, what happened?" and I told him. He was walking with a cane and he jabbed this old man and said, "Your horses have been eating up these boys' crop every year—now get out of here." He told mother not to whip me and went away. After a while he came back and said to me, "Marion, I expect you had better get out of here for a while. The fire has burned up forty sheep for one man. It's an awful fire." I got on my pony that night about ten o'clock and the next night I rode into Montague County. There I got a job with a cow outfit and worked on west with ranches until I went to work on the Circle Ranch for Rufe O'Keefe, where I worked for some years. I have been back home only once since the woods burned. They were having a camp meeting and I went, and stood around, but I felt so guilty I didn't have a good time, so I left and never went back.

MOVING THE HALE CITY SCHOOL HOUSE
By N. M. Akeson

The two towns of Hale City and Epworth, only two miles apart, flourished during 1891 and 1892 as each had hopes of securing a railroad. The drouth caused some of the people to leave, however, and in 1893 the people in both towns got tired of keeping up two towns and wanted to go together as one. They decided to select a new townsite and move all the buildings from both towns to the new site which they named Hale Center. In the summer of 1893 the men from both communities got together with their teams to move the Hale City School House to Hale Center. They got it on wheels and started across the unbroken prairie from northwest to southeast. When they had almost reached the edge of the townsite, the sheriff arrived with an injunction enjoining them from moving the school house off of the Hale City townsite. It seemed one of the citizens who had helped to build the school house opposed the moving of it until he should be reimbursed for what he had put into it. It remained standing for some time on the corner of the townsite. The time came to open school and still not a man could touch it. But the Epworth School had burned down and this was their only school house. Finally they fell upon the idea that the women were not enjoined from moving it, so on a day selected, all the women from both towns turned out and moved the school house to Hale Center.

Of course, you understand, the men attended to the horses, but the women were all there commandeering the men, and they got the job done.

EARLY SOCIAL LIFE
By Mrs. L. A. Knight

In the early days here all ranches gave big dances, or house parties as we would call them now, usually when the cowboys were getting ready for their round-ups, or had just finished. I remember best one at the XIT Ranch. The news of the dance had spread from person to person, for everybody was invited. The young men made their dates with the young ladies to take them and on arrival were free to join any amusement desired. For there was a dance in one room, "42" or cards in another and in still another all sorts of games to amuse those that didn't want to play cards or dance. They had good music, for usually among the cowboys there was someone that played the violin and the banjo. At the dinner hour they opened the dining room and there was a long table loaded with an abundance of food—roast beef, baked hams, potatoes, beans and all kinds of cakes. I remember that the ladies all ate first, and then the men, though the dining room was kept open all during the evening, and anyone that wanted to could eat, no matter when. In the wee small hours a few who wanted to rest did so, the ladies in one house and the men in what they used to call the bunk house. There were very few of them that slept very much, though the party lasted three days.

Another dance I well remember was at Frank Norfleet's, just after George Callup's wedding. It began to snow on us just a little bit before we got there, and by the time supper was ready, the ground was covered with snow. The house was open to everybody and I guess everybody in the country came, and we danced and played games until nearly morning. The next morning the ground was covered with eighteen inches of snow as level and pretty as could be. Mr. Norfleet had a lot of grayhounds, so someone suggested we have a rabbit hunt. We got out all the horses and quite a crowd of us chased the rabbits. They could not run very well in the deep snow but the dogs were so long legged they could get over the snow and they caught a lot of rabbits. That night we danced the same as before, with eats all through the evening. The morning after, we took our departure, having had one of the most pleasant times I can remember.

A CHRISTMAS FESTIVITY
By Mrs. W. A. Lowe

In the early nineties, I lived in the community of the Progress School which is the school now called Ellen. The young folk used to like to get together and as there were very few homes large enough to have parties in, we used the schoolhouse for gatherings of all kinds. Our early homes were dugouts and it was difficult to have a party on a dirt floor. Whenever we did, the young folk all had to sit around and play games that had little action so they wouldn't raise too much dust. I think it was the Christmas of 1892 that we all went to the Progress School house to eat Christmas dinner together. The whole neighborhood for seven miles around brought their dinners and we all ate together. One of the important features of a Christmas dinner was to have cake, for we had very little sweets and a cake was a real treat. Harrison Portwood had given my little boy a leghorn hen and a rooster and the hen had been laying, so I was saving the eggs to make a cake for Christmas. Mrs. Portwood didn't have any eggs as her hens were not laying, and I thought I could save up enough eggs by Christmas to make both her cake and mine. But a coyote caught my hen when I only had two eggs saved up and there was no way to get any more. The day before Christmas I baked a one egg cake and walked a mile to take Mrs. Portwood the other egg to make her cake with. Mattie Matsler had come over to stay all night with the Portwoods so she baked the cake. A cowboy named Tommy Harral who was working at Amarillo on a ranch, was coming down to spend Christmas with the Portwoods. On his way, he stopped at a house and bought a dozen eggs for Mrs. Portwood, paying a dollar for them. He tied them up in a red bandana and carried them on his arm all the way, arriving at midnight. The girls got up when they heard about the eggs and baked cakes until daybreak. When I got over to the Portwoods' on Christmas morning, Mrs. Portwood had a big surprise for me when she showed me all the cakes the girls had baked. That was a happy Christmas, for we all had plenty of cake with which to celebrate.

EARLY ROMANCE
By B. H. Towery

No one living on the Plains now can imagine what the country was like forty years back unless they were here then. I often wonder what the young people of today would do if there were no more way of entertainment than there was at that time. We sometimes would gather at some nester's house and have a party and find that some had ridden horseback twenty to thirty miles to get there. How would a young man feel today if he had a date with a young lady to take her some place and she were to go out and rope a wild mustang and saddle it to ride? This was often done during that time. I remember one time I went to a young lady's house to invite her to a party and she told me that she was going to a party that night and if I wanted to go along with her it would save me quite a lot of riding for I would see all the young people in that neighborhood at that party and could invite them. I agreed to go, so she asked me to go out on the range and get her a horse. I did so, bringing up a small herd of ponies. She opened the corral gate and I penned the horses. She roped the one she wanted, saddled it and when she was ready to go, she had me get on my horse and draw the head of her horse up to the horn of my saddle until she could mount. I did not speak half a dozen words to her from that time until we arrived at the place about ten miles from her home for the party, for I could never get closer than forty or fifty yards of her.

I had come to the Plains to take care of a small ranch stocked with cattle which my father had bought in the summer of 1893, near what was then the Post Office of Whitfield. Having lived with the stock for more than three years, I began to tire of the life and want to be back with the folks at home, but one day while riding across the prairie I happened up on a dugout from the rear. Imagine my feelings when a very pretty girl came out of the place and invited me to lunch! After this visit I began to lose the longing to go home, for my visits to the dugout became regular and after a time, I convinced these people that it was not good for a man to live alone and talked them out of this young lady.

THE FIRST CHURCH WEDDING
By Mrs. Mary V. Dye

The first church wedding in Hale County was that of Miss Eugenia Welter and Mr. William H. Beyette. Miss Welter was a teacher in the Plainview School and Mr. Beyette was a young preacher. The ceremonies took place in the little Methodist Church in Plainview on October 31, 1894, and the Methodist pastor, Rev. J. T. Bloodworth, officiated. The entire town was greatly excited over the event and everybody wanted to have a part in the preparation for it. But what to do with the church was a question. It was not painted, had bare walls and floors of rough lumber, and home-made pews. We all put our heads together and decided what could be done to beautify it and make it suitable for a wedding. We bought cheese cloth and made curtains for the windows. Mrs. R. C. Ware had been to St. Louis and had learned how to make paper flowers and she showed us how. We made a bell of white morning-glories, which we suspended from a large coaloil lamp which hung from the ceiling in front of the pulpit. I had a rag carpet that I had brought with me from Tennessee, and we took that up off the floor, ripped the strips apart and carpeted the aisles with it. The church was lighted with coaloil lamps. The bride wore a white satin wedding dress with a long train. She was a beautiful girl and the groom was tall and dark and they made a handsome couple. Ione Burch was bridesmaid. The wedding went off beautifully, after which all repaired to the parsonage next door and cut the wedding cake. Mrs. Beyette is now living in Downey, California.

STARTING THE TOWN OF PETERSBURG
By Ed M. White

The starting of the town of Petersburg was not an accident, but it grew out of an accident in which I was crippled and paralyzed from the fall from a horse. Old Captain Peters, who was a captain in the Union Army during the Civil War, got a post office which was kept in his home in Floyd County, four miles north and one east of Petersburg. He was moving away and wanted someone to take the Post Office off his hands. The settlers wanted me to take it. I didn't want to but my wife told me I had better take it, as I couldn't do anything else and it would take my mind off of other things. So I took it and moved it to Hale County. My first quarterly payment was $5.00 for keeping the Post Office. Afterward it ran up until we got about $200 per quarter. My wife persuaded me to get a stock of goods and keep a store in connection with the Post Office. We did pretty well with it, though Jesse Boyd said he could have carried my stock of goods on his shoulder. It wasn't long until I was keeping two or three wagons on the road hauling goods from Amarillo for my store. People had to go to Plainview, Floydada or Lubbock to trade, so my store was at a location best situated to supply those in the community. I added a stock of hardware to my general store, but later I went into the hardware business. In spite of the serious accident that changed the course of my life, I regained my health and have passed my ninetieth birthday. Petersburg is still my home, though the antelopes and the wild horses that once raced about the prairies near my home have vanished and the motor cars race past my door in their stead.

EARLY GRAIN BUSINESS
By L. F. Cobb

I got started in the grain business in Odessa, Missouri. I was working for an elevator man at one dollar per day, and when business got slack, he put me to hoeing sweet potatoes. I told him I thought I was too smart to hoe sweet potatoes, and so I fired myself and went into the grain business for myself. I moved to Happy in 1906—my two daughters and I— and built a grain business there. At that time there was nothing but the prairie. In those days we had to go fifteen or twenty miles to find a little crop to load in with another shipment to make out a car load. I often had some grain to ship and in order to make out a car load I would take my horse and buggy and drive all over the prairie to find a little bit of grain to complete a carload shipment. I was at Happy when the first railroad came to Plainview. We built elevators at Happy, Tulia and Plainview and when the railroad built to Lockney and Aiken, we built there. The business was known as Cobb and Elliott. We came to Plainview in 1907 soon after the railroad came. The first wheat we shipped out of Plainview was hauled from down about old Emma, some sixty five miles. A fellow named Leatherwood sold me a car of wheat that was three years old. He said he had been waiting three years for the railroad to haul his wheat off. When we dumped the wagon, we took out the endgate and dumped the wheat out, lifting up the front wheels to do so. He stood and looked at it and said: "Broke end, just as I expected." He had never seen anyone dump a wagon and he thought the end was broken and had spilled the wheat out. He couldn't understand the elevator. He couldn't see why the wheat went down and went up again. One fellow asked what that big coal chute was and I told him it was an egg renovator and that the railroad put it up to keep eggs in, and he believed it. The Banks in those days stayed open till nine or ten o'clock at night. They were not uneasy about being robbed and nobody ever bothered them. We didn't have a chance to deposit any money until late at night and lots of times we would bring up $1,000 to $1500 to deposit.

A FULL MEAL
By R. W. O'Keefe

In 1883 I took charge of the Circle Ranch, better known as the Runningwater Land and Cattle Company. When I came, there was only one settler, Mr. Horatio Graves, though about 1886 more settlers began to come in. A funny thing happened one day in the summer of 1887. One of my men had been down along the Runningwater Draw and came back and reported that they were going to start a town down at the Hackberry Groves. The owner of the ranch had written me to discourage all that I could the settlement of the country and to use any legal means possible to prevent it. I didn't think there was any need of opposition. I told him I would eat all the town they ever built there. I think I'd have a good big meal now, though I like Plainview mighty well.

THE COMING OF THE RAILROAD
By Emma Grigsby Meharg

For years the early settlers dreamed and worked to secure a railroad into Hale County. The early years of struggle had been lightened by this vision and hope spurred them on to realization. The Santa Fe Railroad at last rewarded them by building into Plainview and the first train was scheduled to arrive on the afternoon of December 31, 1906. When this news came, plans were made for the greatest celebration the county had ever known. The citizens had busied themselves for weeks and months in preparing to keep up the Plains reputation for feeding everybody that came to see them. For days prior to the event, the Committee on Foods distributed to the housewives of the town dray loads of food stuffs that had been freighted from Amarillo. This they cooked into delectable dishes which were collected on the morning of the celebration and taken to the barbecue pits to be served with the barbecued beeves, mutton and "goat." Coffee was made in wash pots containing from 20 to 40 gallons each. Long tables were constructed on the site of the present Sante Fe depot, upon which the foods were distributed. Toward noon it was learned that the train would not make it into the station by noon, so the pick and choice of all the foods was loaded into cartons and tubs and sent up the road to where the workmen stopped to eat. There was a dray load—I mean packed. The people who came to witness the incoming of the train were served in quantities almost unheard of, until the thousands had eaten.

When the workmen finally sent word that they would be down to the site of the present station by four o'clock, many of the people, eager to see the arrival of the first train, started out in droves to meet it, on horseback, with buggies, wagons and canvas covered hacks. They were strung out along the right of way for possibly two miles. When the train whistled for the first time, it brought such a thrill that even people who came from countries where they had known and seen trains were almost frightened. Needless to say, the horses which were hitched to the vehicles had never seen a train and never heard a whistle. They broke and ran in every direction over these prairies. They fairly flew as there was nothing to stop them. That was so much fun for the train crew that they added steam and blew the harder to see the horses run. Many of the local citizens had never seen a train before. The crowd lingered until the twilight scattered them. All the South Plains and even many counties of the north plains were represented.

It was a red letter day for Plainview and the surrounding country. They were realizing their dream of the years and felt that much had been accomplished by their efforts and years of waiting. At last the South Plains was getting a gangway opened to other ports of the world and was getting the recognition that only a country rich in natural resources receives. No longer would supplies have to be freighted from Amarillo. No longer would mail be conveyed in canvas covered hacks drawn by little mules—which sometimes were held up for days at a time by heavy rains or snowstorms. No longer would our grocery stores run shy of necessary supplies, compelling us to borrow sugar, coffee and flour from our neighbors. Those who have never traveled miles with a horse and buggy to borrow food from a distant neighbor, or the proverbial "coal of fire," can fully appreciate what it meant to us— the security we felt, and the freedom from many privations— when we heard that first train whistle.

THE LANTERN ON THE WINDMILL
By Rev. J. H. Abney

In the year 1907 I was in the Sunday School work in Hale County, organizing Sunday Schools in the rural communities over the plains. On one occasion I was spending the night with one of my Superintendents out on the plains. Suddenly, breaking into our conversation, he called: "John! John, go hang the lantern on the windmill tower." When I asked, "What's the idea?", he replied, "The boys have gone out after the horses and we always hang the lantern on the windmill so they can see the light and find their way home."

We had been discussing the problem of keeping our little Sunday School alive and going. After a few moments thought, I said, "Brother, that light on the windmill tower reminds me of our little Sunday School. If the light on the tower should go out, there would be nothing to guide the boys home, and if we let that little Sunday School in the School House go out, the boys and girls of the plains will have nothing to guide them to their Heavenly Father's home." He was silent for a moment; then in tones most reverent, he said, "It must not go out," and it did not.

The words of this Superintendent express clearly and simply the ruling purpose in the minds and hearts of that group of men and women which many years ago, in that little "Upper Room," covenanting together in prayer, constituted themselves "The First Presbyterian Church of Plainview, Texas." For that little church, which began in the "Lantern on the Windmill" stage many years ago, has now grown into a great Tower Light for our Master's cause on the South Plains of Texas. May its light shine so brightly that all those who come within its light may see clearly the way to their Heavenly Father's Home.

LOOKING BACKWARD

By Captain R. G. Carter

(*Author of "On the Border with Mackenzie"*)

Yes! I was one of Mackenzie's right hand officers. I marched and ate and slept with him. When I think of that vast Panhandle area and the "Staked Plains," of which we were the first Cavalry Column to traverse in 1872, going as far west as Forts Sumner and Bascom, and no living creature except Indians, buffalo, wolves, rattlesnakes, jack rabbits and prairie dogs nearer than old Fort Griffin 130 miles distant, I marvel at its almost miraculous growth and expansion—towns springing up right upon our trails, railroads, schools, hotels and prosperous business enterprises. I wish to express my high regard and esteem for the hardy pioneers of the Texas Panhandle who, following the Mackenzie Trail after we had driven the marauding savages out of that section, made it possible for all of that once desolate region to blossom like the rose. I most sincerely congratulate all of the pioneers and citizens of West Texas on their achieving the accomplishments of these results within a period of sixty years, or since we routed the Comanches, Kiowas, Cheyennes and Arapahoes.

www.ingramcontent.com/pod-product-compliance
Lightning Source LLC
Chambersburg PA
CBHW030547080526
44585CB00012B/291